SINGING YORUBA CHRISTIANITY

SINGING YORUBA CHRISTIANITY

Music, Media, and Morality

Vicki L. Brennan

Indiana University Press

This book is a publication of

Indiana University Press
Office of Scholarly Publishing
Herman B Wells Library 350
1320 East 10th Street
Bloomington, Indiana 47405 USA

iupress.indiana.edu

Manufactured in the United States of America

Library of Congress Cataloging-in-Publication Data

Names: Brennan, Vicki L., author.
Title: Singing Yoruba Christianity : music, media, and morality /
    Vicki L. Brennan.
Other titles: African expressive cultures.
Description: Bloomington : Indiana University Press, 2018. | Series:
    African expressive cultures | Includes bibliographical references
and index.
Identifiers: LCCN 2017018457| ISBN 9780253032096 (pb : alk. paper) |
    ISBN 9780253032072 (cl : alk. paper) | ISBN 9780253032089 (e-book)
Subjects: LCSH: Church music—Nigeria—Lagos. | Singing—Religious
    aspects—Christianity. | Singing—Social aspects—Nigeria—Lagos. |
    Yoruba (African people)—Nigeria—Lagos—Music—History and
    criticism. | Yoruba (African people)—Nigeria—Lagos—Religion. |
    Cherubim and Seraphim Church Movement.
Classification: LCC ML3151.N547 L34 2018 | DDC 782.2209669—dc23
    LC record available at https://lccn.loc.gov/2017018457

1 2 3 4 5 23 22 21 20 19 18

In Memory of
  Bàbá I. K. Dairo, M.B.E.
  (1930–1996)

Contents

Preface

I VISITED THE Cherubim and Seraphim Ayọ̀ ni o Church in Lagos on the first full day of my first visit to Nigeria in 2001. Though I was headed for Ibadan, where I intended to scout out potential sites for my dissertation research on religion, music, and urban experience, I was taken to the Lagos compound of the Ayọ̀ ni o Church by my host, who earlier that day had informed me that the "center" of Cherubim and Seraphim music was not in Ibadan but in Lagos. Jet-lagged and a bit groggy from my travels, I nevertheless agreed to visit the church before leaving for Ibadan. After a whirlwind tour of Lagos, made possible because there was little traffic on the road that Sunday morning, we pulled off of the Oshodi-Apapa Express Road and slowed down to enter the church compound. Our first stop was at the gatehouse to collect a tally from a smiling man wearing an orange safety vest over his white prayer gown, who greeted us with a hearty "*Ayọ̀ ni o!*" (It is joy!).

We drove into a compound filled with dozens of churchgoers wearing their white church uniforms and clutching Bibles. They were all rushing to enter the already packed church building to attend the service that had already begun. Music blared from loudspeakers positioned on the corners of the buildings, broadcasting what was happening inside the church to all those that were outside. We parked the car just outside of the building that was marked as housing the Church Secretary's office and, slipping our shoes off, we walked through the sandy compound toward the door. A churchgoer stopped us, asked us what our interest was, and after explaining our purposes we were directed to the "Public Affairs Unit." After introducing ourselves, we were ushered into a carpeted room with sofas lining the walls. Pictures of Jesus, the Last Supper, and elders in the Cherubim and Seraphim Church—including one of Prophet G. O. Fakeye, the general leader of the Ayọ̀ ni o Church—were hung on the walls of the room. We sat for a moment while someone was sent to bring soft drinks for us and listened to the broadcast of the service that was taking place in the church. Boisterous music could be heard, featuring sung choruses, drums, and guitars. As I learned later I had arrived during the offering portion of the service.

The public affairs officer echoed my friend's assertions that the Ayọ̀ ni o Church was the center of Cherubim and Seraphim music and strongly suggested that my research would be better served by studying his church's choir. "They have many, many cassettes available," he explained, "They are at the forefront of gospel music in Nigeria today." I indicated that I had made plans that required that I stay in Ibadan, but would try to see if I could fit in another visit to Lagos during the six weeks I would be in Nigeria. The public affairs officer recommended some of their "sister" churches that I could visit in Ibadan, and said that when I came back to Lagos, he would make arrangements so that I could interview the church's General Leader Prophet Fakeye.

On the drive to Ibadan that day I quizzed my friend Toyin about the Ayọ̀ ni o Church choir: Was she familiar with their music? What could she tell me about Fakeye? Were there other Cherubim and Seraphim churches as large as the one we had just visited? Was there a church like that in Ibadan? Toyin, who attended a Pentecostal church, answered my questions patiently, and although she admitted that she was a bit suspicious of some of the smaller Cherubim and Seraphim churches, she was confident that Fakeye was a true Christian and a "man of God." Later that week she confided that although she wanted me to do my research in Ibadan so that I would stay with her, she also thought I should do my research with the Ayọ̀ ni o Church choir because their music was really "the best." She took me to a cassette vendor who specialized in gospel music so that I could buy some of the Ayọ̀ ni o Church choir's cassettes, in order to familiarize myself with their songs. There were ten recordings by the choir for sale, and after I asked him which one was his favorite, I purchased that along with their latest release.

It was based on this experience that I intended to focus my research on the Ayọ̀ ni o Church in Lagos when I returned for a longer field trip in January 2002. However, it was six months before I received permission from church leadership to join the choir. During those six months I lived in Ibadan and visited a number of churches in that city and its surrounding locations. My time during this period was not limited to the sister churches that the public affairs officer had recommended, nor solely to Cherubim and Seraphim churches. Instead I visited a variety of congregations, including a number of Yoruba independent (Aladura) churches, orthodox (Methodist and Anglican churches), and Pentecostal churches (Foursquare, Redeem). This research in Ibadan was a good contrast to my future research in Lagos, as it helped me to better understand Yoruba Christianity and the negotiations between various Christian denominations in a different urban setting than that of Lagos.

Living in Ibadan also gave me a good perspective on the kinds of urban experiences to be had in Nigeria. Ibadan was a stark contrast from Lagos, and most people distinguished the two by noting that Ibadan was "dull," "slow," "quiet," or "peaceful." Although these words do not precisely describe the nature of urban life in Ibadan which, like most cities, has a distinctive hustle and noise, they do help to place Ibadan in contrast to Lagos, a city like no other. Not only is the urban experience multiplied exponentially in Lagos, but the cosmopolitan nature of the city was quite distinct. English, Pidgin, and Yoruba remained the most commonly spoken languages in the city, but people from all over Nigeria, and indeed all over

Africa called Lagos their home. Furthermore, the "expatriate" population in Lagos was significantly larger than that in Ibadan, and Mercedes-Benz cars and Toyota Rav 4s containing families from India, Lebanon, the United States, and Europe were scattered throughout traffic, their homes clustered in certain areas of the city.

The sense of familiarity and openness palpable on the streets of Ibadan did not obtain in Lagos. This was brought home to me one day when my roommate, a Yoruba woman who attended a Pentecostal church, teased me because every morning as we left the compound I greeted the woman who ran a small kiosk selling household goods at the gate. "Do you know her?" she asked me. When I explained that in Ibadan it seemed as though one greeted strangers as a matter of course—particularly those who were part of one's everyday routine—she laughed and said, "I forgot that you just came from the village." Indeed, the famous Yoruba greetings were still required to open transactions or conversations as one went about one's daily business; yet they took on a more terse nature in Lagos, used in a perfunctory manner except when greeting one's friends or family. Lagos, as many Nollywood films depict, could be isolating and alienating, with little time for the niceties of life as everyone scrambled to make a living.

Once established in Lagos I visited the Ayọ̀ ni o Church a number of times each week, attending Sunday worship, Saturday vigil, choir practice, Bible study, and other services in addition to talking with prophets in between counseling sessions and interviewing church officials in the course of their work day. I also met with church members in their homes and occasionally in their places of work. Toward the end of my stay I began to be invited to social events—weddings, funerals, naming ceremonies—held by church members. I also occasionally attended services at other churches in Lagos, both Cherubim and Seraphim as well as Pentecostal churches, including attending the Pentecostal Redeemed Christian Church of God's monthly revival service, Holy Ghost Night.

My access to the church, particularly to joining the choir, was due to a personal connection I made while attending a wedding ceremony in Ibadan. When I was telling one of the groom's brothers about my research, because he had asked why I had come to Nigeria, he exclaimed, "You are in luck today. My big auntie is a member of that church and she sings in the choir. I will introduce her to you immediately." It was indeed my lucky day, as Prophetess Wright not only was a member of the choir, but she was a particularly influential member of the church. She soon arranged for a meeting with the church's choirmaster and the other officers of the choir. The meeting was cordial, but I left feeling uncertain that I would be allowed to join the choir after all. They told me to come back in two weeks. However, Prophetess Wright took me out to the church's parking lot where she had arranged for a tailor to meet us to take measurements for my church uniform. "Don't worry," she said. "They just need to pray to make sure God wants you to join us. You should pray too so that they will hear his wishes." Two weeks later

I was told to come to church by 8:30 a.m. prompt so I could sing with the choir during Sunday worship services.

Most Sundays I sat in the main church with the choir, arriving before 8:30 a.m. The Sunday service usually lasted five to six hours. I sat beside Prophetess Wright toward the back of the choir stall with the other percussionists, and played the casaba, an imported Chinese-made handheld shaker that consists of loops of steel ball chain wrapped around a cylinder with a handle attached. Occasionally I was given a ṣẹ̀kẹ̀rẹ̀ (gourd rattle), or a tambourine, though I never did master playing those instruments to the satisfaction of my fellow percussionists. Prophetess Wright always played the maracas. On occasion, especially during choir practice, I would be invited by one of the drummers to play the conga drums. I also took lessons on how to play the *gángan*, a Yoruba talking drum that was able to "speak" fragments of the Yoruba language, with the choir's lead drummer. In addition, I studied the choir's songs one-on-one with one of the group's lead singers; we would meet before choir practice for our singing lessons.

Even though I was singing during much of the church service, there was ample opportunity to take notes during worship. People often would encourage me to write something down that they thought was significant, and often if I appeared to be struggling with understanding the Yoruba being spoken they would come stand behind me and whisper in my ear in English. I had also brought a video camera with me intending to document worship services, but I often found it intrusive. Fortunately, however, the church had a video unit that documented nearly all services and I was allowed to purchase duplicate copies of their videotapes for my use. I did occasionally record choir practices, mostly audio but some video, and I recorded all of my singing and drumming lessons.

It is based on these opportunities and experiences that I have written this book. This is a book about how religious music, understood both as forms of media and practices of mediation, not only produces a moral community of people that are bound to each other through a set of meaningful and aesthetic practices, but also links that community to a set of ethical guidelines that are themselves expressed and experienced via aesthetic media. The analysis I present here emerged out of my observations of and participation with a group of Yoruba Christians in Lagos and is thus primarily an ethnographic one.

Ethnography as a method of both research and writing enables certain arguments and conclusions and, more important, advocates a particular claim for the veracity of its findings. Ethnographic research is often intimate and personal, based more on a reflection on one's experiences and conversations during fieldwork rather than on a simple transfer of information from research subject to researcher. It is a process and an exchange, one that leads to relationships, obligations, and ideally to reciprocity (Buggenhagen 2012). In doing so, ethnography emphasizes the subjective, building up a sense of what a given community is and how it is perceived by recognizing the diverse standpoints that particular members of that community take toward it. As such, the presentation of an ethnographic perspective is also a political act, one that acknowledges that the kind of thought that is usually deemed "theoretical" by scholars in the North Atlantic tradition is not limited to universities but is an aspect of human thought more generally (Comaroff and Comaroff 2012; Trouillot 1991).

A key part of doing and writing ethnography is acknowledging that my discussion here is subjective in a second way—it emerges from my own perspective and understanding based on my conversations with and observations of members of a specific Yoruba Christian community. That is not to say that this is a book about me, or about my own personal transformation or awakening. Rather, in this book I present the events and lives of those who spoke with me from their perspective. This entails an attempt to understand that perspective on my part, all the time realizing the absolute impossibility of such an endeavor. Thus, my claims here about how music works in this context or what people are doing with religion are certainly partial, built up from ongoing conversations and questions that continue up until the present day.

Though my account here is admittedly subjective and partial, that is not to say that it is fictional. I have tried to represent the events that I participated in and the lives that people shared with me as honestly as possible. At times this has meant that I have left certain details out, to protect the privacy of those who shared their stories with me. The names of some of the people who appear in this text have been changed to protect their privacy, but no composite characters were used to exemplify an abstract church member's perspective.[1]

What I present in the chapters that follow then is a narration of what I learned about religion and music from those who spoke and interacted with me during my time in Lagos and Ibadan. This representation of their perspectives is for scholars of religion and music, as well as for Yoruba Christians, who will see themselves in the pages of this book. Over the course of more than a decade of research and writing with and about members of the Ayọ̀ ni o Church I have sought their comments and feedback. This ranged from viewing videos of church ceremonies together and then recording the comments and discussion that ensued, to sending portions of this text as I wrote it to both clarify questions that I may have had but also to see their reaction to being written about. At times they have found what I have had to say about them surprising, but most often they confirmed my interpretations and analysis. The most frequent comment I have received from church members who have read my writings about them is that I have not been critical enough in my writing; that I affirmed their practices rather than pointing out their faults. Though I do not perceive my role here to evaluate their practices—to ask if they are good or bad, effective or useless—such comments did force me to think more carefully about the conclusions I make at the end of this analysis. The discussion of social inequality at the end of chapter 8 is a result of this urging by certain members of the church for me to consider more critically what I had to say about their community and their experiences.[2]

Although I have said that this is not a book about me, there is an aspect of my positionality in relation to the church that invites comment here. That is my own claims to religious belonging; my own perspective on the place and veracity of religion in the world.[3] Such questions are especially fraught given anthropology's long avoidance of and perhaps even hostility toward Christianity, even on the part of researchers who may have been devout Christians themselves. I entered the field as a young woman who had been raised in a Catholic family and who was ambivalent at best about my own need for religion but curious about why and how others saw religion as a fundamental part of their existence. My attitude has mainly remained the same, further tempered and refined both by my conversations with my Yoruba Christian friends throughout the years and by a decade of teaching courses about theories of religion and religious traditions to mainly secular and skeptical students at the University of Vermont. I have always represented myself as such to those about whom I write, and my skepticism was even acknowledged and welcomed by the choirmaster during one of my first meetings with him when he assured me that he looked forward to reading a critical study of the church.[4]

I am not sure whether this book was what the choirmaster had in mind when he invited me to join the choir. However, a chief concern in writing this book has been to take the Christian perspective of my informants seriously and not to see it as ideological justification for the place of Nigeria in the world or alternately as an escape from their reality. Rather, inspired by the example of my dissertation advisor, Jean Comaroff (1985; see also Comaroff and Comaroff 1991) as well as by the way in which the anthropology of Christianity developed as a subfield while I was writing this text (Cannell 2005, 2006; Robbins 2003; see also Comaroff 2010), I have instead attempted to represent the ideas and practices of members of the Ayọ ni o Church in their own terms and as constituting a critical theory about Christianity itself—one that attempts to make sense of their place in the world as Yoruba people, as Nigerian citizens, and as Christians. It is for this reason that each chapter begins with an epigraph taken from the bible, a religious tract, or from a song sung by church members; these quotes represent the way in which members of the church grounded the particularities of their experiences in relation to the purportedly universal texts of Christianity. In this way the Yoruba Christians that I write about here make their own theological discourse, one that is abstract and generalizing as well as specific.

In January 2004, after I had been regularly attending choir rehearsals and Sunday services at the Cherubim and Seraphim Movement Ayo ni o Church for more than twelve months, I interviewed Bàbá Ogunbiyi. An older man, in his mid-sixties, he typically sat in the back row of the choir stall next to the choirmaster and the choir secretary. Over the course of my research I had noticed that although Ogunbiyi did not play a central musical role—in other words he was not a lead singer, instrumentalist, or composer—he was nevertheless well-regarded by members of the choir. He attended choir rehearsals regularly, and was often consulted for his guidance and advice. During Sunday church services he would often receive messages from other church members; slips of paper folded over with his name written on the front that were either brought to him by one of the ushers, or passed to him through the windows at the back of the choir stall. He frequently was involved in intense discussions with the choir's spiritual and administrative leadership. Outside of the church he was a successful business-owner, who owned and operated a printing press. His shop was responsible for producing many of the pamphlets, programs, brochures, collection envelopes, and other printed materials distributed by church members as part of their religious practice.

Ogunbiyi always made sure to exchange greetings with me during choir rehearsals and church services. If he noticed that I was struggling to understand what was happening he would often send someone to stand beside me to help translate what was going on. I had decided to interview him as part of a series of life histories of choir members that I was collecting, so we made an appointment to meet in the Choir Hall following worship one Sunday. We sat in a corner of the large open room, as other choir members bustled through discussing the coming week's plans with each other, collecting personal belongings they had stored in one of the choir offices for safekeeping during services, and laughing and joking about recent events. For more than an hour Ogunbiyi patiently answered my questions about his personal biography, his church membership, and his role in the choir. As I took a last look at my notes, and began to pack up my recorder, he looked at me and said, "Can I ask *you* a question?"

"Of course," I replied, not sure what to expect.

"I want to know what you are doing in church. I've been watching you. You don't sing. You don't dance. So what is the point? What are you doing here?"

Flustered, I began repeating the purposes and questions that drove my research. I told him that I was interested in understanding how the music in the church worked. That I wanted to know what makes the music sound good to the members of the congregation and how they used music to communicate with God.

"I know that," he said. "But how can you know if you don't *really* sing or dance? I want you to try harder."

Humbled, I agreed with him that I needed to work on singing and dancing more during worship services. This practical action constituted my initial response to his question, but I would now also respond to him by asking him to read this book. I hope that it will let him as well as others in the church know more about what was the point of our collaboration and exchange during the past fifteen years.

Notes

1. Most of the names used throughout this text are pseudonyms. However, because of their role as public figures in Nigeria, I have used the real names of prominent church leaders, specifically Prophet G. O. Fakeye, who was the general leader of the Ayọ̀ ni o Church until his death in 2015 and Prophet S. F. Korode, who was the choirmaster of the Ayọ̀ ni o Church Choir until he was named Fakeye's successor.

2. There are two moments in particular that stand out for me that led directly to the conclusion for chapter 8. The first was a visit with a member of the church's public relations unit during a short trip back to Nigeria in 2010, soon after I had defended my dissertation. He asked me what I had written about, and after I had read to him the conclusion of my dissertation he said that I still had more work to do. As he did so, he shuffled through a stack of papers on his desk and handed me a copy of the United Nations Human Development Report for Nigeria, stressing that I should be sure to take such data into account. The second moment was after a member of the church who also holds a PhD and is a professor at a Nigerian university gave me feedback after reading my dissertation that specifically urged me to be more critical of the church.

3. This is not to say that other aspects of my position as a white, educated, middle-class, American woman did not inform my research, creating both the possibility for me to travel to Nigeria to ask such questions as well as shaping how those who interacted with me responded to my very presence.

4. I was introduced to the congregation during Sunday worship by the church leadership soon after I was invited to join the choir. I was brought to the front of the church and informed those present of my name, where I was from, and what I intended to do while I was visiting. However, given the size of the congregation as well as changing patterns of attendance over the course of my research, it is likely that many church members did not know who I was or why I was there. I overheard a conversation between two women who were shocked to see me exiting the church wearing a choir uniform, speculating as to why I was there: either I was married to a Nigerian or I was a missionary. I suspect that many other people in the church with whom I did not have direct contact made similar assumptions about me.

Acknowledgments

THE SEEDS OF this project were sown during my first year of graduate study in ethnomusicology at the University of Washington. It was there that I met Bàbá I. K. Dairo, the renowned jùjú musician who was also the leader of a Cherubim and Seraphim congregation in Lagos. I learned my first Yoruba hymn from Dairo and it was because of his influence on me as a musician that I decided to focus on Cherubim and Seraphim music for my dissertation research. At the University of Washington Chris Waterman also played an important part in my scholarly development, by encouraging me to pursue research in Nigeria and also to broaden my training by pursuing a PhD in anthropology at the University of Chicago.

If the project germinated at the University of Washington, it came into full flower at the University of Chicago. I was fortunate to have a diverse network of professors, colleagues, and friends who helped me traverse the arduous road leading from "systems" to the dissertation defense. The largest debt is due to my dissertation committee—Andrew Apter, Jean Comaroff, Danilyn Rutherford, and Martin Stokes—for their generosity of time, intellect, and support during the various stages of this project. I also received valuable feedback on chapters from the African Studies Workshop, the Interdisciplinary Christianities Workshop, and the Ethnoise! Workshop. The ideas in this manuscript were further shaped by conversations with colleagues and students at the University of Vermont. The religion department continues to be a supportive environment in which to further develop my understanding of the interrelationships between religion, ethics, and performance.

This research was generously supported by a number of financial sponsors. The University of Chicago African Studies Workshop provided funds for Yoruba language training as well as for a short preliminary research visit to Nigeria in 2001. I also received funds from the Committee on Institutional Cooperation's FLEP program for a summer of intensive Yoruba training at the University of Wisconsin in Madison. The financial support of the Wenner-Gren Foundation, the National Science Foundation, and the Fulbright-Hays doctoral dissertation research abroad program made it possible for me to complete eighteen months of field research in Lagos. The Carter G. Woodson Institute at the University of Virginia provided funds and resources to support the initial writing stages of this project. Subsequent research trips have been funded by the University of Vermont, including through the Joan Smith Award from the College of Arts and Sciences dean's office and a REACH grant from the provost's office.

Dee Mortensen and Paige Rasmussen at Indiana University Press have been patient, supportive, and helpful at bringing this project to publication. I also am grateful for the insightful and constructive comments provided by Elisha Renne who reviewed the manuscript for the press. Thanks are also due to Beverley Wemple and Chris Burns at the University of Vermont for their technical assistance in producing image files for this publication.

Material in several of the chapters has been published previously. A version of chapter 3 was published as "Mediating 'The Voice of the Spirit': Musical and Religious Transformations in Nigeria's Oil Boom," *American Ethnologist* 37, no. 2: 354–370. Parts of chapter 2 were published as "Up above the River Jordan: Hymns and Historical Consciousness in the Cherubim and Seraphim Churches of Nigeria," *Studies in World Christianity* 19, no. 1: 31–49, and parts of chapter 4 as "Take Control: The Labor of Immediacy in Yoruba Christian Music," *Journal of Popular Music Studies* 24, no. 4: 411–429.

I am indebted to the leaders and members of the Cherubim and Seraphim Ayọ̀ ni o Church for welcoming me into their congregation. The following were central to the success of my research: Prophetess Sarah Toyin Wright, Prophet S.F. Korode, Most Senior Apostle G. O. Ogunleye, Most Senior Apostle H. O. Atansuyi, Senior Apostle Balogun, Pastor Ogunbusola, Senior Mother in Israel Yemi Akiremi, Senior Apostle J. O. Dairo, Senior Apostle Simbo Ogunnubi, Prophet Niyi Adeyemi, Pastor Mrs. Tinu Oyenuga, and Mrs. Ola Toyo. The members of the Seraph Voices choir made me feel welcome and helped me learn the ways of the Ayọ̀ ni, and while I cannot thank them all here by name they are the most important part of this project. Special thanks to Ayan for teaching me the rudiments of playing gángan, Aunty Ṣola for taking care of business, Mummy Dairo and Mary for helping me to find the beat, and Febi for making me sing. I am beholden to Prophet Oluṣesi for his assistance in transcribing and translating many of the song lyrics and other Yoruba texts I analyze in the pages that follow.

The list of people in Nigeria who were essential to the success of this project is long. In Ibadan I am especially grateful to the following people who provided hospitality, friendship, and answered (or at least took seriously) my ridiculous questions: Toyin Alalade and family, the Eyituwi sisters (Toyin, Wumi, Funke, and Ṣola), and Dayo Atunrase (Daddy Bolu). For their assistance with my research I thank Laolu Ogunniyi, Professor J. F. Ade-Ajayi, Professor Obadike, Professor Abogunrin, Bode Omojola, Wole Adetiran, Olapade Ogoro, and Mr. Fadipe.

I am grateful to Toyin Ajayi-Frankel and Andy Frankel for coming to my rescue when I was unable to find housing in Lagos. Thank you for graciously inviting me into your home and reassuring me that I would be able to complete my project. Yemisi Ajayi introduced me to the fine art of negotiating taxi prices in Lagos, shared her love of textiles and fashion design, and has been a wonderful friend. Harrison Adeniyi helped to arrange for my affiliation with Lagos State

University and has since become a valued colleague and dear friend. Thanks also to Toun Ilumoka, Wale Aderemi, Patrick Oloko, Jimi King, Lucky, James, Arinola, Ayo, and Titi for friendship, conversation, and support.

I must also express my gratitude to my wonderful Yoruba language teachers, Akinloye Ojo and Dayo Laoye, who have made themselves available throughout the research and writing of this project in order to answer questions about the intricacies of translation. I am also grateful to Dayo for making me a part of his family in Ibadan.

I am grateful to my colleagues, mentors, and friends over the years who read drafts, provided inspiration and advice, helped me to develop my thoughts into paragraphs and chapters, and provided much-appreciated encouragement and support: Sareeta Amrute, Jayson Beaster-Jones, Anya Bernstein, Tom Borchert, Mieka Brand, Beth Anne Buggenhagen, Melvin Butler, Anne Clark, Rosalind Hackett, Sherine Hamdy, Cindy Hoehler-Fatton, Travis Jackson, Kelda Jamison, Anne-Maria Makhulu, Emily Manetta, Adam Mohr, Ilyse Morgenstein Fuerst, Kennetta Perry, Lorri Plourde, Hanan Sabea, Noah Salomon, Jesse Shipley, Lisa Shutt, Sarah Silkey, Jonah Steinberg, Kabir Tambar, Todne Thomas, Kevin Trainor, Andrea Voyer, and Thabiti Willis.

Marina Peterson deserves special recognition for reading draft after draft of this text and encouraging me to finish the manuscript because she wanted follow the argument through to the conclusion. Gretchen Bakke helped revive my enthusiasm for this project during a low point of writing by reading the manuscript in full and providing incisive and supportive feedback and advice.

I am especially grateful to my mother, Elizabeth Haahr, for her unconditional love and support. Thanks also to my sister, Carrie Brennan, who led by example and completed her PhD while I was still working on mine. Various members of my extended family have encouraged me throughout this process and I appreciate their patience.

Ben Eastman has been a constant source of love, patience, careful criticism, and inspiration. Thank you for helping me see this project through to its conclusion; it would not have been possible without you.

Note on Language and Translation

Yoruba is a tonal language, with high (indicated by an acute accent), middle (unmarked), and low (grave accent) tones. In addition, there are three letters in the Yoruba alphabet that have diacritical marks—Ẹ (pronounced as "eh"), Ọ (pronounced as "aw"), and Ṣ (pronounced as "sh"). I have indicated tonal marks and diacritics for all Yoruba words appearing in the text, with the exception of proper names and place names.

Much of the research for this book was conducted in two languages: English and Yoruba. As the two dominant languages spoken in southwest Nigeria—but not the only two, given the cosmopolitan nature of the city of Lagos—it was fairly easy for people who interacted with me to switch to English when they felt that they had reached the limits of my knowledge of the Yoruba language. Thus interviews were conducted in a combination of two languages. Most speech and song that occurred in the context of church worship was in Yoruba (some speech, especially sermons and announcements, was translated from Yoruba into English or vice versa during the course of performance). All songs and other religious texts that I initially encountered in Yoruba have been translated into English for the purposes of this book, with key Yoruba terms indicated in parenthesis. Many of these terms also appear in the glossary at the back of this book.

SINGING YORUBA CHRISTIANITY

1   Singing the Same Song

Make a joyful noise to the Lord, all ye lands. Serve the Lord with gladness, come before his presence with singing.

—Psalm 100:1–2

For the word of God says, if we live in Spirit as we claim we do in the Cherubim and Seraphim Church, let us also walk in Spirit. The Church must set for the whole world the perfect pattern of spiritual worship by worshipping God, in Spirit and in truth. We should proclaim His Holiness, Might, and Dominion, day and night, ceaselessly through all eternity in our words, speeches, actions, and deeds.

—S. F. Korode, *Cherubim and Seraphim Legacies*

THRONGS OF CHURCHGOERS wearing their white prayer gowns and clutching Bibles scurry toward the main hall of the Cherubim and Seraphim Àyọ̀ ni o Church in Lagos, Nigeria early each Sunday morning in order to attend worship services. As they move toward the building they encounter the sound of voices singing, amplified through a system of loudspeakers strung throughout the compound. To the soundtrack of voices, guitars, organ, and drums, they enter the church, take their places in the pews, and join the singing. The volume of the music increases and people begin swaying back and forth and smiling in anticipation of the service. At precisely 8:45 a.m. the tempo of the music slows down and the organ sounds the chords of that day's opening hymn, a signal that the service is about to start. As the worship leaders for that day's service process into the building from the back entrance, the rest of the congregation joins voices and bodies together in song. The procession moves toward the sanctuary in the front of the church, drawing everyone's attention to the altar at the front of the church hall. Once they have arrived everyone in the church faces forward, a sea of people clad in white flowing gowns singing together. Worship has already begun.

It is this scene, repeated by churchgoers each Sunday morning, that serves as a point of departure for the arguments about music, media, and morality that I undertake here. This book is an ethnographic examination of the ways in which music—together with other elements central to church worship such as speech, dress, and movement—was a crucial tool for the making of self and community for members of a large, independent Christian church in Nigeria's largest city. As a prophet at the Ayọ̀ ni o Church explained to me, "Music can connect thousands of people at a time and create the same mind. When we are singing the same song, our minds cannot change." In other words, church members saw singing together as a means of creating unity and cohesion around a shared set of values. By "singing the same song" an individual church member became part of a larger imagined social collectivity, one that extended across time and space.

It was by singing the same song, and thereby producing the same mind—a shared ethical orientation toward the world—that one would be able to achieve a "good life." Church members sought to create a community of people oriented around the same moral and ethical values through their religious musical practice. A good life included health (*àlàáfíà*), joy (*ayọ̀*), happiness (*inu didùn*), wealth (*ọlà*), and success (*iṣẹ́gun*). All of these elements that make up the good life can be glossed with the Yoruba word àlàáfíà, which not only refers to physical health, but more generally describes a person at peace due to the presence of all of these elements. At the same time as participation in church worship enabled such prosperity, it also provided protection (*ààbò*), mercy (*àánú*), and salvation (*ìgbàlà*). For church members, singing the same song was a means to achieve these ends, and to do so in the right way: a moral way, an ethical way, rather than through corruption, or by buying one's way to happiness or stealing and cheating in order to become wealthy. These negative behaviors were of central concern to church members, and indeed to many in Nigeria who, as Daniel Smith puts it, "see corruption at work in every aspect of social life" (Smith 2007, 5). To counteract the perceived pervasiveness of such negative behavior, church members emphasized that hard work and "correct behavior" according to agreed-on social norms and values were necessary to achieve a good life.

But there was something more behind church members' admonishments to go to church and sing each Sunday. Singing the same song was not only figurative but was also technical, in the sense that doing so involved techniques of the voice, body, and self, as well as the belief that these techniques needed to be perfected (Mauss 1973). One had to actually sing the same song as everyone else—the same lyrics, the same melody, the same rhythm. And this singing had to be done in accordance with rules and expectations that shaped how church members understood singing to be emotionally affective as well as religiously effective.

Singing the same song together correctly was more difficult than it might initially seem, given the nature of music itself. A song is composed of discrete musical parts (such as harmonic layering or interlocking rhythms) that when brought together produce a cohesive and recognizable whole. These discrete parts of a song, in performance, produce a trajectory over time, whether it is from one rhythmic or melodic motif to another or a cyclical repetition. Such aspects of musical performance are often performative and context-dependent. In other words, choices made about whether to lengthen or shorten a musical phrase, or to repeat a section of a song, are often made in the moment of performance for particular needs or desires. Thus, the potential for each performance of a song to be unique is constrained by "tradition"—by rules that govern how to sing, who sings, and what and when to sing—but a given performance is not limited by these rules. Any performance of a song is both a repetition and an innovation at the same time.

How, then, did the congregation sing the same song? This is the question I set out to answer in this book through an examination of the technologies, media forms, disciplinary practices, and cultural theories about what constitutes the right kind of singing, through which church members saw themselves as singing the same song. I argue that it is the gap between the rule-bound nature of music that allows it to be repeatable and recognizable as a repetition, and the transformations, large and small, that happen in any given performance of a song, that allows song to not just be expressive of shared values and practices but also to be productive of ethically informed ways of being in the world.

My analysis of the sounded aspects of Cherubim and Seraphim worship speaks to larger anthropological concerns with the tensions between conventionality and spontaneity in ritualized action (Drewal 1992; Mahmood 2001), and between normative and innovative aspects of affective states (Bloch 1974; Tambiah 1985; Turner 1967). To accomplish this, I examine musical and ritual performance in the context of Cherubim and Seraphim worship. Through this analysis I demonstrate how church members articulated and embodied the moral and ethical prescriptions and attitudes necessary to be "a good Christian" via musical participation. Music served as a highly stylized and aesthetic participatory form, one that allowed church members to create "the right kind of worship." Church members understood music to be capable of enhancing the spiritual power of the singer, of producing a unified body of worshippers, and of effecting material changes in the world. The efficacy of musical participation was usually evidenced by the visible or audible presence of the Holy Spirit during musical portions of church worship. It was this capacity of correct musical performance as part of worship that made church members emphasize singing in order to create a social context in which they were able to achieve prosperity and success.

Church members saw singing in church as an efficacious and ethical mode of acting in the world. I focus on two aspects of church music: first, how music helped church members to reproduce themselves as Christian subjects, and second, how musical performance in the church extended outwards to shape a Yoruba social world. Members of Cherubim and Seraphim churches did not just sing with their voices, but also used musical media such as hymnbooks and cassette tapes to reproduce themselves as Christian subjects. They danced and moved their bodies in coordination with songs. They attended choir rehearsals, Bible study classes, and lectures on religious topics regularly. They prepared themselves outside of church to do all of these things correctly and properly. These musical forms and practices mediated religious experiences for church members, connecting people to God, to church history, and to each other. At the same time, music provided a means through which church members developed an ethical self, one that enabled them to interpret and apply the lessons learned by singing in church to issues and situations that they faced in their own lives. It was the work of attempting to sing the same song that provided church members with their ability to achieve success in the midst of economic and political transformations and uncertainty that characterized Nigeria since 1999.

The Right Kind of Worship

For church members "singing the same song" was central to navigating the transformations of Nigeria's political economy in the early twenty-first century, especially between 2001 and 2004, a time when the majority of the ethnographic research for this book was conducted. Nigeria's transition to democracy in 1999 was seen by many Nigerians as holding the best promise for undoing many of the social and economic problems that had plagued the country during the years of General Sani Abacha's military dictatorship (1993–1998). Under Abacha, a small fraction of Nigerians, particularly those with connections to the military regime, had been able to amass vast wealth from oil revenues, while the majority of the population continued to live in extreme poverty. According to United Nations, in 1996 more than 60 percent of Nigerians survived on less than $1 per day. By the time of Abacha's death in 1998, the middle class had been nearly squeezed out of existence.

The shift to democracy—marked by the election of Olusegun Obasanjo as president in 1999, as well as his successful reelection in 2003—represented a moment of possibility for what remained of Nigeria's middle-class, who looked forward to the "democracy dividends" that were owed to them in return for years of suffering and deprivation under military rule. For many Nigerians "democracy meant better paid jobs, education, health care, modern amenities such as affordable homes, motor transportation, pipe borne water and electricity, and above all, a better future for children" (Ojo 2004, 77). Some of these improvements seemed to materialize quickly, in particular the introduction of digital cellular telephone technology and infrastructure that brought access to wireless telephone service to a significant portion of Nigeria's population. However, other services lagged behind. Electricity remained inconsistent and generators were prevalent across urban Nigeria, especially in middle-class residential and commercial districts. Roads and highways were in a prolonged state of disrepair, making travel difficult as cars, busses, and trucks navigated around massive potholes and obstructions.

The most visible sign of the failure of democracy to ensure prosperity for Nigeria was the scarcity of fuel. People spent hours waiting in long lines outside of service stations so that they could fill their gas tanks in order to travel from home to work, or to purchase a jerry can of diesel in order to run a home generator when the electric utility failed. Adding to the frustrations of the Nigerian middle class, who sought to create a comfortable life for their families in the midst of the chaos of Nigeria, the Obasanjo administration introduced new regulations on the import of consumer goods. The intent of the government was to increase the consumption of consumer goods produced within Nigeria rather than imports and to encourage local businesses to expand their offerings. However, these restrictions were understood by the middle class as a deprivation because they restricted their ability to purchase items such as used cars, refrigerators, and air conditioners (generally referred to as *tọkunbọ* [lit.: from overseas]) as well as imported textiles, poultry, and manufactured items from Europe and China. The price of such goods increased in response to the limited supply available making it more difficult for those on middle-class salaries to afford such amenities. Universities were underfunded, and between 2002 and 2004 were frequently closed due to strikes by lecturers and other university staff who sought to improve both their wages as well as learning and living conditions for their students.

The Ayọ ni o Church attempted to step in to fill this gap in public services that the state failed to provide. This often took the form of providing free meals, clothing, and medical assistance to impoverished church members, or serving as an informal employment network, but it also promised to deliver to church members a morally sound form of social organization through their participation in church services. Cherubim and Seraphim worship practices worked to produce a social imaginary fashioned according to what they deemed to be Yoruba and Christian values. Indeed, church leaders stressed that theirs was a particularly Yoruba form of Christianity, one that joined together Yoruba and Christian values and practices. By attempting to sing the same song, and learning how to do so, church members were able to create a particular vision of an ideal society that brought together traditional Yoruba social orders with Christian moral codes. In particular, church leaders emphasized the importance of hierarchical directions of respect organized according to seniority, as well as wealth redistribution from senior patrons to junior clients, as crucial to ensuring moral order and ethical behavior.

Singing made this social imaginary tangible, accessible, and applicable. Church members sang the same song in new contexts, affecting both the meaning of the song as well as their interpretation of current events. It was in this way that the moral ideals of Cherubim and Seraphim Christianity were brought to bear on church members' understandings of their everyday lives in the context of political and economic transition. Furthermore, music and musical performances enabled particular modes of mediation and circulation so that Cherubim and Seraphim social values and imaginaries contributed to cultural politics and public culture in Nigeria more generally.

The Ayọ̀ ni o Church choir played a crucial role in creating and circulating musical forms that linked religious values to everyday life. In addition to opening up communication between heaven and earth in order to bring down God's power, the Ayọ̀ ni o Church choir's musical performance was used to create a relationship between divine power and the congregation. As a prophetess explained to me: "The choir sets an example for the church. If the choir makes noise, the church will make noise. The choir is a service department in the church, a ministry which is necessary in order to carry the congregation and to produce unison so that the congregation recognizes before whom they are coming." Church members understood music to be required by God in order to draw down his power, as well as to produce unity in the congregation. This was further seen as a practice of angelic mimicry. In his history of the church, Omoyajowo quotes a member of a Cherubim and Seraphim Church in the 1970s who described practices of angelic mimesis: "using the Bible as authority, members believe that 'Cherubim and Seraphim are the names given to the angels around the throne of God in heaven singing praises unto Him continually day and night'" (Omoyajowo 1982, 114). Singing was thus not just about the music itself but also a bodily practice; worshippers did what they could to sound like, look like, and move like angels, which created a link between church members and the divine. This link was crucial to transforming individuals into recognizable worshippers of God who, through their religious efforts, were able to be successful in the world.

For participants in church worship, musical performance was an engagement with and taking on of divinely inspired and thus morally correct subjectivities and social relations. As a church prophet explained to me, "Music is a mode of happiness by which the order was founded. Music and dance are required by God, because they make him happy." Indeed, church members believed that good musical performance, especially when combined potently with other ritual modes such as dance, dress, and oratory, ensured that their prayers would be heard by God, that the Holy Spirit would descend into the space of the church, and that the church prophets would experience visions, all of which promised to change material circumstances for believing members. The transformations of self, community, and materiality effected via singing were usually evidenced by the visible or audible presence of the Holy Spirit in the church during musical portions of worship as members of the congregation fell into a spiritual trance or began to speak in tongues.

Although singing was a necessary part of Cherubim and Seraphim worship, it could not be done haphazardly. Musical performance in the context of worship had to be done correctly in order to be effective at transcending space and time, linking human and divine, and creating unison amid difference. Church members attempted to sing the same song, not just in the same way, but more importantly in the correct way (see Engelhardt 2015; Rommen 2007). Singing in the right way mitigated the risk that music might distract participants from the true purpose of worship, which was to reproduce and circulate Cherubim and Seraphim Christian values. This was how church members' affective connections to music, their feelings of happiness and joy that emerged out of musical participation, became connected to the ethical practice of Christianity.

Thus, Cherubim and Seraphim worship practices were both a structure of ideal social forms and relationships, represented to the congregation via hymns, sermons, and sacred texts, as well as an active process of inhabiting these ideal forms via dressing, singing, dancing, and acting as angels. Cherubim and Seraphim musical performances allowed church members to inhabit an idealized form of personhood, one that offered the promise that church members would be able to achieve success in their lives on a personal as well as a collective level. Indeed, church members themselves understood imaginings of Christian community and the moral forms of action that constituted Christian practice to be primarily accomplished musically. It was because of this that church members understood singing in church to be an effective means of ensuring health, prosperity, and happiness. As church members often explained to me, "music is a magnet." The magnetic powers of music attracted people to the church, and through repetition in worship and disciplinary actions such as choir practice and Bible study, remade individuals in line with the ethical and moral imperatives of the community. It was this new community, one produced by singing the same song together and organized around Cherubim and Seraphim values, that promised to help church members to achieve a good life in the midst of the political and economic uncertainty that characterized Nigeria.

Musical performances reproduced religious community; they not only organized life on this plane, but they also enabled access to the divine. Church members acknowledged that music, a magnet that drew people to the church, also attracted God's attention. Musical performances made spiritual power tangible and available to participants, and it was via this spiritual power that moral forms of subjectivity and desired modes of social organization became perceptible. In this context music, worship, performance, and the utterance of religious texts were creative acts that summoned up the divine rather than just registering its presence. Church members understood that it was during lengthy musical performances that God's power entered the church, and the evidence that this had happened became visible and audible as people began to appear ẹlẹ́míì (in the spirit) by convulsing and speaking in tongues.

Church prophets and prophetesses, along with those trained in interpreting spiritual messages provided by God through those who were in the spirit, transmitted God's messages to the congregation. These messages may have been directed to the entire congregation; for example, frequent announcements were made to church members during the worship service that God had revealed that they should not take a particular route home from church that day to avoid danger or that everyone should pray that night using a particular Bible passage in order to ensure success in their week. Other messages were intended for individual members of the church, and were delivered to the selected person either in writing or through a personal consultation with a prophet. These messages usually pertained to a specific issue or problem a person was facing, and often offered a practical means through which the person's problem could be addressed. For example, one afternoon after the Sunday service, as I was walking through the church compound a prophet stopped me and said he had a message for me. He said he did not know my name, but that God had told him that there was a white woman in the church that day who he assumed was me, and that I was expecting news from home. The prophet told me that I would hear from my people at home in two days, and that I should pray and fast for the next day to make sure that the news would be positive. Church members regularly received such messages from God through the church prophets as a result of their participation in church worship.

Further evidence that God's presence was summoned through church members' worship practices was given when people provided testimonies of prayers answered or miracles performed on their behalf. A portion of each Sunday's service was devoted to testimonies, and people would come forward to attest to the work that God had done in their lives, from healing illness to enabling financial success. Music was also embedded in such statements, as those giving testimony would break into song at moments when words seemed to fail them. Alternately, a person's testimony would be interrupted with a song from the choir, so the feelings of joy and gratitude expressed by the person could be taken up and reaffirmed by the congregation. As these examples indicate, musical performance in the context of religious worship was thus an agentive intervention that brought into being contexts for divine encounter, healing, and moral transformation.

Aesthetic and Ethical Formations

In her influential work on Ghanaian pentecostalism, Birgit Meyer has suggested that scholars of religion build on Anderson's (1991) conception of the nation as an imagined community by conceiving of religious communities as aesthetic formations, connected by shared images, mediated cultural practices, established modes of interpretation, and agreement about their meaning, as well as "the capacity of these forms to induce in those engaging with them a particular common aesthetic and style" (Meyer 2009, 9). Meyer's formulation leads away from conceiving of religious communities as stable, tradition-bound entities, but rather forces us to consider the ongoing nature of their reproduction as embodied and materialized processes. She argues that it is through shared styles and a common aesthetic orientation to practice that religious communities reproduce themselves (see also Warner 2002 on publics).

Crucial to my analysis here is Meyer's (2010, 749) identification of an "aesthetics of persuasion" that underlies religious forms and the communities oriented around them. The aesthetics of persuasion that characterize a religious community further become objectified in heightened material configurations, which she deems "sensational." Meyer (2009, 13) argues that such sensational forms are transmitted and shared, that they bind believers together with their idea of the divine, and help create religious practitioners as moral subjects. For members of the Cherubim and Seraphim Church, their aesthetics of persuasion was wrapped up in singing the same song, and music was the key sensational form through which religious ideas were made real and immediate and religious experiences made possible and effective at changing people's lives for the better.

I examine musical and ritual performance in the context of Cherubim and Seraphim worship in this book. Through ethnographic and historical analysis, I demonstrate that songs are media through which religious experiences and beliefs were materialized and made available to church members. In this way, church members were bound to each other and to a set of moral ideals as articulated via church authority through the means of aestheticized sensational forms. At the same time, these aesthetic forms connected the lessons and ideals of Yoruba Christian practice to church members' understanding of their everyday lives, thus allowing them to achieve their ideals in the world. Through this analysis I show how via musical participation church members articulated and embodied the moral and ethical prescriptions and attitudes necessary to be "a good Christian."

In the chapters that follow, I provide a detailed ethnographic analysis of the relationships between musical sound, the texts produced in and about music, and the social contexts for musical performance, in order to understand precisely how music was seen as an efficacious practice for church members. This analysis entails more than a consideration of musical lyrics and the visual images associated with music, but also requires attention to the details of musical form and practice, the dynamics of performance, and the context within which performance occurred. Music is thus understood as a specific kind of semiotic form—as a tool for enacting change in and on the world. I attend to the particularities of music by exploring the theories about musical practice that shaped Cherubim and Seraphim understandings of the efficacious power of music and how these musical ideologies were put into practice by church members in their daily lives.

The focus on the musical practices of this particular Yoruba Christian community and their religious experiences in this book builds on anthropological and ethnomusicological studies which place sound at the center of how religious communities constitute themselves: from Charles Hirschkind's (2006) analysis of an "ethical soundscape" of Islamic cassette sermons in Egypt, whose listeners cultivate particular modes of hearing that enable them to acquire religious knowledge and sensibilities in accordance with a changing political context; to the comparative insights Judith Becker (2004) offers into the ways in which participants in religious ritual use music to profoundly manipulate sensory stimuli in order to bring the presence of unseen forces into being via practices of trancing and spirit possession.

Conceiving of music as a sensational form through which religious communities are produced and religious ideas made tangible also speaks to issues of ethics and morality. A main theme in the anthropological study of religion concerns the importance of understanding how notions of morality organize social life (Durkheim 1995; Fassin 2008; Lambek 2000; Robbins 2004). The aesthetics of persuasion enacted via singing together serves to connect people forcefully to their moral ideals. At the same time, the emotional and affective experiences that emerge out of participation in the sensational forms of religious worship allow for contingent and contextual understandings of how moral rules are applicable to particular instances of lived reality. In many ways, this formulation echoes the emphasis in the anthropological study of ritual on the way in which systemic ethical norms are reproduced within stereotypic and stylized cultural practices (Comaroff 1985; Fernandez 1986; Lambek 2010; Turner 1967, 1969)

With codes of conduct perhaps more accurately reframed as the *coding of conduct*, ethics become less exclusively confined to the domain of sociopolitical reproduction. Instead, issues of performance, skill, and creativity become salient, as morality is no longer simply conformity to prevailing norms but instead hinges on how well one understands one's commitments, obligations, aims, and ambitions as well as how well one prioritizes and acts on them in ever-unfolding relationships and circumstances. As Lambek (2000, 315) argues, "morality cannot be simply an act of commission or an acceptance of obligation but includes the reasoning behind choosing to do so and the reasoning that determines how to balance one's multiple and possibly conflicting commitments." Such an orientation invites us to consider how people gain access to the resources on which such moral reasoning is based; to seek out moments when and where the "ought" and the "is" are brought together and assessments made of the overlaps or gaps between them; to inquire into what people then do to or with themselves and others on the basis of such assessments; and, finally, to be attentive to the ways in which these processes are continuous, requiring ongoing commitments to the evaluation of the self and others, rather than an isolated and stagnant achievement of virtue.

Musical performance is a key medium through which moral ideals and ethical deliberations are articulated and made relevant to current situations. Some analysts have emphasized the conventional nature of musical performance and extended it to ritual participation more generally—most famously Maurice Bloch (1974) who argued that the requirements of singing the same song limit the possibility for debate and the emergence of alternate ideas—whereas others emphasize the procedural, performative nature of musical and ritual performance

(Askew 2002; Bell 1992; Drewal 1992; Tambiah 1981). Rather than privileging either the structuring, persuasive force of musical performance or its creative and potentially transformative aspects, my analysis of how members of the Ayọ̀ ni o Church attempted to sing the same song captures how ritual is both conservative and critical (Apter 1992; Basso 1985; Turner 1967). Ritualized musical performance does this through its ability to transcend space and time, by creating a separate space outside of the everyday world, via aesthetic forms and practices that engage people at emotional and bodily levels. Indeed, even the adoption of conventional moral ideals, such as the emphasis on seniority or hard work in Cherubim and Seraphim practice, may itself be understood as an agentive, creative act in a moment such as the neoliberal transformation of Nigeria in which the people I write about in this book found themselves.

Understood in this way, then, religious performances in the Ayọ̀ ni o Church—particularly affective, compelling, sensational musical performances—were one of the key media in which the "ought" of Yoruba Christianity and the "is" of contemporary Nigerian realities were brought together. Worked out in rehearsal, church members "sang the same song" in order to "produce the same mind." As I describe in more detail in chapter 4, choir members were asked to consider what the message of the song to be sung in church on a given Sunday meant at that moment. Each performance thus reproduced practice according to a recognizable norm, and yet was calibrated to the moment of the performance. Through such disciplined work choir members rehearsed the necessary actions that made singing together able to summon correct emotional and ethical actions that constituted religious experience (Csordas 1997; Luhrmann 2012). In this way, by singing together church members were inspired to think about the "ought" and to consider the "is"—themselves and their lives—in relation to it. The aesthetics that bound together members of Cherubim and Seraphim churches were thus constitutive of the very processes of ethical work that served as the basis on which moral actions in the world could proceed.

The examples discussed here suggest that this ongoing formation of ethical selves is always social, involving others as exemplars and teachers. Figures of religious authority—particularly church elders, prophets and prophetesses, and those understood to have other spiritual gifts—played an important role in shaping ethical discourses and orienting church members toward them through disciplinary practices. As already noted, music was seen as capable of activating divine power and enacting moral authority. Thus music was an especially potent means by which the members of the church modeled a form of social interaction that articulated their vision of how society should be organized. In the church choir the charismatic authority of the choirmaster served to structure and organize the modes through which musical practice shaped an ethical Christian self within this ideal of moral community. While authority figures served to discipline and socialize church members toward ethical orientations, such attitudes and dispositions were also understood to be intersubjective, arising out of interactions through which people were inspired, encouraged, and empowered through their relationships to and reliance on others.

The perceived efficacy of church worship was linked to the agency of church members and their ability to act in the world. Evidence of efficacy was apparent through a change in one's material circumstances, such as promotion at work, passing an exam, or conceiving a child. Àlàáfíà, the general state of well-being that encompasses health, happiness, wealth, power, and prestige was evidence of success. Salvation (ìgbàlà) thus promised both this-worldly and otherworldly gains. One achieved eternal life in heaven as well as success in this world. Participation in worship also produced a change of mood. This too was àlàáfíà, not just a state but also a feeling. In this way worship provided church members with a new way of seeing the world. This new way of seeing the world was both evidence of the efficacy of church worship, and part of what made one effective in achieving àlàáfíà. This dynamic was crucial to the making the ethical self of Cherubim and Seraphim subjects via musical practices.

Underlying church members' certainty in the morality of their worship practices was the understanding that there were other, immoral means of being efficacious in the world. These include what were seen as the corrupt practices of politicians, who siphoned money from state coffers to benefit themselves and their associates. These unethical ways of being effective in the world also included criminal practices such as armed robbery, or the use of magic and witchcraft to acquire prosperity, success, or health (see Smith 2007). This critique of immoral ways of achieving wealth and happiness was also frequently directed against the perceived excesses and corruption of certain pastors of prominent Christian churches, especially those who were seen as using the church to support their own luxurious lifestyles. Such Christian leaders also came under suspicion of misleading their followers and using church monies for their own personal gains; their corrupt practices evidenced by their purchase of private jets or luxury cars.[1] From the point of view of church members—and of most Nigerians—these practices were unethical and immoral, and did not lead toward àlàáfíà. Instead, they led to a false sense of happiness, to a facade of joy that could not last. Furthermore, unethical and immoral actions, even though efficacious in the short term, resulted in serious trouble for those who practiced them—the loss of one's job, family, and happiness.

Corrupt and unethical practices were not about salvation as articulated by Christians, but about ensuring material happiness on an individual level, and this is why they were an inadequate and non-efficacious means of ensuring àlàáfíà. This is part of what the choir sang about on their first album (discussed in chapter 3), and was a theme emphasized in sermons and Bible study sessions:

The way of salvation is so sweet
Come and taste it, it is as sweet as honey
Christ gave it to us free of charge
We shall not purchase it with money

Religion and Mediation

An analytic focus on mediation allows us to better understand how religion and music enabled church members to make authoritative claims about morality and experience in the context of Nigeria's transition to democracy and economic liberalization. An anthropological conception of religious mediation refers to the practices through which religious communities create meaningful connections between cosmological principles, moral values, and social realities (Engelke 2007; Keane 2007). Thus, a key conceptual focus of the book is organized around questions of mediation, as they analytically shape a model of cultural negotiation and transformation. I argue that a focus on material, musical, and religious processes of mediation is one way of making analytically visible the linkages between individuals, forms of material culture (including songs, rhythms, technologies, religious texts, and clothing), and forms of disembodied agency (including God, the Holy Spirit, religious authority, and political economy).

In employing this framework, I bring together literatures concerned with the semiotic analysis of media forms (Boyer 2007; Fox 2004; Mazzarella 2004), religious processes of mediation (Meyer 2004a, 2006), and the mediatization of African cultures (Larkin 2008; Schulz 2012; Spitulnik 1993, 1998) to understand how these processes of mediation make church worship efficacious. Media may be understood to refer to a variety of objects and practices, from electronic forms of mass media, to religious symbols, sounds, or musical styles. These objects and practices index modes of sociality. Mediation is a process that creates meaningful links between these various media, forms of social organization, and cultural meanings. William Mazzarella notes that "'mediation' is a name that we might give to the processes by which a given social dispensation produces and reproduces itself in and through a particular set of media" (2004, 346), a description that references the semiotic definition of mediation as "any process in which two elements are brought into articulation by means of or through the intervention of some third element that serves as the vehicle or medium of communication" (Parmentier 1994, 24).

As a general cultural process, mediation is thus a way in which social practices are constituted by virtue of their relationship to cultural forms; in other words, "the discursive production of conceptual and intuitive links between domains of social experience" (Fox 2004, 346). This sense of mediation is particularly helpful for understanding how music, as a cultural form that is experienced in real time through performing or listening, can help create linkages between moral values, historical events, and everyday experience. The use of affective musical techniques (including rhythm, musical form, and lyrics) helps to bring certain cultural values and ideas into focus and thus enables people to connect their everyday practices to them.

This is of particular interest for the study of music in the context of religious practice as it helps to foreground how the mediated nature of religion is often erased and experienced by practitioners as immediate. As many scholars who examine practices of mediation in religious contexts have noted, religious mediations tend to take on a reality of their own (Eisenlohr 2007; Engelke 2007; Meyer 2006, 2011; Schulz 2006). Music is key to both the mediation of individuals and religious ideas as well as to the erasure of the mediating nature of these formations so that they seem immediate. For example, the Cherubim and Seraphim understood music, and especially singing, to be capable of enhancing the spiritual power of the performer, producing a unified body of worshippers, and having the capacity to effect material changes in the world. In addition to opening up communication between heaven and earth in order to bring down God's power on earth, the choir's musical performance was also used to create a relationship between that power and the congregation.

In a review article on media and globalization, Mazzarella identifies nodes of mediation as "the sites at which the compulsions of institutional determination and the rich, volatile play of sense come into always provisional alignment in the service of (and always, in part, against the grain of) a vast range of social projects" (2004, 352). He suggests that attending to such nodes enables anthropologists to make sense of the cultural implications of social dynamics without relying on essentialized notions of culture or on attempts to describe them in relation to various overdetermining processes (such as modernization or globalization). Seen in this light, musical performances in the context of Cherubim and Seraphim worship can be understood as a node of mediation that brought together musical aesthetics, affective experiences, ethical discourses, moral modes of practice, and conceptions of spiritual efficacy that led to political action. These practices enabled members of the Ayọ̀ ni o Church to remake and act on their possibilities for success and happiness in contemporary Nigeria.

Singing in the City

The majority of this book is based on ethnographic research conducted since 2002 with members of the Cherubim and Seraphim Ayọ̀ ni o Church in the city of Lagos, Nigeria. With a population that numbers between 17,000,000 and 20,000,000 people and growing, Lagos is the largest city in Nigeria, and one of the largest cities in the world (Campbell 2012; Rosenthal 2012). The city is made up of a number of islands located in a coastal lagoon along the Atlantic Ocean, as well as expansive urban sprawl on the mainland, which extends more than twenty-five miles northwest of Lagos Island. The majority of the population of Lagos lives on the mainland. Lagos is the commercial and economic center of Nigeria, due largely to the presence of Nigeria's primary seaport through which foreign goods are imported and domestic products—mainly petroleum—are exported. Most financial institutions and major corporations, local and foreign, are located in the city as well. Finally, the city is a major site for the production of cultural media, particularly music, television, film, and publishing.

Since the beginning of the twentieth century, the population of Lagos expanded rapidly through rural-urban migration from across Nigeria and other parts of West Africa. Because of this, the city is characterized by vast ethnic diversity. Indeed, Lagos is one of the most diverse cities in Nigeria and includes ethnic groups from all over the country. However, because it is located in the Yoruba-dominated southwest region of the country, members of the Yoruba ethnic group make up the majority of the population, and Yoruba and English constitute the two languages most often heard in the city. The influx of migrants into Lagos has also contributed to urban crowding and exacerbated economic inequality. As such, the city includes a variety of neighborhoods, from the densely populated, rough-and-tumble district of Ajegunle, to the famous floating slum of Makoko, to exclusive communities featuring shopping malls and gated compounds in areas such as Victoria Island, Lekki, and Ikeja.

The frenzied nature of life in Lagos, often commented on by residents and visitors, requires that one cultivate a particular way of being in the city. Next to impossible traffic conditions and unequal access to sanitary living conditions exacerbates the everyday contingencies that characterize life in Lagos. At the same time, this urban milieu is a key site for the reassertion of vital community values. "Lagos, city of the wise. If you go there, watch out," the lines of a popular song warn, "If you stay in Lagos and are not wise, you will never be wise for the rest of your life."[2] These lyrics serve as a warning about the dangers of Lagos, and the wisdom necessary to navigate the city; if one does not acquire such wisdom, the song suggests, one is doomed to a life of suffering at best, and an early death at worst. At the same time Lagos is called the city that is elastic and changing. Thus, Lagos is understood by its residents as necessitating both wisdom and flexibility in order to make one's life there.

For many residents of Lagos religion is a chief mode of navigating the city and creating connections with others. Religious belonging helps to provide stability in the chaos that characterizes everyday life. Christianity, Islam, and indigenous religions coexist with more secular institutions and social formations and create both alliances and tensions between neighbors and strangers around the city. In most areas of the city adherents of different religious communities live among one another. Every neighborhood is peppered with a variety of religious institutions, from large churches and mosques that can accommodate hundreds, if not

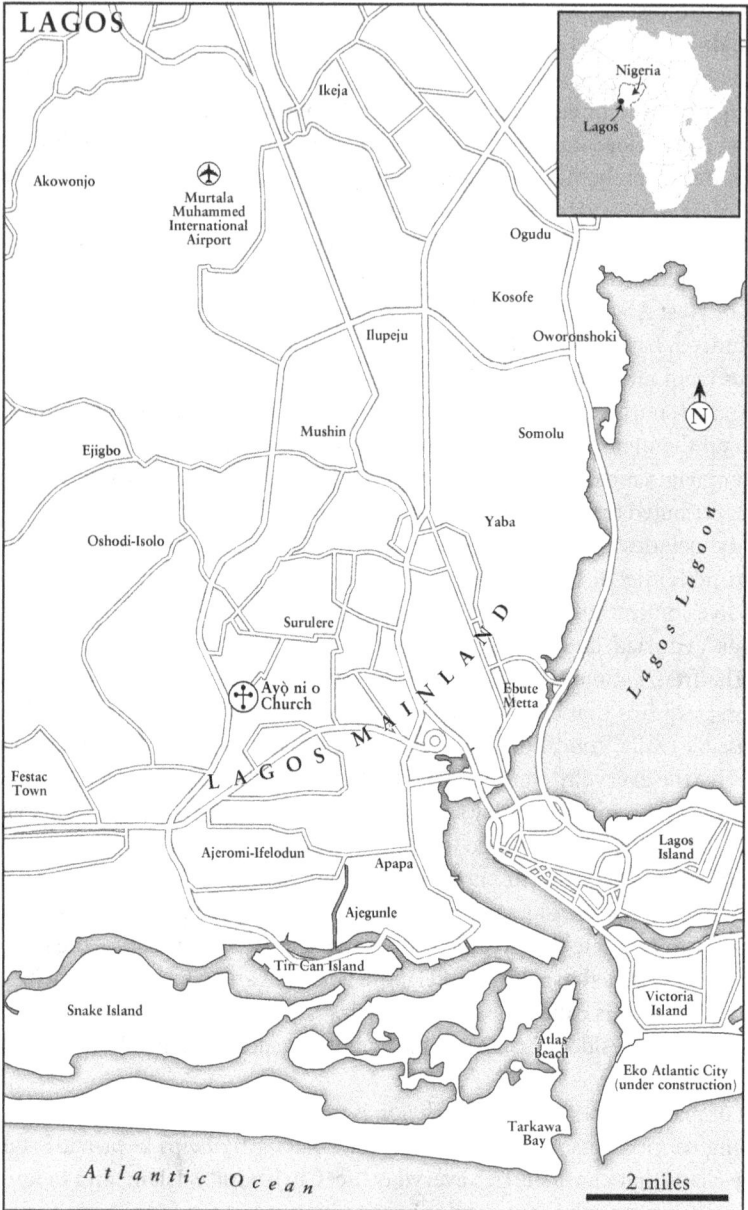

Map of Lagos showing location of Ayọ̀ ni o Church

thousands, of worshippers, to smaller, storefront locations and impromptu spaces where intimate prayer groups meet. Sound is a key medium through which these religious groups make their presence known in a variety of locales and differentiate themselves from one another. Loudspeakers on churches and mosques call adherents to prayer and to worship, speakers outside of market stalls alternate between the latest gospel recording or a recent recording of a sermon from a prominent Muslim imam, and televisions and radios broadcast religious programs throughout the day. In this way, religious sounds circulate via mass media and the movement of people through the city (see Brennan 2015).

A variety of Christian denominations have emerged and expanded to serve Lagos's growing population both historically and more recently. These range from conventional Catholic, Anglican, Methodist, and Baptist churches that date back to the arrival of European and American missionary societies in southwest Nigeria, to the boisterous, upstart Pentecostal congregations that dominated Christian public life in Nigeria during the time of my research (see Marshall 2009; Ukah 2008; Wariboko 2014). Most of these Pentecostal churches emerged in the 1980s and have become a prominent part of Yoruba Christian life in Lagos (Ojo 2006). These churches use billboards and other forms of media to advertise their worship services to Christians all over the city (Marshall 2009; Ukah 2008). The larger Pentecostal congregations also regularly hold massive, open-air revival services that attract thousands of worshippers to a variety of locations in the city such as stadiums, concert halls, and at retreat centers located just outside of the city along the express road.

The Cherubim and Seraphim churches that are discussed in this book belong to a category of churches known among Yoruba Christians as Aladura churches. Aladura refers to Yoruba Christian denominations that broke away from mission churches in the first half of the twentieth century to establish separate congregations with distinct doctrines and practices. As described in more detail in chapter 2, Cherubim and Seraphim churches first appeared in Lagos during the 1920s in response to demands for greater autonomy in church leadership on the part of Yoruba Christian converts, as well as a desire for Christian practice to serve the immediate spiritual and material needs of church members living in a world that was rapidly changing due to colonialism, urban migration and expansion, and the transformation of daily life in the early twentieth century (Omoyajowo 1983; Peel 1968, 2000). Early in their history, Cherubim and Seraphim churches were subject to fragmentation along issues of leadership, doctrinal orientation, and worship practices. For this reason a number of Cherubim and Seraphim denominations exist in Lagos, including the Cherubim and Seraphim Society, the Eternal and Sacred Order of Cherubim and Seraphim, and the Cherubim and Seraphim Church Movement. It is to the latter denomination that the Ayọ̀ ni o Church belongs.

The majority of the examples discussed in this book are based on ethnographic research with a large branch of the Cherubim and Seraphim Church Movement in Lagos frequently referred to as the "Ayọ̀ ni o Church." This name is taken from a greeting used among church members: "Ayọ̀ ni o!" (lit. "It is joy!"). The Ayọ̀ ni o Church is one of the largest Cherubim and Seraphim churches in Nigeria, and during the time of my research approximately 5,000 people attended worship services there each Sunday. The church was well known by most residents in the city, due not only to its size but also because of the renown of its leader at the time, Prophet Gabriel O. Fakeye. Fakeye, who died in February 2015, was an important public religious figure known in Nigeria for his spiritual healing abilities. However, the Ayọ̀ ni o Church was also renowned among Yoruba Christians of all denominations for the musical offerings of its choir, popularized through recordings and music videos. Many people I spoke with about my research identified the Ayọ̀ ni o Church with Cherubim and Seraphim music.

The Ayọ̀ ni o Church is located on the Lagos mainland in a large compound off the Apapa-Oshodi Express Road, a busy four-lane divided highway that links Apapa, Lagos's main commercial port, to the city and the rest of southwestern Nigeria. In the other direction the road connects to the Badagry Expressway leading to the Benin Republic. The area surrounding the church is dotted with a variety of industrial and commercial operations, including a soft drink plant, a large commercial bakery, and a massive construction yard. In addition to the Ayọ̀ ni o Church compound, a few Pentecostal mega-churches have set up places of worship in between the commercial endeavors along the road. During the week, the express road is filled with motortrucks and other commercial vehicles. Sunday mornings however, most commercial traffic is replaced with minivan busses and private cars carrying churchgoers to their worship services. Automobile traffic enters the church compound through the front gate located on the expressway service road, and footpaths connect the rear of the compound to the densely populated middle-class suburb of Surulere. Waves of worshippers enter the compound via these paths, and make their way to one of the buildings in the compound where worship takes place: the Main Church, the Youth Chapel, the Disciples of Christ Fellowship, the English Chapel, or Sunday school for the children of church members.

The Main Church is the primary worship hall and the oldest worship space in the compound, where adult church members attend worship services each Sunday. Most of my research activities focused on the Main Church where I was fortunate to be invited to join the choir even though I was not a church member. Under the name "Seraph Voices" the Main Church choir was responsible for the majority of the commercial musical recordings and videos made by the church. Another important site within the church compound was the Youth Chapel, a worship space for unmarried church members between the ages of eighteen and thirty. The youth were encouraged to start their own fellowship in the mid-1990s, in response to what church elders saw as a threatening loss of young members to Pentecostal congregations. One of the reasons that many church members gave to account for this need for a separate space for youth had to do with the different spiritual needs of young people as well as the youth's desire for greater autonomy in the church. These needs were often described in terms of different worship practices, including music. The Youth Chapel has its own choir, puts on its own revival services that feature large-scale musical productions, and even has recorded an album of its own. There was also an English Chapel in the Ayọ̀ ni o compound, featuring services performed primarily in English, in which a small fellowship met each Sunday. In 2005, a new group, the Disciples of Christ, was added to those who worshipped in the compound. The Disciples of Christ was created to appeal to churchgoers who were too old to attend the Youth Chapel but who felt out of place in the Main Church. All of these groups considered themselves to be a part of the Surulere branch of the Ayọ̀ ni o Church, even though they held separate and simultaneous worship services.

In addition to the development of the Disciples of Christ, the Youth Chapel and the English Chapel, groups known as *egbẹ́* were part of the organization of the church. Ẹgbẹ́ is the Yoruba word for a club, society, or association and can be used for any grouping of people outside of kinship relations: professional, regional, age mates, and so on. Although the word "band" is used by many Yoruba to translate ẹgbẹ́ into English, it is important to note that it is used in the sense of "band of brothers" rather than a musical group. Cherubim and Seraphim churches are divided into a number of ẹgbẹ́ for the purposes of organization and spirituality. The ẹgbẹ́ system creates subsets of the congregation. This organization of the large congregation into smaller groupings created a structure of responsibility and obligation among church members that could be enforced through personal contacts. Churchgoers conceived of belonging to a particular ẹgbẹ́ as a spiritual connection to other church members because membership was determined by a spiritual directive (chapter 8 discusses the ẹgbẹ́ system and their worship practices in more detail).

In addition to worship spaces and church offices, the compound also included a number of facilities such as a canteen, which prepared and served fresh meals of jollof rice, stew, and pounded yam, and a kiosk that sold soft drinks and snacks such as meat pies and popcorn. To the right of the entrance to the compound was a small shack selling Bibles, hymnals, lectionaries, and other popular Christian publications, some of them written by elders in the church. Another shop in the church compound sold plastic water bottles that people could fill at a tap in the compound and then pray into during church service to bless it, small bottles of olive oil for use in anointing, fringed sashes used to tie one's prayer gown at the waist, handkerchiefs, and a selection of packaged biscuits and other sweets. Behind the main worship hall was a long narrow building housing the church's offices, including the secretary's office, the public affairs officer, the General Leader's suite, and the offices of other church elders. Low structures around the circumference of the main worship hall housed small chapels used by different sections of the congregation. Finally, a series of buildings at the back of the compound made up the church's educational facilities and included a theological seminary to train pastors and prophets, as well as a primary school.

With its focus on a large independent Christian congregation such as the Ayọ̀ ni o Church, this book adds historical and analytic specificity to recent ethnographic accounts of media use by religious groups in contemporary African contexts. In particular, there are a number of parallels between the examples discussed in this book and the use of media by neo-Pentecostal, or born-again, churches in Africa since 1990. In recent anthropological studies (Gifford 2004; Hackett 1998; Marshall 2009; Marshall-Fratani 1998; Meyer 2004b, 2006; Ukah 2003), scholars have discussed how neo-Pentecostal churches in Ghana and Nigeria use mass media to circulate, promote, and localize ideas related to political and economic globalization in an ever-widening public sphere. However, this link between Pentecostalism and the global, as opposed to the local, is also found in Pentecostal discourses that characterize how Pentecostalism differs from other forms of Christianity in West Africa. Pentecostals often portray earlier forms of Christianity, such as those practiced in the Cherubim and Seraphim churches that I focus on in this book as potentially evil, demonic, occultic, or spiritualistic, and they speak of the dangerous and "un-Christian" practices of those who attend such churches.

A focus on how religious practitioners in Nigeria from different denominations or congregations draw various forms of mediation together and make them articulate contemporary realities might provide scholars with better analytic purchase on the use of media by a variety of religious groups. Although membership in Cherubim and Seraphim churches has declined in the past decade, not everyone has left to join Pentecostal churches. And although Pentecostals are the predominant users of media, they are not the only religious groups to make use of it. To understand the reasons for this, as well as the complexity of religion in Nigeria's public sphere, scholars must look at the interactions between different churches and examine the shifts in church membership and Christian practices in Nigeria in relation to each other. My analysis suggests that one way of making sense of the complexity of these interactions is to pay attention to the particular media forms used by religious groups and the ways in which those forms make connections between particular aspects of social and cultural life (see Meyer 2004a). An analysis that explores how various forms of mediation are drawn together in particular contexts will help scholars better understand the way in which people use religion to act on and make sense of their lives and to construct identity and moral community. Investigating these questions is relevant not only for study of

Christianity in Africa but also for understanding the relationships between religion, culture, and media, more generally.

The Plan of the Book

This book examines the musical media and worship practices through which members of a specific Yoruba church in Nigeria articulated and embodied the moral prescriptions and attitudes necessary to be a good Christian. These embodied practices enabled church members to transform the ethical message elaborated by religious authority—enshrined in history, texts, and people—into ritual practice. Effective ritual practice brought the space of the church closer to heaven and produced a connection that gave church members access to the spiritual power of God through the Holy Spirit, thus allowing them to make a tangible change in their everyday lives and circumstances. In doing so the book unpacks exactly how "singing the same song" achieved the moral and ethical ends of a large group of Yoruba Christians in Lagos, Nigeria.

The chapters in this book explore how members of Cherubim and Seraphim churches used musical and religious media such as hymn books (chapter 2), cassette tapes and other recordings (chapters 3 and 4), and clothing and architectural space (chapter 5) to reproduce themselves as Christian subjects. These materials mediated religious experiences for church members, connecting people to God, to church history, and to each other. At the same time, religious and musical media provided a means through which church members developed an ethical self that enabled them to interpret and apply the lessons learned through embodied and affective participation in church worship to issues and situations that they faced in their own lives. The practices through which church members cultivated such moral and ethical dispositions, which included attending choir rehearsals and Bible study sessions, are discussed in chapters 6, 7, and 8.

Music served as a highly stylized and aesthetic participatory form, one that allowed church members to create "the right kind of worship." Performing music during church worship was an important means through which connections between heaven and earth, between humans and God, and among members of the congregation were produced. Church members understood music to be capable of enhancing the spiritual power of the singer and of producing a unified body of worshippers. Musical performance in the context of worship was understood to have the capacity to effect material changes in the world. This was usually evidenced by the visible or audible presence of the Holy Spirit during musical portions of church worship.

During a break in choir practice one evening, a member of the choir explained why he thought music was central to the church: "Most members of this church, if you have the privilege to ask them why they decided to join this fold, they will inform you that the initial and first thing that made them to be a member is music before salvation." While emphasizing the importance of music, his statement also revealed that the place of music in Cherubim and Seraphim conceptions of their Christian practice is not one that is taken for granted. The statement acknowledges the way in which music is able to engage church members and to connect them to the church community. However, the latter part of this statement also provokes a concern that engagement with the music leads people away from the central purpose of Christian practice, salvation. Thus, the challenge becomes how to move people from their initial attraction to the music and the emotional responses it provokes, to ensuring that church members understand and correctly enact main elements of Christian doctrine, such as salvation. Throughout this book, I look at how various musical media, from hymn books to cassette tapes, from the repetition of choir rehearsal to the stereotypicity of ritual performance, are used by the Cherubim and Seraphim to reproduce themselves as properly Christian subjects. I do so in order to understand how exactly engagement with music leads to salvation. Or, to put it another way, how do church members' affective connections to music produce the ethical practice of Yoruba Christianity?

Notes

1. These suspicions are based both on ambiguous rumors that circulated in Nigerian popular culture about pastors taking advantage of their leadership positions to exploit their followers as well as on high-profile stories of Christian leaders who have been caught in scandalous situations. For example, in 2014 Ayo Oritsejafor, the president of the Christian Association of Nigeria, was accused of transporting more than US$9,000,000 from Nigeria to South Africa for the purpose of acquiring weapons. For more on this controversy, see Sam Oakford, "Pentecostal Pastors in Nigeria Are Rolling in Money—and Political Power," Vice News, October 17, 2014, https://news.vice.com/article/pentecostal-pastors-in-nigeria-are-rolling-in-money-and-political-power.

2. From the song "Eko Akete" as sung by the highlife musician Fatai Rolling Dollar. The lyrics are an adaptation of Yoruba praise poetry for Lagos.

2 Onward Christian Soldiers

The songs of the Alàdúrà, which match the emotionalism of their worship—
again a distinctly African element—are not the compositions of Europeans
and Americans, nor are they sung to alien tunes. They are evocative,
sometimes spontaneous compositions.

—E. A. Ayandele, "The Aladura among the Yoruba"

Amidst the darkness there shone a great light
Among the Seraphim
Michael is the Captain of this Band
He will guide us from this day

—Cherubim and Seraphim Hymn #727

A NUMBER OF miraculous events are attributed to Moses Orimolade, the founder
of the religious movement that would become the Cherubim and Seraphim. One
in particular speaks to the way in which music and musical performance was to
become central to Cherubim and Seraphim worship practices: near the turn of
the nineteenth century, the pastor at St. Stephen's Anglican Church in Orimolade's hometown saw a strange light in the church building and heard a sound
"like the voices of about a hundred people" singing (Famodimu 1990, 31). When
the pastor investigated the source of the light and the music, to his surprise he
discovered the young boy Orimolade sitting alone on the floor of the church bathed
in "a kind of bright phosphorescent illumination" and "singing as though he
were a whole choir" (Omoyajowo 1982, 120). The missionary, who had "never heard
any melodious song like this before" (Famodimu 1990, 31) was so moved by this
performance that he asked Orimolade to teach his "spiritual songs" to the other
Christians in Ikare. However, unlike the pastor, the Christian converts in Ikare
were not transfixed by Orimolade's song. As Famodimu writes, "Orimolade sang
his song but they were not interested. The song was not as melodious as the pastor
had described to them. They did not understand and even care to know the wording
and the meaning of the words. The people despised the singer and his song"
(1990: 32).

This interaction between the young Orimolade, the Anglican missionary, and
the Christian townspeople of Ikare places music at the center of the negotiation

through which the Yoruba actively refashioned both themselves and Christianity in the Nigerian colonial context (Peel 2000). At stake was the construction of a subjectivity that was both Yoruba and Christian and that provided Yoruba Christians with a means of acting in a world that was changing around them. Conversion to Christianity certainly represented one of the ways in which many Yoruba individuals attempted to both remake and redefine their community in order to make sense of these changes. However, the inability of Orimolade's townspeople to recognize the beauty and message of his song suggests that much cultural and social work remained to be completed before Orimolade's vision of Christianity could be seen as a valid model for Yoruba identity and community formation.

The song that Orimolade was singing when discovered by the pastor of Ikare's Anglican church has been made a permanent part of Cherubim and Seraphim historical memory through its inclusion in Cherubim and Seraphim hymnal. One biographer claimed that Orimolade wrote it "from the very moment of his conversion to Christianity" and that "it became the evangelical song of Saint Moses Orimolade Tunolase whenever he went, singing it alongside his gospel messages" (Atansuyi 1988, 23–24). The lyrics appear in the hymnal as Hymn #807, with the caption that it is the "Traditional Song of Holy Cherubim and Seraphim Founded by our father Moses Orimolade":

> Up above the River Jordan
> I am called, I am called
> By my beloved ones that have gone, that have gone
> I want to enter into the house of glory with them
> We shall meet and there will be no more parting forever
> Come home, come to the home of love.
> The book of Jesus told me that
> Angels carry me to know the place of joy
> And Jesus carries me in.

It is impossible to know exactly what this song might have sounded like when Orimolade sang it alone in the church that evening. However, it is worth noting that most narratives of this event emphasize the song's compelling melody as well as the implied presence of more than one voice singing. Such descriptions emphasize a sound distinct from religious musical styles that would most likely have been heard in Ikare at that time. Yoruba religious music, particularly songs sung in the context of òrìṣà worship (part of Yoruba indigenous religion), tended to take the form of poetic chants performed to a free rhythm and often accompanied by drumming (Euba 1967).

Additional musical elements may be deduced both from an analysis of the form and content of the lyrics themselves, as well as from how this song is performed in the present. Formally, Orimolade's song is unlike that of European and American Christian hymns, which for the most part follow a strophic, or verse-refrain, pattern. By contrast, "Up above the River Jordan" is sung in a non-strophic, continuous format. In this way the song differs from most of the other hymns in the church's hymnal, which consist of translations of European or American hymns, newly composed lyrics set to European or American hymn melodies, or hymns that consist of both newly composed lyrics and melodies that nevertheless follow European or American melodic, harmonic, and formal conventions.

The song features poetic lyrics that make allusions to main Christian symbols. In particular, the River Jordan was where Jesus was baptized by John the Baptist, which emphasizes the importance of baptism and rebirth in Orimolade's conception of Christianity. Furthermore, the lyrics articulate a Christian cosmological conception of heaven ("the house of glory," "angels carry me to know the place of joy") that is emphasized in Cherubim and Seraphim worship practices, which use song and dance to emulate angels worshipping in heaven before the throne of God. The line referring to the "beloved ones that have gone" was alternately interpreted by contemporary church members that I spoke with as referring both to biblical prophets but also to deceased Cherubim and Seraphim prophets, fusing the history of the Cherubim and Seraphim churches to a wider biblical Christian history.[1] Finally, the lyrics emphasize the centrality of the Bible—the book of Jesus—as a source of religious authority, one that Orimolade was said to have mastered even though he was unable to read and write.

Although the song is supposed to be sung annually on the anniversary of the founding of the Cherubim and Seraphim, I have heard it performed only once by a Cherubim and Seraphim congregation, in August 2002, at a small church in Ibadan during the anniversary service that celebrated the founding of that particular church.[2] The choir performed this song after a long sermon in which the pastor narrated the history of their church in relation to the Cherubim and Seraphim as a whole. He concluded the sermon by noting that the Cherubim and Seraphim were blessed because they followed in the example of Moses Orimolade. It was with this mention of the founder of the Cherubim and Seraphim that he called on the choir to sing the hymn.

The group's performance provided some clues as to how Orimolade and his music were understood by contemporary church members. It also articulated a historical sense of Cherubim and Seraphim musical practice. Performing "Up above the River Jordan" required the use of only certain instruments. Instruments such as organ, electric guitars, trumpets, and drums, which had been used during most of the other musical performances that day, were silent. Instead only a single long-handled bell accompanied the singers. The person holding the bell struck the clapper on the side of the bell, creating a rhythmic timeline pattern underneath the singing. The rest of the congregation clapped their hands in unison with the bell, though some members improvised their own rhythms that coordinated with that played on the bell.

It was clear from the stilted nature of the performance that this hymn was not often sung during church worship, and was certainly not rehearsed to be sung that day but rather had been spontaneously called for by the pastor as part of his lesson. Most people followed the lyrics closely in their hymnals. However, it provoked a great deal of emotion from many in the church, some of whom burst into tears while singing. Others sang with their faces turned toward the ceiling of the church, looking down only to read the next line from the hymnal.

When I asked the pastor afterward why the choir did not use the organ or guitars when they performed Orimolade's hymn, he replied that it would not be appropriate to do so, given that Orimolade himself did not need any instruments in order to sing his message. He explained the significance of the hymn to me by reciting the story of Orimolade singing it in the church in his hometown, and then told me that it was important for everyone in the church to know about it, because otherwise the memory would be lost. He explained, "There is a value in our past that we must hold on to. Our fathers had a certain kind of power. They could heal sick people, make women fertile, all kinds of things. We remember the past, so that we too can access that power. This is what Orimolade saw, and why he carried the Christian message to the Yoruba people." The pastor told me that he would make sure that all members of the church could sing the song, "just as it was sung in Orimolade's time," so that what he saw as the efficacy of Cherubim and Seraphim Christianity—its ability to heal and to ensure people would have a good life—would continue to be passed on.

This chapter explores the history of the Cherubim and Seraphim churches with an emphasis on the development of its musical repertoire of hymns. Hymns served as a repository of history for church members, and hymn performance was a way of bringing the past into the present as part of religious practice (see Muller 1999). Rather than seeing the past as backward or as the source for the contemporary moral breakdown of Nigerian society as many Pentecostal churches did (Marshall 2009; Ojo 2006; see also Meyer 1998), the Cherubim and Seraphim resuscitated the past, and integrated what they understood to be powerful and efficacious about Yoruba history into their version of Christianity. In this way, most members of the Ayọ ni o Church saw themselves as practicing a form of Christianity that was particularly suited to their needs; in other words they saw themselves as both Yoruba and Christian at the same time.

Hymns and related media served to both objectify and circulate a form of historical consciousness central to Cherubim and Seraphim ways of remembering the past and drawing on it in the present. Thus the history of the church was accessed through a variety of media forms and these forms shaped religious practices as well as the interpretation of such practices as originating in the past. Songs, hymnbooks, printed materials, and other documents narrating the history of the church or biographies of church founders all served to objectify the past for church members. These versions of the past entered into Cherubim and Seraphim worship when sung, performed, or discussed in sermons. Such performances entailed both a recreation of history as well as a reinterpretation of it in relation to present circumstances. Thus contemporary events could be interpreted in light of past events, from the understanding of how large-scale national politics would affect members of the church, to how everyday choices and decisions made by church members should be made through reference to the past. In this way church history and the lives of the founders of the Cherubim and Seraphim served as an ethical framework within which church members could model their own lives. This too was accessed via musical media when songs known to have been sung in the past were performed in the present.

Music is a key medium through which to examine such processes of historical memory and performance (see Emoff 2002). I bring together historical and ethnographic research on musical practices in the Ayọ̀ ni o Church in order to emphasize the centrality of musical performance for Cherubim and Seraphim practice as well as indicate a means through which Christianity was adapted and made relevant by African converts in their own terms. I examine how members of the Ayọ̀ ni o Church narrate Cherubim and Seraphim history, focusing on moments in which musical practices played a central role in the development of the religious movement. This history was not only narrated by church members, but it was also sung; the performance in the present of the same songs sung in the past enabled church members to access power that was understood to be available to early members of the church. In particular, as the examples I discuss below demonstrate, this power of the past was connected to how church members understood their worship practices to be efficacious, able to produce happiness and well-being (àlàáfíà), as well as capable of healing both physically and spiritually.

"Music has a powerful power"

Members of Cherubim and Seraphim churches today believe that Moses Orimolade established a form of Christianity that was suited to the spiritual and material needs of Africans in general, and to those of the Yoruba in particular. Members of the Ayọ̀ ni o Church saw their musical practices, inherited from Orimolade, as central to the shaping of Yoruba Christianity. This can be seen in the following explanation of the role of music in worship given by a pastor during a baptismal training session that I attended at the Ayọ̀ ni o Church in Lagos in 2003. In this statement, the pastor identified that music was central to the origins of the church and outlined a conception of how cultural and religious factors of Yoruba Christianity are currently understood by contemporary Cherubim and Seraphim congregations:

Orimolade was sent by God to preach the gospel to the Black community, especially in Nigeria. Orimolade wrote songs which did a lot in transforming the life of the people. The way the whites showed us Christianity there was not a lot in it to make their faith to be steadfast. They didn't put it in a way that would stimulate the interest of the people. Orimolade knew that music could be used to invoke the Holy Spirit by adapting classical music with indigenous music.

Let me explain: in òrìṣà, our deity, when they are doing their music you will see a woman who will go into spirit (ẹlẹ́mìí). She will start going like this [*shakes shoulders up and down in imitation of someone under spiritual trance*]. It is the music that has actually elevated her to go into spirit. Music has a very powerful power. Music has got power in the Cherubim and Seraphim Church to elevate the spirit of people up.

It is a supernatural thing that you cannot express. And it is only our church. It is to the Cherubim and Seraphim that God gave this gift, and it was used by Orimolade.

The pastor identified Cherubim and Seraphim music as embodying a special kind of spiritual power, one that was understood to be transformative and agentive. He argued that music connected people profoundly to their Christian faith; it made them "steadfast" and stimulated their interest, thus enhancing their participation in worship. But more than this, musical performance during Christian worship invoked the Holy Spirit, thus making possible an intervention of the spirit in the lives of church members.

Of particular interest is the pastor's analysis of the spiritual power inherent in musical performance. According to the pastor, the power of music in Cherubim and Seraphim worship originated in Orimolade's deep Yoruba insight, based on musical practices in òrìṣà worship that music elevated the spirit of humans up and drew the spirit of God down. What the pastor called "classical music"—referring to European styles of Christian music that make use of four-part harmonies and minimal rhythmic patterns—was insufficient in the Yoruba context because it was not able to engage the people in order to draw their spirit up. Neither was "indigenous music" sufficient because this music attracted the òrìṣà rather than the Holy Spirit. As the pastor asserted, it was by bringing these forms together and producing a distinctive musical style that Orimolade produced an efficacious form of Christian worship for Yorubas.

Musical Media and Historical Memory

The Cherubim and Seraphim hymnal provides a material lens through which to view the ways in which church members remembered the origins of the Cherubim and Seraphim churches. However, the insights that it provides can be limited. It is difficult to hear how the past sounded, and even more difficult to write about it, given the kinds of evidence left to analyze in the present (Corbin 1999; Sterne 2003). In many cases, and particularly in the context of religious worship, the sound of musical worship may only be available in the moment of performance. Even notation systems, which are usually designed to guide a song's future performance, are limited in their ability to capture what a performance actually sounded like at a given moment. Thus while a hymnal contains useful information for reconstructing how Christian songs emerged and were heard in the past, it only provides certain types of information about how hymns should be sung and performed.

Admittedly, the ability of the scholar to reconstruct the musical past using the hymnal is limited, but my ethnographic research suggests that members of the Cherubim and Seraphim churches understood their hymnal to be a historical document. One member of the Ayọ̀ ni o church told me that it was important for me to pay attention to Cherubim and Seraphim hymns if I wanted to understand the church. "I hope that you have bought a copy of the hymnal," she advised, "Everything that you want to know is in there. The hymnal contains the wisdom of our daddies, who started this church." Other church members made clear that hymn singing traversed intellectual, emotional, and historical levels of worship. For example, another woman told me, "if you go through the hymn book, you will notice that it is inspirational, composed by our fathers when they go into trance. The wordings are well-selected, showing us God through Jesus, and are emotional." Similar comments were frequently made by church members, and speak to the centrality of hymns in Cherubim and Seraphim worship. These comments also revealed the hymnal to be an important part of worship and a text that preserved church history so that church members could access it in the present. Church members thus used the hymnal to connect to the spiritual wisdom of the past in order to produce particular kinds of religious experiences.

For these reasons, we can approach hymn performance and the use of the hymnal by church members as a node of mediation, a site in which religious, institutional, cultural, and musical media come together to produce connections between individuals, histories, and contexts (Mazarella 2004). The hymnal itself is a form of material culture that contains the history of Cherubim and Seraphim Christianity and that allowed church members to activate and bring that history into the present. The history contained in the hymnal is one of Christian missionization together with Yoruba conversion.

Christian missionaries to the Yoruba used a variety of Anglican and other Protestant hymnals. Among them were the *Hymnal Companion to the Book of Common Prayer*, the *Church Missionary Society Hymn Book*, *Hymns Ancient and Modern*, *Sankey's Sacred Songs and Solos*, the *Congregational Cottage Hymn Book*, and Charles Kemble's *The New Church Hymn Book*. Missionaries and early Christian converts translated many of these hymns into Yoruba. Converts and missionaries also began to compose new hymns in the Yoruba language, beginning in the middle of the nineteenth century. In 1923, the Church Missionary Society in Nigeria published the first Yoruba-language hymnal.

Songs from these Protestant hymnals were also a part of Cherubim and Seraphim worship practices during the early days of the religious movement. Mrs. Josephine Adesola, the society's first choir leader, compiled the first collection of Cherubim and Seraphim hymns in the late 1920s (Omoyajowo 1982, 61). This collection included hymns that were composed by early members of the Cherubim and Seraphim, hymns drawn from the Church Missionary Society hymns, as well as songs from other books used in mission churches in Nigeria at that time. During the time of my research a number of different hymnals were used by various Cherubim and Seraphim denominations, though the most common was the *Ìwé Orin Mímọ́ fun Àpapọ̀ Ẹgbẹ́ Mímọ́ Kẹ́rúbu àti Sẹ́ráfù Gbogbo Àgbáiyé* (Hymnal for Assembled Cherubim and Seraphim Churches Worldwide), in its second edition.

Most of the hymns included in the Cherubim and Seraphim hymnal are either taken from European and American hymnals used by missionaries, or date back to the group's formal establishment in Lagos in the 1920s and 1930s. The hymnal is organized into sections based on the appropriate use of the hymns: there are sections for hymns that are to be used at a certain time of day (morning, night), at a particular time of year (Advent, Harvest, Lent, Easter), in the context of certain occasions (baptism, marriage, birthday celebrations, housewarming), in combination with specific worship activities (prayer, thanksgiving, sanctification, revival), or to achieve desired spiritual effects (protection, mercy, healing, victory). Each hymn is numbered, and there are over eight hundred entries in the most recent version of the hymnal.

Only the lyrics are printed in the hymnal. Indications for musical elements of the hymns are limited to the following: For some hymns the melody is indicated in the header through reference to one of the foreign hymnals. For example, the header for Hymn #89 in the Cherubim and Seraphim hymnal includes the following text: "Tune: S.S.&S. 134 Near the cross," which refers to a hymn in *Sankey's Sacred Songs and Solos*. The only other musical details included in the hymnal are dynamic markings indicating the desired volume in performance on a handful of the hymns.

Other than indicating that a hymn's tune may be the same as that of one of the foreign hymns, the hymnal does not indicate anything else about a given hymn's origins. Only a handful of the hymns are attributed to a particular composer. Furthermore, it is impossible to tell from the hymnal whether a hymn's lyrics have been translated from English to Yoruba, or whether members of the Cherubim and Seraphim movement composed the lyrics. In addition, because of the fixity of printing and the need to standardize the hymnal for ease of use in worship services, especially to facilitate the numbering system by which hymns are announced before their performance during worship, the hymnal contains very few contemporary additions.

The Boy Who Could "Sing Himself to Heaven"

Much of what is known about Orimolade, particularly his early life, is derived from oral histories and reconstructions of the time period collected from those around him: residents of his home town and early members of the Cherubim and Seraphim Society. In addition, a number of Orimolade's biographies have been written and published by church members. I have relied primarily on three such texts here: (1) *Moses Orimolade Tunolase: Supreme Founder Cherubim and Seraphim Worldwide (From When He Was in the Womb to His Death)*, written by Dr. E. Olu Famodimu, a member of the Cherubim and Seraphim Church Movement, and published by the church in 1990; (2) *God of Orimolade: The Life, Times, and Evangelical Works of St. Moses Orimolade Tunolase*, written by Dr. H. Oludare Atansuyi, also a member of the Cherubim and Seraphim Church Movement; and (3) *More Than a Prophet: The Adventures of Moses Orimolade Tunolase, Founder of the First Indigenous Church in Nigeria*, written and published by Moses Oludele Idowu, a self-described Pentecostal historian, in 2009. In these publications Orimolade's life is presented in hagiographic terms, with an emphasis on demonstrating how his founding of the Cherubim and Seraphim churches was predestined from the time of his birth.

Moses Orimolade was born in the late 1870s to a royal family in the town of Ikare, located in the northernmost area of the Ondo region of Yorubaland.[3] He came from a family that was deeply connected to Yoruba political and religious structures in Ikare. Orimolade's father, Tunolase, belonged to the royal lineage of Ikare and was a descendent of the mythological progenitor of the town. Tunolase was a noted herbalist and warrior, and biographies of Orimolade emphasize his father's immersion in traditional Yoruba religious practices.

These accounts of Orimolade's early life make clear that he came from a family that was deeply connected to Yoruba political and religious structures in the small village of Ikare, located in the Ondo region of Yorubaland. They emphasize that Orimolade was intimately familiar with indigenous Yoruba religious and cultural practices both as a matter of his genealogical lineage and through his exposure to such practices in his youth. However, Orimolade is also described as being something of an outsider to the religious practices of his contemporaries whether they had converted to Christianity or not. In documents written by church members that narrate the history of the Cherubim and Seraphim churches, an argument about the past was constructed that claims that both Yoruba "traditional religion" as well as mission Christianity were not sufficient religious modes of addressing the needs of the Yoruba. In doing so, church historians further emphasized what church members see as the oracular quality of Orimolade's inspiration to create the Cherubim and Seraphim churches.

This historical and hagiographic construction of Orimolade as both insider and outsider to Yoruba and Christian communities encapsulated within the life of an individual the tensions and negotiations experienced by Yoruba communities in the colonial period. As described in church histories and biographies, Orimolade's conception and early life foreshadows the impact he was to have on Yoruba Christian practice. Music and singing were significant parts of how Orimolade is remembered and commemorated in the present and for this reason music is seen as both providing a lens through which to access the past as well as a means to bring that past into the present.

Before looking specifically at claims about Orimolade's musical practices, it is worth examining the stories told about Orimolade's birth in order to understand both the nature of the stories themselves, and how Orimolade is positioned in a telling of the history of the Cherubim and Seraphim churches. One event connected to Orimolade's birth that is uniformly told by his biographers is revealing of how Orimolade himself is made to stand for both the rupture and continuity produced by Christian conversion. Drawing on a biography produced by a Cherubim and Seraphim congregation in Ikare, Omoyajowo writes: "It is said that the new child 'stood up in its birthblood' desiring 'to walk out three times'" (1982, 27). This event is often said to account for the physical impairment that Orimolade apparently suffered from throughout his entire life.[4]

Furthermore, for Cherubim and Seraphim historians, Orimolade's disability is symbolic of his particular subject position between a pagan past and a Christian future. As most biographers detail, the infant Orimolade's attempts to walk upon birth were prevented by the physical force of the midwife who was present as his birth as well as through the efforts of his father, Tunolase, who is said to have used what is described as "juju, charms, and incantations"—in other words, the spiritual practices of harming and healing that formed a key part of Yoruba indigenous religion—in order to restrain the child's movement. Tunolase's use of his knowledge of such "native medicine" to restrain his child's miraculous efforts to walk—these efforts themselves seen as evidence of his being chosen by the Christian God—reinforces a conception of Orimolade himself as a symbol of the struggle and negotiation that characterized the confusion of the colonial period. Here indigenous religion is understood literally as an impediment to Orimolade's progression in life. Furthermore, practices which Yoruba Christians would soon learn to refer to as "pagan," "heathen," or "idolatry" are identified as the source of the conflict and displacement of the time. In other words, Orimolade's disability stands for the inability of Yoruba communities to draw on and access spiritual and invisible forms of power necessary to reproduce themselves in the face of the social changes taking place during this period.

When the Anglican Church Missionary Society came to Ikare in the mid-1890s, Orimolade was among the earliest converts, despite the objections of his father. Orimolade was typical of early Yoruba converts to Christianity, who for the most part were low status or socially marginal individuals who were drawn to this new religion because they were unable to access conventional social modes of self- and community-making (Peel 2000). Women, slaves, young men, and migrants tended to make up the majority of Christian congregations during this period. The stories of Orimolade's youth, particularly those that emphasize his disability and ostracization by his father, suggest that like many other converts at the time Orimolade was drawn to the church because he was seeking to access the new power represented by the mission church. A main aspect of Yoruba religious practices concerned a search for healing, and missions were seen as providing a competing source of "medicine" for those for whom "native medicine" had failed (Peel 2000, 219–223). Orimolade's conversion to Christianity can be understood as an attempt to access new forms of spiritual power to replace the existing forms that had marginalized him socially.

Many accounts of Orimolade's early life include references to his affinity for music. For example, Famodimu (1990) emphasizes that as a young boy Orimolade was constantly singing. Drawing on interviews conducted with Orimolade's age-mates in Ikare, Famodimu (1990, 30) writes, "Songs that had never been heard from anybody would be rendered by him." He reports that Orimolade would sing to his brother while he worked on the family farm, and after his brother refused to carry him to the farm "for he always sang on the farm and he could one day sing himself to heaven like that"; Orimolade would sing to his age-mates in town which "at times led many to forget eating their food [*sic*]."

These stories suggest not only that Orimolade was a talented musician, but that he had also begun to compose original songs. The authors also attribute a certain transformative and transcendent power to singing; it was capable of transporting the performer (who could "sing himself to heaven") at the same time as listeners were moved out of time and place so that they were distracted from everyday tasks. This conception of music, written back onto Orimolade's life by Cherubim and Seraphim historians, emphasizes the centrality of music for the church.

However, as the story discussed earlier of Orimolade singing like a choir all by himself makes clear, his Christian message articulated through music was not appreciated by other Christian converts in Ikare during his lifetime. Orimolade was unable to find a place for himself in either traditional or Christian social and religious spheres in Ikare. As Cherubim and Seraphim historians tell it, after the Christian townspeople of Ikare rejected his "spiritual song," Orimolade is said to have prayed over what he should do. In response, God sent him a vision that prompted him to evangelize and preach the gospel of Jesus Christ. Thus, at some point in his late twenties or early thirties Orimolade left Ikare and began to wander around preaching in nearby towns and villages, eventually ending up in Lagos where was called to minister to a young woman named Christianah Abiodun who had reportedly been in a coma-like state for two weeks. It is to her place in the historical memory of Cherubim and Seraphim hymns that we now turn.

Christianiah Abiodun's Celestial Vision

With her connections to emerging social networks and her location in Lagos at the beginning of the twentieth century, Christianah Abiodun represented a vastly different sort of social subject than Orimolade, the itinerant Christian prophet from a rural Yoruba village. In contrast to Orimolade whose lineage connected him to traditional Yoruba social hierarchies and religious orientations, Abiodun was a Christian from birth and "of an extremely well-connected Creole family which had, like many other nineteenth-century Christian families, links along the West African coast" (Peel 1968, 71). Abiodun herself embodied many of the political, economic, and social transformations that took place in colonial Nigeria.

Abiodun was born in 1907 in what was then called Dahomey (present-day Benin Republic) and came to Lagos as a young girl in 1913. Unlike Orimolade, who received no Western-style education, Abiodun attended a number of mission schools, completing her primary school education at the Baptist Academy in 1920. She was confirmed at St. Paul's Anglican church on May 24, 1925 (Omoyajowo 1982, 41). Thus, unlike Orimolade, whose Christian conversion was a deliberate choice to seek an alternate foreign spiritual power in the context of a small Yoruba community, Abiodun's ties to Christianity were unquestioned and assumed.

In Lagos Abiodun was exposed to many of the new forms of social and cultural life that had developed in the colony's metropolis. This included not only a variety of Christian denominational practices (Anglican, Methodist, Catholic, and Africanist churches, among others) but also diverse forms of musical practices found in these churches and in the streets of Lagos. In particular, distinct religious and musical forms existed in Lagos' communities of repatriated slaves. As Waterman (1990, 31–32) describes, the Amaro (also referred to as the Aguda or the Brazilians) were emancipated slaves from Brazil and Cuba who had returned to Lagos. They were primarily Catholic but also familiar with the syncretic forms of Yoruba religion (i.e., Santeria and Candomblé) that had emerged in new world settings. Their musical practices were equally diverse and they introduced innovative uses of European musical instruments, new song forms, and dance genres to Lagotian audiences.

It was in this cosmopolitan urban space, where a multitude of distinct ethnic, religious, and cultural communities existed side-by-side, that Abiodun had a religious experience that was to bring her together with Orimolade. On June 18, 1925, Abiodun went to the Brazilian district in Lagos to watch the Catholic Corpus Christi procession. There she claimed to have seen an angel near the chalice carried by the bishop. The angel spoke to her and followed her home where he stayed with her for a week before she fell into a coma-like trance.

According to Abiodun's account of her experience, published in 1962 as a pamphlet titled *Celestial Vision*, she had often been visited by an angel while she slept who would take her to celestial places and return her back to bed just before dawn. However, after attending the Corpus Christi event in 1925, the angel became a permanent fixture in her waking life. After she accused the angel of being a devil, she was told that she would soon know the truth of his heavenly provenance as well as receive her call to service from God in heaven. The angel left her, but she soon found herself taken to a celestial region: "After passing through five gates, she came to a garden where she found a host of angels, who, arrayed in white robes, were singing from hymn books they held in their hands" (Omoyajowo 1982, 6).

Abiodun's visionary description of heaven and its denizens is highly evocative of the Cherubim and Seraphim Church's use of religious imagery and sounds in their worship practices. Thus in her retelling of her visionary experience Abiodun emphasizes that the current worship practices of the Cherubim and Seraphim—particularly their use of the white robes during worship as well as the prominent role of singing from hymnals in their practice—were inspired by and in imitation of the practices that she saw among the angels in heaven. Abiodun further elaborated on the use of music by angels in heaven when she describes them calling on her familiar guardian angel using songs, "because angels call one another with songs" (Omoyajowo 1982, 6).

During her time in heaven, Abiodun underwent a spiritual test and received spiritual training: "she was asked a series of questions to test her knowledge and faith, which she answered correctly with the aid of her angel friend" (Renne 2004, 121), and "was commanded to renounce traditional herbalism and was taught prayers for healing and the blessing of water" (Hackett 1995, 264). She also was taken to see heaven and hell by the angels that accompanied her on celestial travels. These angels had refused to allow her to leave until somebody who knew how to pray came and prayed for her. That person was Orimolade.

To heal Abiodun, Orimolade used a combination of prayer and music (Omoyajowo 1982; Peel 1968). "Abiodun, as the angel had commanded, asked Orimolade three Biblical questions, which he answered. Orimolade bade people clap and sing, as the Holy Spirit was in the house" (Peel 1968, 71–72). In this way Orimolade brought Abiodun out of her trance. This event is a defining moment in the founding of the religious movement that produced the Cherubim and Seraphim churches. Orimolade's use of song to heal Abiodun, as well as her own musical experiences with the angels in heaven, further served as a model for Cherubim and Seraphim musical practices. Music was understood to be a medium of communication between the angels, but also and important, a means by which humans could communicate with celestial beings, from angels to the Holy Spirit. In addition, music was a crucial tool that could be used both to cause people to enter into a spiritual trance but that could also serve to heal people.

The hymn that is reported to have been used by Orimolade in order to help Abiodun transition back to the human world appears in the Cherubim and Seraphim hymn book as #105, "*Ẹ je ka f'inu didun,*" the Yoruba translation of John Milton's hymn "Let Us with a Gladsome Mind" (Atansuyi, 36; Famodimu 1990, 39). According to most biographical sources, this hymn was a particular favorite of Orimolade who sang it frequently during prayer healing sessions. As Famodimu writes, "Any time a sick man was brought to him he would start this song in his room and his followers would sing it. This would be followed by a sign of the cross on the sick and he instantly would be healed" (1990, 140). Thus, Orimolade made use of a popular Anglican hymn for specifically Yoruba purposes: to heal physical and spiritual ailments. The hymn became reinterpreted through a Yoruba model of spiritual efficacy and practice.

Musically, the hymn differs from "Up above the River Jordan" in a number of ways. First, "Let Us with a Gladsome Mind" is a translated hymn, rather than an original composition of Orimolade's. As such, it takes the strophic form typical of most hymns, with a verse-refrain structure. The lyrics are based on Psalm 136, and each strophe begins with two lines that alternate followed by the refrain, "For His mercies aye endure; Ever faithful, Ever sure." The same music, particularly the melody and harmonic progression, is used for each repetition of the verse-refrain unit, in contrast to "Up above the River Jordan" which features a continual melodic development.

Many of the narratives that describe Orimolade singing this song at Abiodun's bedside note that he not only sang the hymn, but also called on the rest of the assembled group to join him by singing and clapping. This suggests that the practice of clapping while singing Christian hymns was being performed by Orimolade, and possibly was in wider musical practice in Africanist and other independent Christian churches. Vigorous clapping is a distinct marker of Aladura musical styles, and many Cherubim and Seraphim Church members noted that clapping was one of the oldest musical techniques used in the church. As one choir leader explained to me, "clapping invigorates the body and draws down the spirit."

I heard "Let Us with a Gladsome Mind" performed frequently by many different Cherubim and Seraphim churches. While the instrumentation often differed from church to church, at a minimum each rendition that I heard was performed to an organ accompaniment. Churches with larger or more elaborate choirs also sang this hymn while accompanied by electric guitars, trumpets and saxophones, and a variety of drums including hand drums (such as conga-style drums), a Western-style drum kit, and Yoruba talking drums (*gángan*). The song was frequently sung to an energetic rhythm, and while church members held their hymnals in their hands while singing, they did not always need to refer to the book. While singing "Let Us with a Gladsome Mind" church members appeared radiant and smiling, embodying the lyrics, which urge church members to praise God with happiness and joy.

The hymn also continues to be central in Cherubim and Seraphim healing practices. One prophet I interviewed claimed that he sang it at the beginning of each session with those who came to him for spiritual counseling. He told me that singing "Let Us with a Gladsome Mind" not only allowed him and the person in need of counsel to discuss their problems with the correct frame of mind, it also attracted the spirit to the counseling session. In addition, singing this hymn allowed healing to begin because it created a link to the moment when Orimolade brought Abiodun out of her trance.

The use of "Let Us with a Gladsome Mind" as a regular part of Cherubim and Seraphim worship in the present, as well as in ongoing practices of healing conducted by Cherubim and Seraphim prophets modeled on Orimolade's practice, speaks to how "Yoruba" and "Christian" religious forms and practices were integrated by the Cherubim and Seraphim as a part of their historical practice and linked to their conception of spiritual efficacy. In my discussion with the prophet of his use of "Let Us with a Gladsome Mind," I asked him why this particular hymn was so effective, given that it was composed in 1623 by an English poet, in a European Christian context removed in time and space from a Yoruba cultural and religious milieus. His reply was illuminating. "This is not a European song!" he admonished me. "[Let Us with a Gladsome Mind] is a Christian song. It is an important part of our tradition. When we sing this song together in Yoruba it is very powerful. The Holy Spirit is sure to intervene in whatever problem that person is having."

In order to better understand the implications of the prophet's argument, I asked about the variable instrumentation used by different church choirs when they sang the song. The prophet often played electric guitar in the church choir each Sunday. I asked him why he used this instrument to perform hymns even though this particular instrument was not available during Orimolade's life. The prophet laughed and said,

> When we perform the hymn in the present, we change it to suit our present tastes and options. If the electric guitar was there in Orimolade's time, perhaps he would have used it. But maybe not. However, we choose to use it because it pleases us. It makes us have that joy, that is what the hymn is about.

Thus, questions of origins were insignificant in understanding how European and American hymns came to be sung in Yoruba contexts; rather the efficacy and use of a particular hymn was understood in relation to historical practice and significance. Instrumentation was thus matter of historical and cultural differences, while the song itself was understood to belong to a religious formation—Christianity—that transcends those differences.

Furthermore, the recontextualization of this historical practice in the present may also entail a transformation of practice. The use of the talking drum in contemporary Cherubim and Seraphim worship is a prime example of how such distinctions are negotiated and transformed over time. The talking drum's use by the Cherubim and Seraphim most likely dates back to the 1970s. When Peel observed Cherubim and Seraphim worship in the early 1960s only single-membrane frame drums such as the *sámbà* were used. He noted that the talking drum was "not used because of its association with *Egúngún* [ancestral masquerade] drummers" (Peel 1968, 163). Negotiation over whether or not particular Yoruba drums may be included in Christian worship continues until the present day. Thus, while it is now acceptable to play the talking drum during church worship, other drums, such as the *bàtá* drum used in indigenous settings to worship particular òrìṣà, are still forbidden.

As the historical narratives and performances discussed thus far suggest, a variety of musical practices—such as using Yoruba language or melodic forms, clapping, and performing to the accompaniment of drums and other musical instruments—came to be a crucial part of Christian worship. These practices contributed to the efficacy of Cherubim and Seraphim worship, particularly in regard to the ability to attract and draw down the Holy Spirit into the space of worship. By categorizing these practices as part of Cherubim and Seraphim history practitioners accessed the powers attributed to a Yoruba past and made use of them in contemporary Christian contexts.

The Seraphim Society's New Musical Forms

The meeting of Abiodun and Orimolade brought together the contradictory experiences of inside and outside, past and present, remade through processes of colonialism and missionization in order to produce something that was new yet relied on older ideas of spiritual power and authority. Combining what she had learned during her celestial journey and his powerful healing abilities, Abiodun and Orimolade went on to organize a prayer society that preached "faith in prayers and a renunciation of the devil and all his works—including the worship of idols, the use of juju and charms and the fear of the power of witches" (Omoyajowo 1982, 8). For many Yoruba Christians in Lagos, the society's practices—especially with regard to prayer and the use of music—filled a perceived gap between mission church practices and their need for spiritual protection from witchcraft and magic in colonial Lagos.

Abiodun and Orimolade's prayer group was named on September 9, 1925, following a three-day fast during which members were encouraged to pray to God to reveal the name of the society. One woman revealed that she had seen the letters "SE" in the sky, but the rest of the word was covered by clouds. Another member said that he had seen the letters "RA." On the following day Orimolade led the followers in a revival service, where they sang a hymn from the CMS hymnal titled "Pleasant Are Thy Courts Above" (Famodimu 1990, 81; see also Atansuyi, personal communication).[5] During the service a third member interpreted these visions to be a reference to the word "SERAFU," a Yoruba transliteration of the English word "seraphim." The group became known as the Seraphim Society; the word Cherubim was added later that year following another vision.

Orimolade organized twenty-four of the influential members of the Seraphim Society into a Praying Band (*Ẹgbẹ́ Alàdúrà*), who would assist him in praying for those needing spiritual guidance (Omoyajowo 1982, 12).[6] Under the leadership of the Praying Band the Cherubim and Seraphim Society held night watch services on the weekends, set up a network of Bible classes that met for two hours on Sundays after regular church services had concluded, and would go and pray for each other as necessary. They also continued Orimolade's evangelical practices and would encourage new converts to join whatever church was convenient for them to attend.

Music was the primary way in which the Cherubim and Seraphim Society attracted new members. Many of the songs sung by the group at this time were taken from hymnbooks used by mission churches in Lagos, including the Anglican, Methodist, and Baptist churches (Famodimu 1990, 140). In addition to standardized hymns taken from the mission churches, members of the Cherubim and Seraphim Society also sang original songs. These songs had been written by Orimolade's followers who were inspired by his use of music in prayer and healing. Many of these early songs were "received" by Orimolade's followers while in spiritual trance. The lyrics of these songs documented the healing and evangelical efforts being undertaken by society members at the time, capturing in their lyrics the circumstances of their composition.

New musical practices were also introduced as a result of the society's evangelical works. In 1927, the society began sending groups of evangelists to the areas surrounding Lagos, traveling to the nearby towns of Ijebu-Ode, Abeokuta, and Ibadan. Abiodun, who had been given the nickname of "Captain" by Orimolade, led these campaigns. The success of these early drives to spread Cherubim and Seraphim practices in the interior was attributed to Abiodun's charisma and youth—she was nineteen years of age at the time and reportedly was quite outgoing and attractive—as well as to sermons in which she testified both to her celestial vision and the success of Orimolade in healing her. During these evangelistic travels, members of the society would march through town wearing their white gowns and singing hymns. When they had attracted enough followers they would deliver sermons and demonstrations of prayer healing, usually in the center of the town's main market (Peel 1968, 78).

Music was key to drawing people to listen to their testimonies and sermons. On their evangelical excursions the Cherubim and Seraphim sang hymns while they marched and used a long-handled bell to draw attention to themselves, beating the bell's clapper against the side of the instrument in order to produce a time line rhythm that supported the singing. Taking inspiration from the Salvation Army Band, as well as from the use of brass instruments in military contexts, the trumpet and the tambourine were also played by society members in their processions.

The effectiveness of music in attracting new members to the Cherubim and Seraphim is made clear in the recollections of an early member in Abeokuta, who was sitting in the Agbeni Methodist Church listening to music being performed on the church organ when he heard the song of the Cherubim and Seraphim as they went by. Drawn to this sound, he rushed out and followed them to the market where Abiodun preached.[7] This suggests that the Cherubim and Seraphim had created a musical style that was particularly compelling to early Yoruba converts, a sound able to compete with the practices of both mission churches as well as with those of traditional religion practitioners.

The Power of Holy Michael

These early evangelical processions throughout Lagos and surrounding towns were effective at attracting new members to the Cherubim and Seraphim Society, but the question of leadership remained central for members of the group. Many wanted to ensure that they would be recognized as legitimate in Lagos' Christian community, a concern given that most members of the society continued to attend mission churches. Although members of the Seraphim Society acknowledged Orimolade's spiritual abilities, some saw his rural village origins and lack of education as a problem. Abiodun, by contrast, was recognized as a vibrant representative of the group, able to attract many followers, but because she was a woman she too was not seen fit to serve as the group's leader. Therefore, soon after the society had been named, they met to settle the issue via prayers, seeking another visionary revelation. Omoyajowo describes the event as follows:

> Twenty days after the society was named the group met to appoint a captain. This was, in accordance with practice, preceded by fasting and praying. Some important people in Lagos were suggested for the position, but were all rejected. Finally a small child, so small that she had to be put on a table for everybody to see her, related a vision in which the Archangel Michael was named as Captain and Jah Jehovah, as Founder of the Society. While the vision was being related (in two stanzas of a song), a red cloud appeared in the west and moved steadily eastward. This was interpreted as God's ratification of their choice, and so Orimolade proclaimed the Archangel as Captain (1982: 11).

This visionary song, which revealed that Michael should be the captain of the society is preserved as hymn number 727 in the Cherubim and Seraphim hymn book, known by the opening line: "Òkùnkùn ṣú ìmọ́lẹ̀ kan si ń tàn" ("There is a light in the darkness"). The lyrics link the ability of the church to act in the world with the spiritual power of Holy Michael, who in his role as Captain of the Church promises that members will be victorious in their own spiritual efforts:

> Amidst the darkness there shone a great light
> In the midst of the Seraphim
> Michael is the Captain of this Band
> He will guide us from this day.
>
> Chorus:
> Michael, Michael, Michael is the Captain
> Of the Seraphim Society
> Jah Jehovah himself founded this holy band
> Not an earthly being

With these two acts, the acknowledgement that it was God ("Jah Jehovah") himself who founded the Cherubim and Seraphim churches and the naming of the archangel Michael as the group's spiritual leader, the issues of leadership and succession that had plagued the group were put into spiritual terms. The visions and songs established the premise that church hierarchy and leadership should always be understood to be determined through spiritual means, and that these spiritual means could also be used to account for the organization of the church.

However, this did not mean that questions of church leadership and spiritual authority within the group were settled. To the contrary, the Cherubim and Seraphim Society split into several factions following this vision and by the time of Orimolade's death in 1933 there existed at least three different organizations that called themselves Cherubim and Seraphim. These organizations exist today as the Eternal and Sacred Order of the Cherubim and Seraphim, the Cherubim and Seraphim Society, and the Praying Band of Cherubim and Seraphim. This pattern of division over questions of religious authority continued to affect Cherubim and Seraphim congregations throughout the twentieth century and up to the present (Omoyajowo 1984).

As a result of this history of schism, each church that identifies itself as Cherubim and Seraphim has its own distinct organizational structure and specific modes of worship. Certain practices, such as the wearing of the white church uniform and the centrality of distinctive ways praying and singing are found across denominational divides. However, the specifics of these elements may differ from church to church. For leaders of Cherubim and Seraphim denominations this is often seen as a source of tension and an obstacle to be overcome in order for the church to be successful in its evangelical goals. Thus certain aspects of contemporary worship practices were designed to remind church members of the theological correctness of their present day practices and the way such practices are in line with the history of the church. The commemoration of the naming of the archangel Michael as the captain of the church is one such example of how the history of the Cherubim and Seraphim is brought to bear on the contemporary organization of the church.

In their celebration of Holy Michael Day, contemporary church members recreate aspects of the Cherubim and Seraphim past by singing hymns that are connected to the memory of the past. Cherubim and Seraphim uses of history as well as their ability to access history through musical performance can be seen clearly in the celebration of Holy Michael Day by members of the Ayọ̀ ni o Church. The Holy Michael Day ceremony brought together multiple historical media in order to reproduce ideas of order, authority, and memory that are central to how the Cherubim and Seraphim understood their worship practices to be powerful and efficacious. Notably, while Holy Michael Day did not involve a recreation of past events, it did feature specific actions that were understood by church members to exemplify the aspects of past religious practice important to maintain and reproduce in the present. Songs, styles of movement, narratives of the actions of the church's founders, and other historical media were brought together in order to reinforce the importance of the link between past and present for church members.

On September 29, 2003, I attended Holy Michael Day at the Ayọ̀ ni o Church in Lagos, making my way to the church in the late afternoon so I would be there on time when the program started at 4 p.m. As the taxi approached the entrance to the church compound I noticed that two wardens were directing car traffic toward an alternate entrance in the back of the church. In order to avoid the delay this alternative route caused in traffic alongside the access road, I quickly exited the taxi and entered the compound on foot.

Once inside, I saw the reason for the alteration to the traffic pattern: rather than entering the church and taking their places in the pews to wait for the service to begin, church members were assembling in the large sandy area in front of the main church where cars were usually parked. The group grew quite large as people streamed into the compound from different entrances, some of them ducking into prayer halls to change from their work clothes into their white church uniform. Amid the confusion, I quickly located and joined other members of the choir who were beginning to line up in rows directly in front of the main entrance to the church. Most choir members carried only their Bible and hymnbook, though the trumpet players and drummers carried their instruments as well. Someone handed me a tambourine and I joined a line of other people holding small percussion instruments: maracas, ṣẹ̀kẹ̀rẹ̀ (a gourd rattle), and tambourines.

An ordered procession began to take place from the chaos. At the front of the procession two wardens carried a large banner on which had been printed the name of the church. The banner was followed by two more wardens carrying a white flag and a Nigerian flag. Behind them a crucifer carried a processional cross before a group of five senior male church elders. After them two men from a group known as the Soldiers of Christ carried another banner with the name of their group on it. The members of the Soldiers of Christ, who wore a special red cassock on top of their white uniform, marched behind the second banner. The singers and instrumentalists from the choir followed the Soldiers of Christ. As the procession began to move, the rest of the church members began to fall in line behind the choir.

The congregation marched around the church seven times while singing a series of hymns, beginning with "Onward Christian Soldiers." As the procession began, and we sang the opening lines of this well-known hymn, a woman marching behind me whispered in my ear to pay attention because this was an important hymn for the church and that it was particularly appropriate for that day, which was about "victory." The singing was accompanied by trumpets and hand drums, which were worn over the shoulders of the drummers as they marched. A female member of the choir carried a bullhorn, through which she shouted the lyrics of the hymn before the congregation sang each line:

Onward Christian Soldiers, marching as to war
With the cross of Jesus going on before
Christ the royal master leads against the foe
Forward into battle see his banners go!

In their performance of "Onward Christian Soldiers," the group reenacted a mode through which early followers of Orimolade and Abiodun established the Cherubim and Seraphim as a religious movement. As noted above, the processional mode of musical performance and movement harkened back to the evangelical demonstrations of Orimolade's early followers in Lagos and surrounding areas during the 1920s. By singing "Onward Christian Soldiers" and marching around the church seven times, the congregation that day indexed earlier forms of religious practice and acknowledged the ability of such practices to achieve their religious goals of success and wellbeing.

After the procession had circled the church seven times the group stopped at the entrance of the worship hall for a series of seven prayers. The prayers called on Holy Michael the archangel, Moses Orimolade, the founder of the Cherubim and Seraphim churches, along with other leaders of the Cherubim and Seraphim to come down to hear the group's prayers that day. When the prayers ended, everyone entered the church.

Once inside the church the lyrics and style of the opening hymn for the service made clear that the point of the celebration was to recognize and call on the history of the church. As people made their way to their seats in the church pews, the choir sang "Ẹ dìde ọmọ ogun 'gbàlà" (Hymn 729; "Army of Salvation, Stand

Holy Michael Day Procession, 2003

Up!"). The hymn was sung in what choir members described as "Cherubim and Seraphim style," one based on an understanding of the church's historical practices. Again a woman lined out the lyrics of the hymn for the congregation, this time into a microphone so that her voice was amplified through the worship hall as well as outside in the church compound. A long-handled bell and hand drums provided a rhythmic accompaniment to the singing, the bell ringing out a repeated rhythm that served as a time line and the hand drums filling in with interlocking rhythms on top of the fundamental beat. This was supplemented by the congregation's clapping. As the congregation progressed through the lyrics of the hymn, the intensity of the group's performance gradually built up; the tempo and volume increased and people started dancing as they stood in the pews, some even circling around in the aisles of the church as the music reached its peak. The lyrics described a moment in the churches' founding when the Archangel Michael was named as the leader of the Cherubim and Seraphim:

> Stand up army of Salvation
> Praise the name of Jesus
> For the great day you've seen today
> Is for Michael our Captain

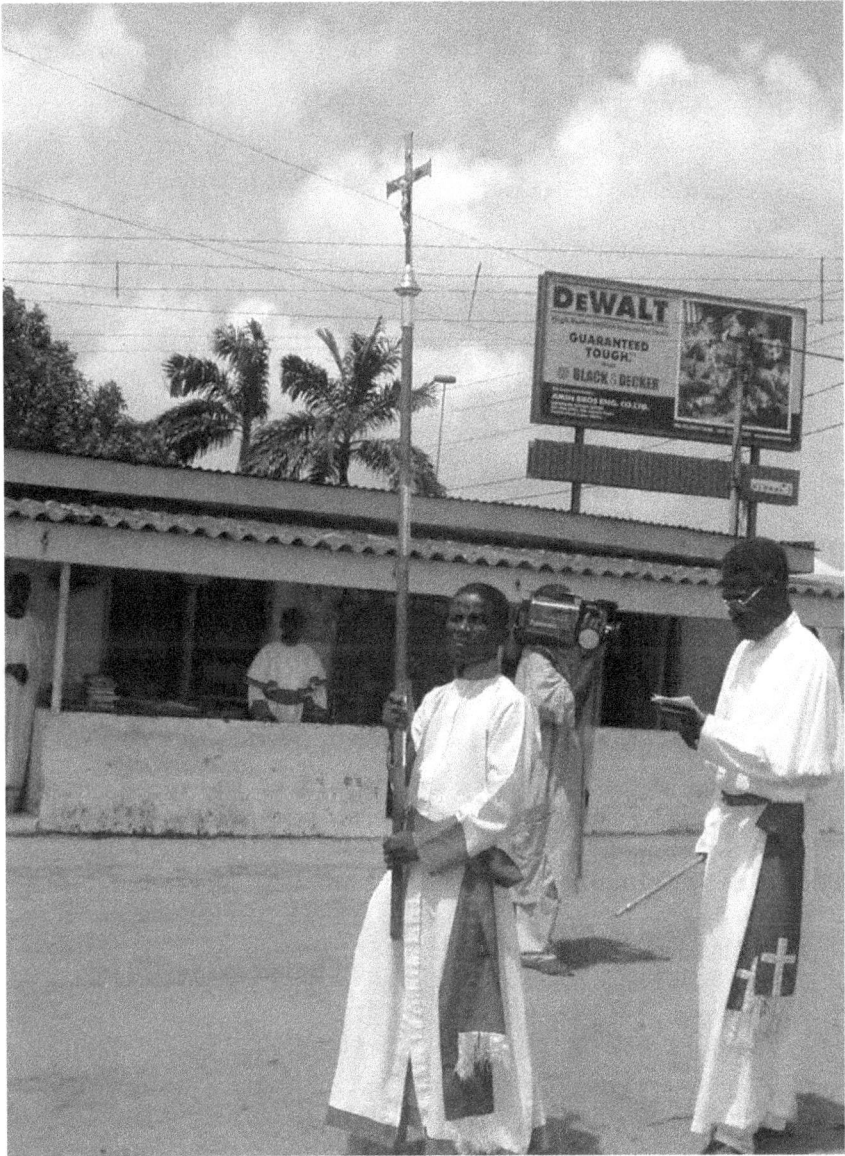

Holy Michael Day Procession, 2003

Chorus:
Holy Michael our Captain
Holy Michael our Captain
Guide us to the end of our life
Conquer Lucifer for us.

We're grateful that he is ours
In the Seraphim band
There is no war that Satan's army can win
Michael will overcome them
[Repeat Chorus]

On the day there was war in heaven
Heaven and earth trembled
The world became filled with great fear
Michael struck down Satan with his sword
[Repeat Chorus]

The performance of this song in this style, using drums and the long-handled bell, with the congregation clapping and dancing, created a proper context in which past and present became linked through performance, and a spiritual connection made to the church founders. Indeed, the song directed the congregation to rise up as one body, creating a directional bodily praxis that further unified the congregation.

Though the historical development of the church was indexed through formal elements of the performance, it was during the sermon that the ways in which the ability of hymn singing to mediate between the past and the present was stated clearly. The sermon that day was given by Prophet G. O. Fakeye, the charismatic leader of the Ayọ̀ ni o Church, who constructed an authoritative historical narrative that used hymns to make clear the relevance of history for the present. Fakeye began by explaining that Holy Michael Day was an important narrative for the church, a day of victory and celebration. Making specific reference to the visionary hymn, received on the day that Holy Michael was named as archangel of the church, he observed, "God has given us Michael as captain of the church as recorded in the song from Christianah Abiodun." He began to sing Hymn 727, "Òkùnkùn ṣú ìmọ́lẹ̀ kan si ń tàn," the visionary song sung by the early members of the church at the naming of Holy Michael as the captain of the church. The rest of the church joined him, singing three verses of the song before the sermon resumed.

Continuing the sermon, the pastor drew on Biblical references, arguing that Michael was sent by God to stand up for the Israelites and restore them to their proper glory, and that he was sent to the Cherubim and Seraphim for the purposes of waging holy war, that Holy Michael will help the Cherubim and Seraphim destroy their enemies. Then he gave an example "in this world" that referred to Abiodun's evangelical crusades in Yorubaland, specifically mentioning her visit to Ota, a town that was a "haven for witches":

> An example in this our world. When Abiodun began evangelism she was warned not to go to Ota because Ota was the headquarters of all the witches in Nigeria at that time. When she got there all the forces of darkness were assembled against her. When she got to Ota she started sneezing. She started singing.

The implication of Abiodun's sneezing when she arrived in Ota is that she was physically ejecting whatever witchcraft was used against her. The pastor then explained that Abiodun sang a song in order to defeat the witches. As he explained this, he immediately started singing the song himself, and the choir quickly joined him:

> Witches are nothing
> The Cherubim will destroy them
>
> Chorus:
> King of Kings
> The God of Eternity
> The Glorious King
>
> The god of smallpox is nothing
> Holy Michael will conquer them
> [Repeat Chorus]
>
> Ifa priests are nothing
> The Seraphim will destroy them
> [Repeat Chorus]
>
> The ancestor masquerade is nothing
> The Cherubim will destroy them
> [Repeat Chorus]

After the song ended, the pastor then spoke of his own experience, in order to create a parallel between himself and Abiodun. Describing a time when he was traveling, he explained that he came to an intersection where there were a lot of "fetish objects" in the middle of the road. His car stopped working as soon as they came to that intersection. Calling on Holy Michael, and singing the hymn Abiodun used against the witches in Ota, the pastor explained that he "prayed away the evil spirits." The engine started working again and they quickly drove away. The next day they read in the newspaper that human remains were found at that place. It was because of the power of Holy Michael, activated through the performance of Abiodun's song, that the pastor was able to defeat those who wanted to harm him. At this point the congregation leapt to their feet and yelled "Praise God!"

"The Secret Power of the Church Is in the Hymns"

During the week following the celebration of Holy Michael Day I met with Dr. Olu Atansuyi, the director of the theological academy at the Ayọ̀ ni o Church. Atansuyi was considered by many church members to be an authoritative source of information about the history of the Cherubim and Seraphim as well as an expert adjudicator in matters of correct religious practice. His authority was derived from two factors. The first, that he was from the same hometown as Orimolade, and related to Orimolade's family by marriage, thus he had a personal connection to the history of the church. In addition, he had received a graduate degree from a religious seminary in the United States, and was the author of a number of scholarly books concerning Christian practice in Nigeria, including his own study of Moses Orimolade and the Cherubim and Seraphim Church.

In my meeting with Atansuyi, he explained the historical significance of the hymns sung during the Holy Michael Day ceremony by beginning with a proverb, a common rhetorical device used when an elder is about to impart important wisdom to a junior. "Orin ni ìṣájú ọ̀tẹ̀," he began, "song leads people to conspiracy." He went on to say that "song is used to do a lot of things in Yoruba culture. In Cherubim and Seraphim music you find a lot of truth, you find the facts of the case in our songs." Linking Cherubim and Seraphim music directly with specific people, places or events from the past, he pointed out several songs from the hymn book and explained their significance to me, noting for example that in one the composer was trying to reveal a dream he had about the goodness of Orimolade, or that another was written during a time of confusion in the church. Atansuyi concluded our conversation with the following observation: "The majority of the activity that is accomplished through our songs is holy war. We are fighting a spiritual enemy. The secret power of the church is in the hymns."

Atansuyi articulated the power of hymn singing as stemming from its ability to join people together. In particular, his use of the proverb "song leads people to conspiracy" indicated that song joined people together for an agentive purpose, causing them to act in the world for a common cause. Here, the idea of "singing the same song" was used to account for how reproducing the songs connected to past events and historical figures is a form of critical agency. Thus conceptualized, songs are powerful weapons that carry messages from the past, which in their present performance produce and embody forms of subjectivity and community that enable one to exert control over one's spiritual enemies. The conception of spiritual power (*agbára*) articulated here is relational, processual, efficacious, and protecting, and linked to a Yoruba conception of religious power (*àṣẹ*):

> The power sought through Cherubim and Seraphim ritual is a proactive force, a power to, generating capacities and capabilities of mind, body and spirit. But

it is also a power over, a protective vitality against the enemies (ọ̀tá) and evil spirits (ẹmí burúkú) who will sap this energy and cause calamity and failure. (Harris 2006: 68)

This conception of power demonstrates continuity between Yoruba and Christian conceptions of power. Hymn performance activates and mobilizes power for use in worship practices to produce well-being, healing, and victory. At the same time musical worship produces continuities by linking Cherubim and Seraphim practices to conceptions of Yoruba culture as well as Christian practice.

Atansuyi also emphasized the politically charged nature of hymn singing for church members. In prefacing his comments about hymn singing with the proverb "orin ni ìṣájú ọ̀tẹ̀" he suggested that there was something potentially transformative in the action of singing together. Indeed, while ọ̀tẹ̀ refers to conspiracy, another possible meaning for the word is rebellion or revolt. Atansuyi's claim that the Cherubim and Seraphim are engaged in a holy war when singing highlights church members' understandings of the conspiratorial and transformational nature of hymn singing as direct and necessary action in the world. Such a perspective was echoed in the congregation's performance of "Onward Christian Soldiers" as they marched around the church seven times during the Holy Michael Day celebration.

These links to the past were echoed in the sermon that day as well. The pastor used a series of hymns to construct a new historical narrative, one that linked the naming of Holy Michael as the Captain of the church, to the defeat of witches and wizards by Christianah Abiodun, to his own victory over evil spiritual forces. As the congregation responded to this telling of church history by performing hymns connected to moments in the past, they indexed the spiritual power latent in the hymns, and in their performance made them a tool for the fashioning of their own subjectivity. In doing so history was actively brought to bear on the lives of church members.

Through hymn singing church members activated the potential they hold within themselves to access the power in song, the "secret power" of the church; linking their own personal histories to this spiritual lineage (from Holy Michael, to the Israelites, to Abiodun, to Fakeye, to themselves). And it was a particular sort of hymn singing practice—one that used the musical practices developed by the early Cherubim and Seraphim members—that came to be associated with Cherubim and Seraphim musical styles that makes this link between past and present possible. Thus the singing of hymns during church worship, especially in the context of ceremonies that were specifically understood to be historical such as Holy Michael Day, placed Cherubim and Seraphim conceptions of power and efficacy at the center of personhood.

The examples discussed in this chapter of how the history of the Cherubim and Seraphim is narrated and sung all emphasize the importance of musical practice, most important those connected to singing songs referred to as hymns by church members. Hymns reinforced and reproduced a certain kind of religious experience for members of the Cherubim and Seraphim churches. They voiced a particular mode of historical consciousness while singing hymns that drew on the church's past. Hymns were understood to be a means through which Christianity was made compelling for Yoruba people, or, as the pastor quoted at the beginning of this chapter put it, of communicating Christianity in a form that continued to attract church members to Christianity and made them "steadfast." This history also allowed church members to understand their hymns to be spiritually powerful and efficacious because of their link to the past. In this way church members were able to attract God's power and to localize it in a particular space. Because of this, hymns continue to be an important spiritual healing practice for church members. These contemporary conceptions of hymns are made possible by reconstructing a narrative of the use of music by the movement's founders but also by transforming certain aspects of hymn performance to suit the aesthetic tastes of the present.

Notes

1. The reference to "beloved ones who have gone before," calling Orimolade from heaven, may also be understood in terms of Yoruba ancestral beliefs. In a pre-Christian Yoruba conception of heaven, ancestors are said to reside there and look out over their descendants. Peel (1968, 153) suggests that such ideas about an "ancestral God" may be incorporated into Cherubim and Seraphim belief, citing the example of certain Cherubim and Seraphim sections having prayers to "Ọlọrun Mose Orimolade," the God of Orimolade. In addition, many church members explained to me that deceased family members go to heaven and join the angels in heaven where they look out for those of us in the world.

2. This date does not coincide with Holy Michael Day, the day in October when most Cherubim and Seraphim churches celebrate the history of the movement. I was unable to receive a satisfactory answer as to why the song was not performed during the anniversary celebrations that I witnessed during the time of my research.

3. There is no official record of Orimolade's birth, but most accounts claim that he was born in 1879.

4. There is some disagreement as to the precise nature of Orimolade's disability and it is unclear if his difficulty walking stemmed from his early life or whether it developed later. However, there seems to be a consensus that Orimolade experienced significant illness during his youth. Most accounts of his life note that for a period of seven years during his childhood he was bedridden and often describe how he was able to miraculously produce food and drink for himself during this period, or that he requested people to bring him water only from a particular source. However, it is clear that he was physically impaired for most of his adult life, as most recollections of his later evangelical campaigns note that he was carried in a stretcher by his followers or that he went around in a makeshift wheelchair (see especially Famodimu 1990). Some of the ambiguity surrounding Orimolade's disability is a deliberate attempt to avoid or sidestep the question of how such a great healer was not able to heal himself.

5. Hymn No. 338 "Bugbe re ti l'ewa to" in the Cherubim and Seraphim Hymn Book.

6. Orimolade would later establish several other bands (ẹgbẹ́) in the church, setting up an organizational structure that is still practiced in Cherubim and Seraphim churches today. See chapter 8 for further discussion of this mode of sociality.

7. This is attributed to Apostle Kuforiji and is recounted both in Peel (1968) and Famodimu (1990). Famodimu's account may in fact be taken from Peel, who interviewed Kuforiji in the course of his research.

3   The Voice of the Spirit

There is no shock
For those who believe
We shall go from strength to strength
Because of the love of our Father
We shall not purchase joy in the world with money

　　—"Ohùn Ẹmí," Seraph Voices

In 1978, the Cherubim and Seraphim Movement Ayọ̀ ni o Church choir, released its first commercial recording, an album containing two songs: "Paradise"
and "Ohùn Ẹmí" ("The voice of the spirit"). With this release, the musical messages
of the Cherubim and Seraphim moved from the hymnal to the grooves of a record—which was quickly replaced by an audiotape—and from a form of written
and oral knowledge passed on within and between congregations to a media commodity that circulated through capitalist modes of economic exchange. Through
its decision to record and release these songs, the choir allowed its music to circulate beyond the church itself, to reach listeners outside of the church's membership, and to enter the Nigerian public sphere through established networks of
commercial music distribution.

The choir's decision to release the recording may be understood, in part, as
made possible by and as a response to political and economic conditions in Nigeria at the time. The Ayọ̀ ni o Church choir released the *Paradise/Ohùn Ẹmí* album
amid significant transformations in Nigeria's political economy; namely, the oil
boom of the 1970s. At a time when the pressures of conspicuous consumption
were reworking middle-class Yoruba identity, the Ayọ̀ ni o Church choir musically articulated its stance toward Nigeria's postcolonial political economy in this
material musical form. The album provided one answer to the question of how a
believer could engage in the oil economy to hold onto his or her middle-class
position while remaining aligned with both Christian and Yoruba values.

However, the release of the recording represented more than a shift in the
materiality of the church's musical practices. By recording and releasing the
songs, the members of the choir also made a decision that transformed the way
in which church music was experienced. As an audio recording of an actual performance, *Paradise/Ohùn Ẹmí* recorded a number of performance details—

including instrumentation, tempo, and timbre—and allowed them to circulate outside of the songs' immediate performance space. A particular sound and style of performance were captured in the recording and fixed to the message and lyrics of the songs.

In this chapter, I explore the creative strategies and choices made by the musicians who created the recording, to understand how shifts in political economy and religious experience in Nigeria during the second half of the twentieth century were related to each other.[1] Those responsible for the recording drew on meaningful cultural forms to make authoritative claims about morality and experience. Their aim in doing so was to engineer a (re)organization of Cherubim and Seraphim churches so that they could better respond to the challenges presented by the oil boom, but they placed this reorganization within morally legitimate historical frameworks of interpretation. Thus, this chapter also provides a discussion of the founding of the Ayọ̀ ni o Church by a group of Yoruba men and women living in the United Kingdom in the 1960s, the growth of the church throughout the 1970s, and the relationship of this church to other Cherubim and Seraphim denominations.

My examination of the creation and production of this recording serves as a means of understanding how members of the Ayọ̀ ni o Church used audio and visual media to create authoritative and meaningful links between political and economic transformations and individual experience.[2] How might the adoption of mass-mediated cultural forms transform the way in which people use religion to act on and make sense of their lives and to construct identity and moral community? As my analysis demonstrates, the church leaders and choir musicians in this case brought together religion, music, and electronic media to create explicit links between political economy and religious experience.

Oil Wealth, Fast Capitalism, and the Morality of Money

The year 1970 was a key moment in Nigerian political-economic history, marking both the end of the Nigerian Civil War and the beginning of the oil boom. The end of the bloody conflict and the reunification of the country promised an increased government focus on national development rather than war. Much of this development was to be funded by the dramatic increase in the export of oil for sale in international markets. By 1970, Nigeria was producing 1.4 million barrels of oil per day—up from 400,000 barrels per day before the war in 1967—and over the next four years production more than doubled. Nigeria joined the Organization of the Petroleum Exporting Countries (OPEC) in 1971, and, as a result of rapid increases in the global price of oil due to OPEC members' unilateral price surges as well as shortages of oil on the world market in 1973–1974, oil revenues in Nigeria increased 350 percent between 1974 and 1979. Oil exports eclipsed those of agricultural goods, resulting in a national economy that relied solely on income from petroleum exports (Kirk-Greene and Rimmer 1981, 83–85). The Nigerian state directly collected the proceeds of this economic boom and distributed the funds through regional and state government channels. The federal government also used these funds to begin a massive reconstruction of the country's infrastructure, which had been weakened by the civil war. The Nigerian state began a number of development projects, including building projects in urban areas (roads, hospitals, schools); increased industrialization (parastatal factories, steel mills, refineries); and attempted to expand indigenous commercial enterprises.

Michael Watts has argued that this influx of oil wealth and the accompanying "rollercoaster economy" (1992, 35), which was tied directly to global oil prices, resulted in a speeding up of capitalism in Nigeria, as a "faster pace and rhythm of life [was] unleashed by oil and state investment" (1996, 271). One result of this speeding up of the rate of monetary exchange and circulation was an increase in socio-economic differentiation. This was especially true in urban areas such as Lagos, where an elite class emerged and the gap between rich and poor grew. Those at the top levels of governmental bureaucracy or with access to government contracts grew extremely wealthy almost overnight. In Lagos, the commercial and political center of Nigeria at the time, a nascent middle class emerged, consisting of educated civil servants working in or servicing expanded government offices.

The expansion of the civil service created new employment opportunities, which resulted in massive migration to Lagos from rural areas, especially from the surrounding Yoruba towns and villages. As a result, competition for urban resources, especially housing, became acute. In addition, the influx of migrants from the Nigerian countryside produced high levels of unemployment, especially for unskilled or semiskilled workers. Those without the influence needed to acquire state contracts that provided access to oil money came to rely on an informal economy characterized by patron-clientage and middleman-type relationships (Barnes 1986, 202). Further, the state-driven distribution of funds exacerbated graft in a governmental organization that was already prone to corruption (see Smith 2007; Watts 1992). Bribes and kickbacks became standard business practices. Many of the funds generated by government contracts and the bribes that helped to produce them were diverted into forms of social capital and conspicuous consumption that were used to support patron-clientage based on kinship and home-village-based networks of solidarity. The need to demonstrate one's class status through the display of appropriate consumer goods (clothing, cars, furniture, etc.) created anxiety for members of, and those aspiring to membership in, the Yoruba middle class.

Discourses addressing how commodification and conspicuous consumption appeared to be unlinked to productive forms of labor became increasingly evident in the Nigerian public sphere. For many, "money seem[ed] to literally appear out of thin air and without the expenditure of effort" (Watts 1992, 54), and this caused wealth and crime to become linked in popular imagination. For example, Karin Barber (1982) describes how during this period social relations of money became central themes in Yoruba popular theater, with plays contrasting legitimate wealth, which derived from productive labor, with illegitimate wealth, which derived from "fake" work such as armed robbery or magical practices. These morality plays emphasized the importance of the Yoruba communal value of hard work. In plays, music, and other popular genres, Yoruba artists articulated a moral economy of value that would be central to the shaping of religious discourses during this period.[3]

The oil boom and the centralization of the postcolonial Nigerian state affected class formations and popular conceptions of money and wealth. For Yoruba, these political and economic transformations were experienced in relation to Yoruba moral conceptions and concerns, as evidenced in popular culture. These concerns about the morality of money were also addressed by organized religion, including churches such as the Cherubim and Seraphim. As a result, many Yoruba cultural and social formations were transformed and renewed through the interaction between religion and political economy. The experience of the oil boom and of the centralized petrostate, as refracted through the prism of Christianity, had an impact on Cherubim and Seraphim churches in terms of both religious practice and institutional organization. The recording that is the subject of this chapter may be understood as produced by, as well as potentially furthering, the political-economic transformations of the time.

Representing the Cherubim and Seraphim Church

The Ayọ̀ ni o Church choir drew extensively on the history of the Cherubim and Seraphim churches discussed in the previous chapter to bring the experiences of middle-class Yoruba church members in line with the new political and economic order of the oil boom. This link to the past may be seen through an examination of the *Paradise/Ohùn Ẹmí* cover.[4] The artwork accompanying the recording featured a blurry reproduction of a photograph of Moses Orimolade (1879–1933), the saint-like figure who, together with Christianah Abiodun, founded the Cherubim and Seraphim churches in Lagos in 1925. The use of Orimolade's portrait—rather than a photo of the musicians featured on the recording or even a widely recognizable Christian image—made a deliberate connection between the present and the past.

Why would the producers of the recording feel compelled to put the face of the old (i.e., the churches' founder) on the cover of something that represented much that was new technologically and musically? Answering this question illuminates what the shifts in technology and circulation meant for members of the Ayọ̀ ni o Church. Orimolade's image—a form of media in itself—created a deliberate connection between the context in which the recording was produced and the context in which Orimolade founded the Cherubim and Seraphim churches.

Album cover for *Paradise/Ohùn Ẹmí* cassette

Looking back to the founding of the Cherubim and Seraphim in the moment of colonial transformations of Yoruba society provides some insight into why the choir members used Orimolade's image to make a link between the colonial context and that of the oil boom.

Recall the centrality of music in the founding of the Cherubim and Seraphim, as discussed in the previous chapter. Orimolade, Abiodun, and the other founding members of the church made frequent public appearances, marching around Lagos denouncing juju and magic, witches, and traditional religious practices. On the first anniversary of the society's founding, they held a large procession, in which, for the first time, they wore white cassocks as their uniform (Omoyajowo 1982, 15). For much of the early history of the Cherubim and Seraphim, the procession was the primary mode through which the church's beliefs and practices were circulated in a growing public sphere in Lagos.

The decision to modify this mode of circulation and to record the church's musical compositions for commercial release in 1978 was made for purposes of both evangelism and promotion. A member of the choir who was instrumental in working with record studios and music distributors in Lagos to produce the first album described the decision to do so as follows:

> Before we started recording, we had songs—soul inspiring songs. Then we said, "Only the church is enjoying the songs." And the songs are actually evangelical. And the church wants to be recognized, wants to be known. So the choir is being used as a tool of evangelizing and promoting the church. . . . That was bringing in people to the church, people of God, who took the soul inspiring songs, and were so moved. Some of them started giving us testimonies, such as "when I was sick I was just listening to the choir music and I got healed."

This use of recording technology and the subsequent distribution of the recording on cassette represented a new way of conceiving of evangelism. It also indexed the church's history at the same time that it expanded it. During the colonial period, the church's founders had organized processions through markets and other public spaces in Lagos and nearby towns, but the expansion of the city in the 1970s limited the effectiveness of such practices in reaching residents throughout the city. The recording was capable of circulating through networks created for the distribution of commercial music, thus potentially reaching new hearers.

The decision by the Ayọ̀ ni o Church choir to record its music for commercial distribution marked the movement of Cherubim and Seraphim evangelism to a mass-mediated level. However, choir members also drew on church tradition in a number of ways, starting with the image on the cover of the recording. They did so to insert a religious message about the dangers of consumption into the very act of consuming. The recording served as a commodity that outlined an approach for dealing with other commodities, one that preserved Yoruba Christian values concerning authenticity and hard work.

Although the recording represented a new use of media by the Cherubim and Seraphim churches, it was made possible by the historical development of Nigerian Christian musical recordings. Most early recordings of Yoruba music were of genres of secular dance music.[5] Some Yoruba social music had been reproduced on 78-rpm discs beginning in the mid-1930s, but it was not until after World War II that Yoruba popular music began to be electronically recorded and distributed on a widespread basis (Waterman 1990, 76–77). By the 1950s, electronic media facilities had been established in parts of southwestern Nigeria, centered in Lagos, including recording facilities and an expanded radio service. Ownership of electronic goods also began to grow as a symbol of elite status and upward mobility (Waterman 1990, 90–93). Genres such as jùjú, which influenced and was influenced by the development of Yoruba Christian music, helped to create a public sphere in which Yoruba values were articulated in relation to modern Nigerian realities (see Waterman 1990).

By the 1970s, an important effect of the oil boom was the import of foreign commodities. Cheap consumer electronics, such as the transistor radio and cassette player, were widely accessible by 1974, and government salary increases made them prominent features of middle-class households. Musical recordings from the United States were also imported and had a significant impact on the development of Yoruba Christian music. Especially influential were country gospel artists such as the Blackwood Brothers, Jim Reeves, and the Speer Family, as well as African American gospel recordings, including those by the Staple Singers and Al Green.

Christian radio broadcasts were begun in the 1960s by the Liberian Evangelical Church of West Africa (ECWA), from its Nigerian base in Kwara state. ECWA created a local Nigerian version of Radio ELWA (Eternal Love Winning Africa), which broadcast sermons and religious programs. Musical performances by musicians from local ECWA churches were important components of these broadcasts. Out of the ELWA broadcasts emerged the first widely known Yoruba gospel performers, Takete Voices, led by M. A. Balogun, the "Singing Bird of Jesus." The choirmaster of the Ayọ̀ ni o Church, Prophet S. F. Korode, whose leadership of the Ayọ̀ ni o Church choir made the recording possible, came from Kwara state and had attended ECWA primary and secondary schools, and Radio ELWA's broadcasts had a formative influence on his childhood.

These examples, combined with the growing number of churches recording and releasing their songs commercially in the 1960s and 1970s, led the Ayọ̀ ni o Church choir not only to enter the recording studio but also to seek a commercial producer and distributor for its first album.[6] This decision can also be understood as a deliberate embrace of a new form of technology, a strategic use of this technology to circulate Cherubim and Seraphim tradition in a package suited to the "modern" present. Electronic mediation allowed the musical messages of the Cherubim and Seraphim to reach a new sort of subject—an educated middle-class Nigerian, rather than a rural newcomer to Lagos—and the listener to imagine him- or herself as part of an audience familiar with new technology and able to purchase the equipment necessary to play the cassette.

Reengineering the Cherubim and Seraphim Church

The shift in the media of musical circulations from processions to recordings can also be understood in relation to the way Cherubim and Seraphim churches, as a network of separate yet denominationally related institutions, were transformed by the oil boom. After Orimolade's death in 1933, the Cherubim and Seraphim Society split into several factions, and thereafter the Cherubim and Seraphim churches continued to be characterized by decentralization and breakaway movements. This structure of fission contributed to the spread of Cherubim and Seraphim in southwest Nigeria between 1940 and 1960, as prophets emerged from within congregations and then left to start new churches. In addition, many church members were sent by the colonial government from the southwest to other parts of Nigeria to work in civil service or industrial positions (e.g., as railway workers). These migrants brought their religious practices with them and started Cherubim and Seraphim churches in non-Yoruba cities, including Kaduna and Port Harcourt.

The Cherubim and Seraphim Church Movement, which is the branch of the Cherubim and Seraphim to which the Ayọ̀ ni o Church belongs, was one of the original factions that emerged following Orimolade's death. The Cherubim and Seraphim Church Movement was established by Yoruba migrants to Kaduna, a predominantly Muslim Hausa city in northern Nigeria, in the 1930s. Kaduna was the capital of Nigeria's Northern Region under the British. Many Yoruba moved to Kaduna during the colonial period to work on the railway or other industrial projects. In church organizational documents and other communications the Ayọ̀ ni o Church is referred to as the "Surulere District Sub-Headquarters" of the Cherubim and Seraphim Church Movement. Notably, the "sub-headquarters" of the church is considerably larger than the church's headquarters in Kaduna.

In the 1960s, Cherubim and Seraphim churches tended to be organized around a charismatic prophet figure rather than a hierarchical bureaucratic administrative structure. The predominant focus of these churches was on spiritual prayer healing and prophetic divination through dreams and visions. In the 1970s, feeling the impact of the oil boom and the shifts in the Nigerian economy described above, many in Lagos's unemployed and lower classes flocked to Cherubim and Seraphim churches as a way of dealing with the pressures of conspicuous consumption and the need to locate themselves within one or more patron-client networks. In doing so, they looked to the visions and counseling of the church prophets as a way of divining the source of and potentially resolving the contradiction presented by the very visible wealth and prosperity that was made possible by the oil boom but that remained out of reach of most Nigerians.

However, the Cherubim and Seraphim also faced significant challenges during this period, both from within and from outside the church. As stories circulated in the public sphere about magical wealth springing from illegitimate sources, many church prophets came under suspicion of asking for monetary payment in return for their prayers. Many criticisms emerged in relation to a new development in Christianity in Nigeria: the neo-Pentecostal revival on Nigerian university campuses.[7] Much as the early members of the Cherubim and Seraphim had done during the colonial period, students at Nigerian universities proposed a new model of Christian practice in Nigeria. In doing so, the students turned to US and British Pentecostal materials and discourses, especially those that emphasized the gifts of the Holy Sprit, such as healing, visions, and spirit baptism.

In the 1970s, Nigerian campuses were the sites of Pentecostal revivals, influenced in part by tours of Nigeria during the preceding decade by North American evangelists such as Billy Graham and Oral Roberts as well as by the growing influx of US-produced Pentecostal literature into the country (Ojo 2006). Students were drawn to this new form of Christianity because it provided them with a stance from which to critique Nigerian elites—many of whom occupied leadership roles in orthodox Christian and Muslim congregations—on the grounds that they were hiding their illegitimate production of wealth behind the religious veneer provided by stagnated mission churches and the Islamic establishment. Many of the congregations founded during this time countered what they saw as out-of-control consumption of commodities with a version of Christianity that emphasized holiness and purity at the same time that it addressed the concerns of the Yoruba middle class concerning the transformation of employment and consumption brought about by the oil boom. These new religious movements presented themselves as alternatives to what they saw as "Africanized," and thus problematic, forms of Christianity practiced in independent churches such as the Cherubim and Seraphim and drew many educated young members away from these churches.

It was to this political, economic, and religious scene that a group of Yoruba men and women returned to Nigeria from the United Kingdom, where they had been studying for advanced degrees in fields such as engineering and business. Highly educated and prepared to take up positions in the new Nigerian government and affiliated industries, together they had formed the first Cherubim and Seraphim congregations in London. Many of them attributed their success in terms of completing their education overseas as well as their ability to find employment in Nigeria on their return to their spiritual strength and religious practice. Their return home to Nigeria was motivated by a desire to assist with the rebuilding process after the civil war and to take advantage of the new oil-driven prosperity in the country.

This group of returnees first joined the congregation of the Cherubim and Seraphim Church Movement branch on the mainland in Lagos, located in a Yoruba neighborhood dominated by railway and other transportation workers. However, disagreements between the returnees and the members of the already established congregation began to grow. Some of the antagonism was due to seniority issues, as the church elders grew resentful of the returnees' suggestions for improving the church. Many of the returnees also saw themselves as bringing "European" values to the Cherubim and Seraphim. In their history of the Ayọ̀ ni o Church, Essien et al. offer the following description of the relationship between the returnees and the established congregations in Lagos:

> Soon after setting up at these local churches, O. A. Jagun [a returnee] clashed head on with the prevailing old viewpoint, tried to sell new ideas, and the controversy spread rapidly to other sister churches. These returnees experienced considerable opposition almost as soon as they got involved in the conduct of church affairs. They were condemned by the Elders-in-Council and finally by the Baba Aladura in Kaduna. But this did not mean the triumph of old values. The Surulere group [of returnees] was out of tune with the "Church of Old." (1999:158)

The returnees were especially critical of church leaders and prophets who took money in exchange for their prayers and visions. Bringing together aspects of the moral critique of wealth articulated in popular culture at the time and the holiness emphasis of the new Pentecostal movements, the returnees were involved in what they saw as a purification of Cherubim and Seraphim practices in relation to the potential danger attending the circulation of money and commodities.

Separating themselves from the more established Cherubim and Seraphim congregations, the returnees began to gather for private prayer meetings at Bar Beach on Victoria Island and in private homes of similar-minded church members. A series of spiritual revelations and visions received by certain members of the group led to the naming of G. O. Fakeye, a communications engineer who also was a charismatic preacher and prophet, as the leader of the group. Other returnees were named as officers, and they decided to establish their own church, although they remained affiliated with the Cherubim and Seraphim Church Movement that was headquartered in Kaduna. They distinguished themselves from other branches of the Cherubim and Seraphim Movement in Lagos through their use of the phrase "Ayọ̀ ni o" ("It is joy"), which the returnees used as a form of greeting with one another. The group built its first prayer house in the Aguda section of Surulere, a middle-class Yoruba suburb of Lagos. In 1979, soon after the choir released its first album, the church moved to its current location, a large plot of land in what, at that time, was an emerging industrial area along the Apapa-Oshodi Expressway.

The use of Orimolade's image on the cover of the recording is relevant here. There are many parallels between the economic and political transformations of Yoruba society in the context of colonialism and in that of the oil boom, from the establishment of new forms of employment and modes of obtaining wealth to the shifts to ever more centralized forms of governance. In both contexts, witchcraft and independent Christianity served as means of making sense of and acting on these transformations. By using Orimolade's image on the album cover, the choir created a deliberate link between the two moments of Nigerian history, pointing to the past as providing an example for navigating current economic and social changes. However, the church leaders—especially those involved in the production of the recording—invoked the church's founding to reorganize the church itself, so that it could better serve the needs of Yoruba Christians in the context of the oil boom. They were also concerned about warding off Pentecostal criticism that Alàdúrà churches were hiding their reliance on magic and other spiritual powers behind a false Christian veneer. They indexed the founding moment of the church to legitimate their claims concerning the corruption of other Cherubim and Seraphim leaders as well as to justify the need to "modernize" the church's "old viewpoint."

This link between past and present was sustained and elaborated through the process of producing the album, from the religious experience of the choirmaster that inspired the recording to the creative musical and aesthetic choices made in composing and recording the songs on it and the decision made by the church leadership to release it. The remainder of this chapter addresses how religion and music, along with the use of media technology, were tools used to make these links meaningful and real for church members.

Dream Visions: Religious Experience and the Mediation of Political-Economic Change

The songs recorded by the Ayọ̀ ni o Church choir for *Paradise/Ohùn Ẹmí* were inspired by a visionary dream experienced by the group's charismatic choirmaster, Prophet Korode. Korode's experience indicates how religion was used to make an authoritative argument regarding moral approaches Yoruba Christians might take to the oil boom. Making this argument also entailed creating meaningful links to the founding moment of the Cherubim and Seraphim Church. Through a process of religious mediation, Korode drew on his religious experience to produce two songs that created affective ties between the experience of political and economic transformation in the context of the oil boom and similar experiences in the colonial context.

Whereas the link to the founding of the Cherubim and Seraphim Church was crystallized in the album's cover art, Korode's experience drew on a specific episode in the church's history. It, thus, indexes a different mode of religious representation and experience than does Orimolade's image. In particular, Korode's dream mirrors Abiodun's "Celestial Vision" that served as the catalyst that ultimately led to the founding the Cherubim and Seraphim movement. In Korode's dream, an angelic guide took him to heaven, where he was subjected to a series of spiritual tests. The dream began with Korode's angelic guide asking him a question about Yoruba kinship relations: "Locally, when you meet a senior sister of yours, what do you do?" Korode responded by saying, "I will prostrate and greet, because that is the local way." He was then told, "You will soon be meeting with your sister. And it will be important that you do just that." After this exchange, he was subjected to what he described as a "trial run" before he was brought to meet his "sister." The trial run consisted of a series of tests.

The first test concerned his knowledge of God's word:

> As we were moving on, I got to a place where [the angelic guide] showed me a certain group of objects, and he said, "Do you see this set of books?" I said, "Yes." "They are supposed to be on the shelves, why are they on ground?" And I said, "Well it will mean that these people are careless, and they have not really stacked them the way they should." He said "OK." We moved on again, we saw some [books] in the shelves, properly arranged. The first set of books, whereas they looked quite all right, were completely disorganized. He said, "The first set of books, I wrote them just as I liked, not as they ought to be." . . . These were deep things.

In this test, Korode was presented with a pile of carelessly jumbled books and asked to compare them to shelves of neatly organized books. A revelation about the way God's word "ought to be," Korode explained, "these were deep things." This part of Korode's dream can be understood as directly taking on a key issue in Christianity concerning religious authority and the legitimate interpretation of the Bible.[8] The books in Korode's dream stand in for this issue and may be understood as nodes of mediation in themselves. The need for them to be properly arranged represented to Korode the need for reality to be organized according to certain rules—not "carelessly" but the way things "ought to be." Guidelines for achieving this proper mode of organization—one that is divinely sanctioned—emerged over the course of his dream.

Korode faced two more tests before he met with his sister. One involved identifying the various groups of people he saw during his journey in heaven: "Then I eventually saw another group of persons moving and they said, 'These who are in the white garment, who are these?' And I said 'These should be the Seraphim.' 'Who are these with the girdle?' I also called those names. They said 'You will know about them later.'" This test examined his ability to distinguish different groups of angels according to their apparel. This test also echoed issues related to the Cherubim and Seraphim Church uniform, which is iconic of angels, with its flowing white robes (the white garment) and sash (girdle) tied around the waist.[9] The appearance of angels in heaven in Korode's dream affirmed this public and sometimes controversial marker of church membership in southwest Nigeria.[10]

The next test asked Korode to verify whether he could determine the authenticity of the sun's light:

> Then the third revelation at that time was putting what you might call the light of the sun, like a ball, in a bowl and putting another light which was not the sun in another container, but also glowing, almost at the same level, and

catapulting the two up. And one got up and just lost its glow, and the other one went straight into the sky and sent another set of rays down. He said, "Do you know the difference between the two?" I said, "Well, one should be the real sun, the other one is mock sun." He said, "Now I will let you see the difference in these things. This is where your people should be going. And this is where they are. What they are doing is all right, but not good enough, so let them know when you get back to them." These were revelations.

In this ordeal, Korode was tested on his ability to distinguish between things that are real and things that are fake. His experience here echoed popular concerns about legitimate forms of wealth and the importance of hard work over fake work, such as magic, that circulated in the Nigerian public in the context of the oil boom. After he proved that he could make this distinction successfully, he was urged to use his ability to discern real from fake to advise his people. Again, religious mediation legitimized and made real particular forms of morality. This lesson, in particular, was understood by Korode as targeting Cherubim and Seraphim prophets who took money in return for their divinatory and healing prayers, which called into doubt the legitimacy of their practices.

Finally, Korode was brought to meet with his "sister," as he was told he would be at the beginning of his dream:

> Now, the next stage was meeting with my supposed sister. But the one that met me was not my sister from what I saw. I said "Ah, you are my brother's wife." My brother's wife should kneel down, regardless of what my age is, and therefore I wasn't supposed to prostrate for her. I said "No, it's you who should kneel down." She said "But you were told that if you should meet someone then you should prostrate." I said "No you are my brother's wife. And the reason is because I got into the home before you so you have to."

> And then she just transformed into something really muscular and there was a fight. We fight, we fight, we would go to the top of a big mountain, and I was assisted by one invisible force to push her down, and thereafter there were appearances of persons who had gone before.

In this final test, Korode was asked to show that he understood proper ethical forms and directions of respect. A Yoruba man should *dòbálẹ* (prostrate himself) to greet his senior sister, but in an encounter with his brother's wife—a "fake" sibling—the woman should *kúnlẹ* (kneel) before him. Affines are typically suspected of witchcraft because they are both stranger and kin at the same time, so it is quite appropriate here that a representation of his sister-in-law became the demon that Korode had to fight to enter heaven. In this case, Korode's knowledge of Yoruba forms of social organization and ethical ideas of respect were put to the test, suggesting that one possible resolution to anxieties about legitimate sources of wealth lay in the maintenance of those forms and ideas. Like the ordeals concerned with the proper and authentic arrangement of books, celestial objects, and people experienced in his dream, this test provided Korode with rules for social organization that were based on Yoruba values.

The dream vision ended with Korode's entrance to heaven, which was accompanied by a song:

> Then from nowhere I heard sounds of heavy drums, clarinets, tambourines, etc. Then a special Halleluiah song. . . . And that was why we started singing about "Those heavenly houses. How glorious they are." Because you saw many that had long gone and were all rising up in a concert of worship.
>
> By the time I woke up the entire bed was really wet. My wife was worried about me. This was a real event. A real event. That was in 1978. So by the time we put all this together, I had the real sound.

Korode mastered the tests put to him, emerged victorious from the battle with his sister-in-law–turned–demon, and was allowed to glimpse heaven, populated by ancestors in angelic form (those who had "gone before"). Through his experience, Korode drew on the Cherubim and Seraphim practice of visionary dreams both to make sense of social transformation through long-standing cultural practices, especially Yoruba kinship relations and the standards of legitimacy thus established, and to create a cultural form of media (e.g., a song) that would further circulate the importance of these values.

This dream, as he explained to me, was a revelation, a message he was to carry back to "his people." It was also, as he said, "a real event"—an authentic experience containing specific lessons that needed to be brought down from heaven to earth. These lessons were made more authoritative by being inspired by a visionary dream—the message was thus made to come from God in heaven rather than from a single individual—and the dream also established Korode's authority by means of the series of tests he successfully completed. The means of mediating these messages from God to his followers appeared at the end of his dream with the sound of what Korode described as a "Halleluiah chorus." This was the "real sound" that would later form the musical basis of the songs recorded for *Paradise/Ohùn Ẹmí*.

The dream itself was a node of mediation that created connections between various social domains—kinship, cosmology, religious symbols, music—and linked them together in a way that was authoritative and meaningful for church members. The recording was another node that translated Korode's dream vision to link religious experience to larger political-economic transformations, by taking an individualized, internal experience and transforming it into a set of songs that could circulate and generalize the main lessons of the experience for church members. To understand how one man's religious experience was able to link religious experience to political economy, it is necessary to examine the form in which Korode presented it to church members: as two electronically recorded songs.

Musical Messages: The Sonic Mediation of Religious Experience

To understand how the songs recorded by the choir were effective in crafting a statement that church leaders thought would help church members navigate the material shifts provoked by the oil boom, the notion of mediation as a semiotic process by which culture is transmitted is most useful. Mediation is thus a way in which social practices are constituted by virtue of their relationship to cultural forms, in other words, "the discursive production of conceptual and intuitive links between domains of social experience" (Fox 2004, 346). This sense of mediation is particularly helpful for understanding how music, as a cultural form that is experienced in real time through performing or listening, can help create linkages between moral values, historical events, and everyday experience. The use of affective musical techniques (including rhythm, musical form, and lyrics) helps to bring certain cultural values and ideas into focus and thus enables people to connect their everyday practices to them.

This capacity of music is particularly important in the case discussed here. Korode's religious experience and the message he received in heaven during his dream vision were transformed into a song titled "Paradise." An act of translation took place: Korode did not reproduce the music heard in the dream exactly. Instead, he took parts of the sound he heard in the dream, elaborated on the revelations of the dream, and, in collaboration with other choir members, composed "Paradise." Similarly, "Ohùn Ẹmí," the other song on the album, further developed Korode's spiritual vision and message, turning the revelations of his dream vision into a lesson for members of the Cherubim and Seraphim Church and Yoruba Christians, more generally.

As this analysis of the recording thus far has made clear, doing so involved indexing the history of the Cherubim and Seraphim Church. The same is true of the musical characteristics drawn on by the Ayọ̀ ni o Church choir in the making of the recording. The founders of the Cherubim and Seraphim churches made two important musical innovations that transformed the musical practices they inherited from the Anglican mission churches. The first involved their use of handclapping, dancing, and, eventually, drumming to accompany their hymn singing.[11] This performance sharply diverged from the typical practice in mission churches of congregational singing with organ accompaniment.

As noted in the previous chapter, Cherubim and Seraphim members also began to write original hymns. These were often modeled musically on Anglican hymns but featured lyrics specific to the context in which they were developed.

Many of these newly composed Cherubim and Seraphim hymns were "received" by society members while in spiritual trance or as the result of a dream vision. For example, Hymn 218, "The New Year Has Come, We Rejoice," includes the following lines: "Those who don't believe in visions are just like hard hearted pagans who could not know one from the other. Ask from Jenny Winful what she experienced before childbirth. Praise God for the new year." This hymn commemorated the experience of Jenny Winful, a Ghanaian woman living in Lagos, who came to Orimolade to seek a remedy for her infertility (Famodimu 1990). It testified to the effectiveness of the spiritual actions of the Cherubim and Seraphim Society, emphasizing the importance of visions. This hymn also represented the effort of early Cherubim and Seraphim members to circulate and popularize their distinctive spiritual practices by using music. Music was a medium through which individual experiences—like those of Jenny Winful in this hymn or of Korode in the songs recorded for the album—were elevated to the level of generalizable experience. Hymn 218 created meaningful links between individual experiences, religious practices, and larger social contexts.

The songs recorded by the choir in 1978 may be understood similarly as documenting Korode's religious experience and communicating it to a wider church membership. The recording built on previous Cherubim and Seraphim musical practices. At the same time, these practices were transformed and made to conform to the requirements and expectations of recorded commercial music, including standardizing the length of the song and using electronic instruments, such as electric guitars and keyboard. It was in this way that connections were made between the musical details of the songs, Korode's religious experience, and the context of the oil boom. The musical characteristics of the songs—in particular, instrumentation, musical form, rhythm, and lyrical content—worked together to create an affective and meaningful cultural form that seamed together these various relationships for church members.

The way in which music is able to create linkages between different domains of experience is something that is explicitly recognized by members of the Ayọ ni o Church. Indeed, the ability of music to educate was often repeated to me over the course of my research: "Music makes the message sweeter," as one musician explained to me. In other words, many Yoruba musicians, especially church musicians, believe that by using compelling rhythms, instruments, sounds, and styles, music can teach a lesson that people might not otherwise be inclined to hear. This understanding of the pedagogical qualities of music, which in the Ayọ ni o Church choir is typically referred to as the "message" of a particular song, connects doctrinal beliefs, political and economic contexts, and individual experience by uniting them in a cultural form that can be experienced at the bodily level when one sings and dances along.

The instrumentation used in the recording of *Paradise/Ohùn Ẹmí* included electric keyboard, amplified lead and bass guitars, and a percussion section that included *sekèrè* (gourd rattle), maracas, and *àkúbà* (locally made, Conga-style drums). The choir included both male and female voices; the lead singer for "Paradise" was male, and "Ohùn Ẹmí" included sections led by a male voice alternating with a male-female duet. The mix on the recording favored the voices and percussion section, which were augmented by the bass guitar. In both songs, the choir used call-and-response variations, and each song progressed from longer verse–chorus exchanges to short, one-line call-and-response exchanges. The melody of each verse–chorus section was introduced by the electric guitars before being sung by the choir. Many of these exchanges consisted of a varying phrase sung by the lead singer to which the chorus's response stayed the same. The àkúbà, sekèrè, and maracas combined to play interlocking cyclical patterns: Both songs started as a slow rumba, an eight-beat cycle, divided into 3+3+2, and shifted approximately one-third of the way through to the *wọ́rọ́* rhythm, a 12/8 Yoruba dance rhythm derived from the Yoruba talking drum ensemble tradition (Euba 1990). All of these musical details worked together to emphasize particular aspects of the songs' messages.

In "Paradise," the melody was first introduced by the keyboard and guitar. The opening lyrics made use of proverbs to describe existence as a problem that Christianity is poised to solve. After this brief introductory section, a series of praises was offered to God ("Exalt Him! Exalt Him!"); these praises, in turn, revealed the gate of heaven ("After all these, I looked, behold, a door opened in heaven"), a direct statement of Korode's experience in his dream vision. The next segment of the song was a verse–chorus call-and-response form in which the lead singer described the twelve gates that lead into heaven and the choir responded with the same textual and melodic phrase ("Paradise, paradise, the glorious land, the abode of the joyful. When shall we see your face?"). "Paradise" ended with a series of exchanges containing millenarian warnings about the impending arrival of judgment day and exhorting "people of the world" to "hear the voice of the prophet" because "today is the day of salvation."

Whereas the lyrics to "Paradise" narrated segments of Korode's dream vision in poetic form, "Ohùn Ẹmí" elaborated on the revelations he received during the dream, turning them into explicit "messages" designed to educate the listener. A version of the "Halleluiah chorus" that Korode heard at the end of his dream was elaborated on during the song's opening phrases. Like "Paradise," "Ohùn Ẹmí" began with lyrics praising God. However, it was after the rhythmic shift from rumba to wọ́rọ́ that the key messages of Korode's dream vision were delivered. This rhythmic shift is significant. It marked the bringing in of "foreign" musical elements and their connection to local musical forms as the musicians shifted from rumba, an African diasporic rhythm brought back to Lagos via recordings of Cuban and other Caribbean musics, to wọ́rọ́, a rhythm recognized as being distinctly Yoruba.

This rhythmic shift may also be understood as an indexical icon of the larger social shifts that the choir members articulated in the recording, a sonic representation of the process of transformation that they called for in the lyrics. The rumba, a rhythm that is both local and foreign, having traveled a diasporic circuit to come back to Nigeria, was made relevant and meaningful through its connection to the wọ́rọ́, a rhythm that is specific to Yoruba music. This is similar to the way in which, in Korode's dream, the symbols of Christianity (books in proper order, angelic beings wearing their correct clothing) were made to resonate with forms of social organization based on Yoruba kinship and moral values concerning authenticity (the battle with his sister-in-law over proper directions of respect). The choir's use of rhythm here might be understood as a performative action that attempted to slow down the speeding up of capitalism experienced during the oil boom by articulating it in local modes of value and exchange.

Such an analysis is also supported by the lyrics of the songs and their relationship to these rhythms. The wọ́rọ́ rhythm is linked to social and political commentary and criticism by Yoruba musicians (Dosunmu 2005). Its use here signaled that the listener should expect a certain type of lyrical content and also be ready to listen in a particular way. The lyrics in the wọ́rọ́ section of "Ohùn Ẹmí" stressed the value of hard work, suggesting that legitimate work will be rewarded and implying that illegitimate work is immoral: "Continue to worship, continue to sing and pray. There is a reward for all our work in the world. Our reward is with Jesus. Endless Joy." Echoing concerns regarding the morality of oil wealth expressed in Yoruba popular theater, the use of the wọ́rọ́ rhythm emphasized that the lyrics should be understood as a commentary on everyday life. As a node of mediation, the song made connections between religion, Yoruba culture, and the experience of the oil boom.

Toward the end of the song, the lyrics directly commented on the relationships between capitalism and Christianity in Nigeria. Drawing on poetic Yoruba metaphors of peace (àláàfíà) and joy (ayọ), the call-and-response segments of the song became more intense as the lyrics warned against those who think that money will buy them salvation. Sung to the wọ́rọ́ rhythm, the lyrics asserted that the Cherubim and Seraphim Church is the means to salvation:

LEAD VOICE:
There is no shock [*Idagiri kan ko si*]
For those who believe
We shall go from strength to strength
Because of the love of our Father
We shall not purchase this joy in the world with money

CHORUS:
The way of salvation is so sweet
Come and taste it, it is as sweet as honey
Christ gave it to us free of charge
We shall not purchase it with money

Stressing that certain intangible items (salvation, joy) are beyond the reach of money, the choir commented directly on the sea of money flowing in Nigeria's oil boom. These lyrics can also be understood as a commentary on the church prophets who took money in exchange for their religious services, a practice that Korode's dream vision affirmed was illegitimate.

The final section of the song outlined the way forward, at the same time that it emphasized the timelessness of the church. It also served as a warning to the leaders of the church that their moral behavior was necessary for the church to move forward, and it urged that the Cherubim and Seraphim churches become unified in purpose and practice. Prominent leaders of various Cherubim and Seraphim denominations, including Christianah Abiodun, the cofounder of the Cherubim and Seraphim, and Fakeye, the leader of the Ayọ̀ ni o Church, were called on by name to pay attention to the final chorus, which warned them to "beware of their conduct" and to "beware in their times of trials" because "we are moving forward."[12]

Together, the two songs delineated the contours of a Cherubim and Seraphim moral community for church members to follow in the midst of political and economic transformation. They did so through a combination of musical innovation and adherence to historical and recognizable forms of musically mediated religious experience. The recordings elaborated on historically sanctioned musical practices and rhetorical strategies that were linked with a particular understanding of Yoruba values their relationship to Cherubim and Seraphim churches in order to creatively make a statement about the role of Christianity in contemporary Nigeria.

Like the hymns written in the 1930s by early Cherubim and Seraphim members, which captured the religious experience of Yoruba Christians in the context of colonialism, this recording documented the congregation's particular experience and interpretation of the moral crisis brought on by the oil boom's "shock of modernity" (Watts 1992). By drawing on the revelations received by Korode during his dream vision, the songs identified a clear means through which to distinguish between real and fake and offered a clear vision of the way things "ought to be." The songs also emphasized the importance of unification and the centralization of church leadership and authority. On the recording the choir sings, "There must be no segregation," emphasizing the moral correctness of the transformations wrought by the Ayọ̀ ni o returnees and their attempts to reform Cherubim and Seraphim practices. Proper order and correct behavior were posited as a solution to the problem of legitimacy in the context of the oil boom. All of this was presented in a package that tied together various stances that church members might take toward the sea of money and commodities flowing in Nigeria but that was out of reach of most of the middle class. In other words, the choir's recordings offered a moral perspective for Cherubim and Seraphim members toward suspect Nigerians who came into wealth by illegitimate means, and they served as a commentary on the improper use of money.

Further, *Paradise/Ohùn Ẹmí*, derived from the revelations Korode received about where his people "should be going," asserted a particular stance toward Yoruba tradition and its relation to modernity: "We are moving forward." However, as Korode's battle with the demon in the form of his sister-in-law makes clear, moving forward can only happen if one knows the proper directions of respect. If fast capitalism with its overwhelming circulation of commodities resulted in an undoing of traditional hierarchies and forms of legitimate power, producing anxiety about those who demanded respect because of their wealth yet were not worthy of respect because that wealth was illegitimately acquired, the choir argued that Christianity—in particular, Cherubim and Seraphim Christianity—was a means of putting things back in order: "The church of Seraphim is the church of life eternal." This life eternal thus contrasted with the everyday experience of corruption and materialism associated with the oil boom.

The Spirit of Yoruba Modernity

The choir's strategy was clearly a successful one. The release of Paradise/Ohùn Emí in 1978 was the beginning of a thriving recording career for Ayọ̀ ni o Church choir members. Since then, they have recorded more than thirty albums, typically releasing one per year. They also created music videos to support their recordings, which are regularly broadcast on Nigerian television. In 2005, their 1992 album Òkè Mímọ (Holy Mountain) was named the Best Evergreen Highlife Album at the Nigerian Christian Music Achievers Award ceremony. This commercial and artistic musical success went hand in hand with the expansion of the Ayọ̀ ni o Church. By the mid-1980s, it had grown to a megachurch with thousands of members attending Sunday services each week, and it produced weekly radio broadcasts and a flurry of pamphlets and other publications. The attempt to build connections to other Cherubim and Seraphim congregations and to unify them within a centralized church hierarchy continues to the current moment. All of this was made possible by the church leaders' strategic use of various media and mediating processes to communicate their message to and legitimate it for an ever-growing population. The success of the choir may perhaps have been due in part to the way in which the message encoded in the recording provided Yoruba Christians with a means to navigate the contradictions of the oil boom.

The linkages traced here between history, religious experience, sound, technology, and social organization are not inevitable or natural. As this analysis has demonstrated, they are actively made and remade through processes of mediation.

The particular church that produced the recording was made possible by the oil boom but also responded to it through religious and musical means. Recall that the Ayọ̀ ni o Church was created by a group of young Yoruba men and women who had returned to Nigeria to take advantage of the possibilities presented both by the influx of money and opportunity associated with the oil boom and by their foreign education. They called for a centralization of Cherubim and Seraphim Church organization as well as for more transparency in relation to the circulation of money in the church. The returnees and their rationalizing practices transformed Cherubim and Seraphim practices and the organization of the church by bringing them in line with new political and economic orientations. Their use of recording technology both enabled and facilitated this process. They created a Cherubim and Seraphim Church as imagined by Fakeye, a communications engineer, and Korode, at that time a young bank executive, rather than by Orimolade, an itinerant, illiterate preacher, or Abiodun, a young, charismatic spiritual leader. They did so not by rejecting the original church but rather by grounding their changes in church tradition. Through the creation of links to church history—from the graphical invocation of Orimolade on the cover of the album to the inspirational nod toward Abiodun's trance—Korode and the choir legitimated their transformation of Cherubim and Seraphim religious and musical practices.

This remaking of the Cherubim and Seraphim Church happened in relation to the political and economic transformations wrought by the oil boom: the pressures and possibilities presented by conspicuous consumption and the overwhelming circulation of wealth; the expansion of Lagos's population as well as its geographic space (from island to mainland); and the influx of new technologies, ideas, and modes of social organization. The Ayọ̀ ni o Church responded to this situation with a musical recording that built on meaningful aesthetic and religious practices to lay out a path that church members might follow to make moral sense of the changes. This moral sense involved full participation in the new political economy but in a way that was deemed legitimate in relation to Yoruba Christian standards, one that provided a means of being in the world, as the ambiguous yet apocalyptic lyrics of "Ohùn Ẹmí" assert: "There is a reward for all the work that we do in the world/Our reward is with Jesus/Endless Joy."

Notes

1. Because of the difficulty of reconstructing the reception of the album after the fact, in this chapter I am concerned with choices and strategies of production, not consumption. I explore the connections between economic transformations and the ways in which religious authority responds to those transformations through a reshaping of religious experience.

2. In doing so, I contribute to the body of work by anthropologists concerned with how the adoption of media technology by religious practitioners in Africa has transformed religious

practice and experience (Hackett 1998; Marshall-Fratani 1998; Meyer 2004a, 2006; Schulz 2006). These questions have also been of interest to scholars of religion and media more widely (de la Cruz 2009; Hirschkind 2006; Meyer and Moors 2006).

3. See Barber (2003) on Yoruba plays. See Waterman (1990) for an analysis of the articulation of such themes in jùjú music. Apter (2005) also discusses similar themes in regard to cultural production in the context of the oil boom, focusing on the Second World Black and African Festival of Arts and Culture,which was held in Nigeria in 1977.

4. It is likely that the recording was first released on vinyl; however, soon after its initial release, it was produced in a cassette version which, because of the economic transformations in Nigeria, made the recording cheaper and more accessible to a wider audience. I have not been able to determine exactly when the cassette version of the album was made available; some choir members have no memory of the vinyl version of the recording, whereas others clearly remember seeing the record. One of the choir members who was involved in the production of the album asserted that it was released on vinyl and cassette at the same time, although this was not supported by Korode who spoke of "waxing" the first album and of a later release on cassette.

5. The earliest recordings of Yoruba Christian music were made by Reverend J. J. Ransome-Kuti, who, in 1921, traveled to London to record his Yoruba Christian hymns for Zonophone Records. Featuring voice and piano, these recordings were most likely popular among the elite Yoruba-speaking classes in Lagos and Ransome-Kuti's hometown of Abeo-kuta. However, Ransome-Kuti's recordings were not available to wider audiences both because of the expense of the technology required to play them and because of the limited distribution networks for recorded music in Nigeria at the time.

6. A handful of recordings were made in the late 1960s by two Catholic Church choirs located in Ibadan; however, the distribution of these recordings was limited primarily to Ibadan Catholic congregations. It was an Aladura church, the Christ Apostolic Church, that was to lead the way in Yoruba gospel music by creating recordings that targeted a mass audience. The first gospel record with significant distribution and influence was recorded by Samuel Akinpelu and the Gospel Choral Singers, who were associated with the Christ Apostolic Church, Oke Ayo, Ibadan; it was released by Decca Records in 1968. In the same year, Prince S. A. Adeosun of Christ Apostolic Church, Alago-Meji, Lagos, released his first album. The Christ Apostolic Church produced the most influential Yoruba gospel music stars of the 1970s and 1980s, including Reverend Sola Rotimi, Bola Are, and Ayewa.

7. The Nigerian higher-education system was one of the main beneficiaries of Nigeria's oil investment. The Nigerian university system expanded dramatically during the years of the oil boom, from five campuses in 1965 to thirteen in 1975 and to twenty by 1980. This resulted in an increase in the Nigerian population of educated young people, who were no longer interested in agricultural work but, rather, sought employment in the expansive government bureaucracy and affiliated service industries, especially banking.

8. Matthew Engelke's (2007) discussion of the relationship between the Bible and religious authority in the Masowe weChishanu Church presents an interesting counterexample to the one I discuss here. The members of this Zimbabwean independent Christian church insist on a "live and direct" relationship with God, shifting religious authority from the text to performance.

9. Elisha P. Renne (2004) discusses how particular designs for individualized white prayer garments are revealed to church members in dream visions and, thus, are divinely sanctioned.

10. Korode would later write a pamphlet titled Cherubim & Seraphim Legacies in which he addressed criticisms of Cherubim and Seraphim practices (especially the wearing of the church uniform) by using both biblical and visionary examples.

11. As already mentioned, drums and Yoruba vocal styles were introduced into Christian worship in churches such as the Cherubim and Seraphim, in contrast to the mission churches'

insistence that such musical elements were "pagan" and not appropriate for Christian worship. Although the use of drums and dancing in the context of Christian worship is now widespread in most Nigerian churches, use of many traditional Yoruba drums was and continues to be expressly forbidden in the context of Christian worship. For instance, the bàtá drum, used during Sango worship, as well as the dùndún, or large talking drum, were not used because their associations with "paganism" were too explicit. Instead, drums with no connections to orişa religion, such as the tambourine and the sámbà, or square frame drum, came to be associated with Christian music (Waterman 1990, 42; see also Thieme 1969).

12. Abiodun led the Cherubim and Seraphim Society until her death in 1994 and was active in the attempt to unify the Cherubim and Seraphim churches.

4 Take Control

It is good to give thanks to the Lord,
And to sing praises to Your name, O Most High,
To declare Your loving kindness in the morning.
And Your faithfulness every night
On an instrument of ten strings,
On the lute, And on the harp,
With harmonious sound.
For you, Lord, have made me glad through your work;
I will triumph in the works of Your hands.

—Psalm 92:1–4

Sᴏᴜɴᴅ ʀᴇᴄᴏʀᴅɪɴɢ ᴀɴᴅ playback technologies facilitated and enhanced religious experiences and worship practices for members of the Ayọ ni o Church. Between 1978 and 2005 the Ayọ ni o Church choir released more than thirty albums. These recordings reproduced and circulated aesthetic values central to producing religious belonging and ethical forms of personhood. The recordings thus played an important role in the everyday religious practices of church members. However, recordings did not replace live musical performance during worship services. While worship without instruments—no guitars, keyboard, or even drums—was acceptable, worship without singing was inconceivable. The idea that there were live people somewhere in the same space as you, participating in the same musical ritual as you were, was important for ensuring the success of worship both in terms of its ability to provoke appropriate emotional responses from the congregation as well as in terms of attracting the Holy Spirit to enter the worship space. Although the songs on the recordings played an important role in church worship, the recordings were never played during worship. Instead the songs from the recordings were performed live by those present.

As scholars working in a variety of contexts have noted, media technologies are increasingly used in religious settings to heighten practices of devotion and worship, to enable interaction with the divine, and to produce various forms of interaction, interconnectedness, and transcendence (Eisenlohr 2009; Greene 1999; Hirschkind 2006; Schulz 2006). As scholars note, the intertwining of mediation and immediacy in electronically circulated religious texts produces a paradox in which the mediated nature of religious practice itself seems to disappear.[1]

Patrick Eisenlohr describes this paradox as follows: "On the one hand, [media] become almost invisible in their function of enabling ever more immediate forms of interaction and interconnectedness through a maximally transparent and therefore disappearing medium; on the other hand, their presence reasserts itself so forcefully as to override the creativity and control of human subjects" (2009, 276). In response, he draws analytic attention to the semiotic processes by which media and their mediations are made invisible. Eisenlohr locates the capacity of media to hide its own workings in the materiality of media itself, noting that "the impression of enabling a more immediate, singular experience is also reinforced by the fact that audiovisual media are able to store singular tokens together with their iconic characteristics" (286).

Eisenlohr's analysis goes a long way in elucidating the techniques whereby immediacy is produced in religious contexts and processes of mediation are made invisible by the materiality of the technology. Indeed, sound technologies enable new possibilities for the entextualization and contextualization of religious music, allowing songs to be materialized as sound-artifacts that can circulate through the community and be recontextualized in a variety of new contexts, from audio playback of prerecorded music to live performances of previously recorded songs.[2] The iterative potential made possible by sound recording allows electronically mediated religious texts to circulate religious values and provoke spiritual experiences of immediacy and transcendence.

An analytical focus on these semiotic techniques whereby media produce immediacy is crucial to analyzing the social processes by which those media themselves are made invisible in experience. However, such an analysis only goes so far in elucidating the "creativity and control of human subjects" that Eisenlohr argues is erased in such processes. In this chapter I emphasize the disciplined and disciplining work as well as the ethical practices that make such cultural and social processes possible. I do so through an emphasis on what I call the labor of immediacy, that is, the practices whereby human subjects discipline themselves and rehearse the necessary actions that allow the mediated nature of immediate religious experiences to disappear. I argue that the perceived spontaneity of musical performance as well as the practical techniques through which religious sound-artifacts are performed in new contexts in order to produce connections and circulate values, all rest on this labor of immediacy.

This chapter examines how the recordings were used by choir musicians in their everyday lives, in individual musical practice, and in rehearsals. Through the musical labor of training, practice, and rehearsal the choir members engaged with the recordings in order to regulate affective and emotional responses and expressions during church worship. The work of choir musicians during practice and rehearsals made possible the recontextualization of recorded sounds during Cherubim and Seraphim worship. Through disciplinary practices of listening and music making that made use of the recordings church musicians attuned themselves to particular sensory responses and modes of behavior and produced appropriate forms of emotionality. These emotional responses were thus available to be summoned contextually by church members in relation to a given situation. Furthermore, these disciplined forms of emotion and embodiment were seen as necessary to survive and thrive in the midst of the uncertainty provoked by political and economic transitions taking place in Nigeria since its transition to democracy in 1999.

An Example for the Church

Most members of the church recognized the important role that the choir played in ensuring the success of the church's worship. Many church elders, particularly those who occupied leadership positions in the choir, argued that the choir played a key role in the church service. As one pastor explained to me, "The choir is there to draw the congregation into the presence of the Lord, and to prepare the mind of the congregation to receive the Lord's blessings for the day." This idea was echoed by Prophet S. F. Korode, the Ayọ̀ ni o Church choirmaster, at a special retreat the choir held for its members. In his lecture Korode described the choir as having a two-dimensional role: the first or vertical dimension consisted of establishing a relationship to God. To achieve this he urged the choir members to "sing praises to God to glorify and worship Him, using the talent that he gave you." At the same time, the horizontal dimension stressed the relationship between the choir and the congregation. In this aspect the choir was responsible for "leading worship, supporting worship, enriching and enhancing worship, and bringing the congregation closer to God in worship." According to Korode, the two dimensions come together during worship. As another pastor explained: the choir is "necessary in order to carry the congregation and to produce unison so that the congregation recognizes before whom they are coming."

For these reasons the choir was seen as an important ministry of the church. A considerable number of material resources were devoted to the choir, from building space to equipment. The choir stall in the front of the church was consistently maintained and upgraded. For example, in 2003 the carpeting was replaced, and in 2007 new benches and chairs were installed. A full-time church employee maintained all of the choir's electronic equipment, including amplifiers, mixing boards, microphones, and cables. Another part-time employee managed the choir's collection of musical instruments such as guitars, keyboards, drums, and a wide assortment of hand percussion instruments.

The choir had also begun construction on a recording studio in the church compound so that they would not have to rent time in a commercial studio when they wanted to make new recordings. While construction remained incomplete in 2008, the plans demonstrated the group's commitment to recording their music. It was also seen as a potential entrepreneurial enterprise, as the choir leadership envisioned renting out the studio to other church groups that wanted to make recordings. Furthermore, the construction of the studio was understood in religious terms as achieving God's will for the group. As Korode noted when asked in an interview about the recording studio, "If we have our own studio, it is just a question of walking into the place and doing the recording, the potentials are there. God has blessed us with the Church, the land, and resources; and he is watching to see what we make out of it. What I am saying is that God wants to establish us and these are things you have to put in place for the future."[3] Thus, church leadership viewed the choir as an apt investment of resources that had been granted to the church by God.

Approximately 150 men and women were members of the choir, though on a typical Sunday only 75–100 performed with the group during church services. A complex organizational structure coordinated the choir's various activities. The choirmaster was at the top of the group's pyramid-shaped structure, with a small group of ten officers of the choir underneath him, and below them an "executive" committee through which most creative and business decisions were vetted. Underneath this were different groups that reflected the sections of the choir: instrumentalists, lead singers, singers, and hymn heralds. There were also groups devoted to particular purposes, such as the spiritualist group, which coordinated special prayers and other spiritual activities related to the choir; the outings group, which organized groups of choir members to visit neighboring churches or other branches of the church as needed; and the publicity group, which created press releases and other promotional materials to support the work of the choir. Most relevant to the discussion in this chapter is the recordings group, which was responsible for determining the theme of each year's recording, working with the choir's composers to select an appropriate number of new songs for each album, arranging and rehearsing the selected songs—usually in conjunction with the choir's annual Festival of Songs, commonly referred to as Choir Day, and negotiating with studios and commercial distributors to produce the new recording.

Church members who were interested in joining the choir applied for membership. After reviewing their application, the choir leadership conducted a spiritual consultation, praying to God for guidance, to help determine whether the applicant should be allowed to audition. Once a prospective member passed their audition, they were then allowed to join the choir. Others joined the choir by means of a spiritual injunction; in other words, they were the subject of a vision or prophecy that said that they should join the choir and once the authenticity and accuracy of the vision had been verified by church leadership they were allowed to join. Most members of the choir received no formal musical training, and could not read Western music notation. Many of them learned to play their instruments in the church, either from those who already knew how to play their instruments, or by picking it up on their own.

A handful of the choir's musicians made their living as professional musicians. A few had drawn on their experiences with the choir to made a name for themselves as solo gospel artists, while others performed with a variety of popular ensembles at parties or concerts. Ensembles comprised of church musicians were often hired by other church members to perform at weddings, funerals, naming ceremonies, and other events. However, the majority of the choir members had professional careers separate from their church-related musical endeavors. Some worked in the financial industry, others were lawyers, teachers, or business executives. Many were engaged in entrepreneurial activities and owned a variety of small businesses, such as printing presses, catering outfits, or industrial laundries, or were engaged in import/export activities. Others worked as petty traders, selling clothing, soft drinks, or recharge cards for pay-as-you go cell phone service in formal and informal venues. All members of the choir devoted a great deal of time and effort to their religious musical activities, making time in their busy professional and family schedules for rehearsals and other meetings.

For choir members their musical activities were understood to be an important part of their religious practice. Furthermore, this religious practice was key to how they understood their professional and personal success outside of the church. As one senior member of the choir, who was both a chartered insurer as well as a barrister-at-law explained, "My membership of the choir and the church has helped me in several ways. Foremost, the choir helped me find a station in life. It was in the choir that I first had a direction and focus, and today I am very grateful to God." As this example suggests, because the choir served as an example for the church, choir members were expected to be exemplary members of the church who constructed themselves as religious subjects through their musical discipline. This in turn has an impact on their life outside of the church as the discipline learned via participation in choir was related to, though not directly determinative of, their career and family success.

The Ayọ̀ ni o Church choir was understood to be an important institution of the larger church that was central to its religious mission and spiritual practices. The material resources, elaborate organizational structure, and systems governing membership and training, all served as an infrastructure in which choir members could produce effective and affective religious musical experiences. This infrastructure enabled the choir to not only contribute to the success of church worship through their live performances, but also to make recordings that circulated and materialized aesthetic values and affective orientations outside of the context of worship itself.

The Three Ms

Members of the Ayọ̀ ni o Church choir talked about the aesthetic qualities and performative efficacy of their songs by referring in English to the "three Ms: music, melody, and message." In this formula "music" referred to rhythm and instrumentation; "melody" to the relationship between the words of the song and the tune of the song; and "message" to the lesson to be learned or critique conveyed through the song. Together these three elements make song an effective mode of pedagogy and religious experience. The three Ms had to be highly developed in a song in order for it to be effective in achieving appropriate modes of religious experience—of bringing church members closer to God, creating a feeling of unison and purpose among worshippers while singing together, and perhaps most important attracting the Holy Spirit to come down into the space of worship. As one choir member explained to me, "Music is a language that every soul understands. When music is played in the church it elevates the member to move the body. This is due to the three Ms in music—the music, melody, and message—which if combined the soul feels satisfied."

When I first began singing with the choir it was suggested to me that one of the best ways I could understand what each of the three Ms referred to and how they all worked together was to listen to the choir's recordings. All the songs on the choir's albums had been conceived of through a rigorous composition and rehearsal practice that deliberately cultivated the three Ms for each song recorded. I was told that through this practice of listening to the recordings on my own, and seeing how the music, the melody, and the message came together in each song to produce a certain kind of feeling—one that was most often described as an "elevation of spirit"—then I would really understand what music in the church was all about. Furthermore, this understanding would help me to better experience and participate in the musical performances during each Sunday service.

When I asked the members of the choir if they too listened to the recordings in order to better enhance their own participation in the church services, most often their reply was "of course." Most church members told me that singing was part of their daily religious practice; many of them started their day by singing a hymn and saying a prayer. In addition, many reported that they often listened to and sang along with the choir's recordings on a regular basis. Those who had access to the necessary playback technologies, such as CD or cassette players, would listen to recordings at home or in the car on the way to and from work.[4] Others reported that they would often listen to the cassettes at home when the power was out—they could not watch television, but with a battery powered tape player they could listen to the choir's albums.

Most church members noted that if they were going to listen to music while going about their daily activities, it was better that it be Christian music than other forms of popular music. Furthermore, listening to the choir's recordings allowed their everyday experiences to be connected to Christian values and orientations (best encapsulated in the idea of the message of a song) and, because the songs on the recordings so perfectly achieved the desired balance between the three Ms, listening to the songs shaped their actions and behavior at an embodied and conscious level. A few noted that they would listen to the recordings as a devotional practice, especially when faced with occurrences that necessitated taking some time to sing and pray. Stress, anxiety, or worry on the one hand, and relief, happiness, or success on the other, could be dealt with by listening to a song that reminded one of God's presence, or that allowed one to express thanks to God for what he had done for them that day. One church member explained to me that she liked to listen to the choir's recordings because it "revived her soul" and made her feel "enchanted." Furthermore, she said, "It allays my worries and moody tendencies."

As this discussion suggests, the repetition enabled by sound recordings reinforced and enhanced the circulation of aesthetic values, such as the three Ms. In addition, recordings enabled and produced particular kinds of religious experiences in church members' daily lives. But more than this they played an important role in the ability of choir members to learn and internalize the three Ms, so that they could better enact the labor of immediacy required during religious worship. As such, they served as a tool for disciplinary practice for church musicians who honed their musical skills in order to achieve an effective performance during Sunday worship services.

Choir Practice: Discipline and Training

Most of the songs sung by the choir on a given Sunday were connected to the theme of that day's service. The theme usually was a condensed Christian message itself, encapsulating in a short word or phrase such as "Thanksgiving" or "God's Love" a larger lesson to be learned about moral behavior and practice. The message was emphasized not only in the songs sung that Sunday, but also in the Bible readings and in the preacher's sermon that day. Many members of the choir saw it as their pedagogical responsibility to enhance the day's message by singing appropriate songs in a proper manner. Hymns comprised much of the music sung during worship; and each Sunday the choir would sing an additional five to seven songs taken from their recordings. These songs were sung at particular moments during the service: first, during the extended praise and worship session that followed the opening hymn; next, during the offering portion of the service, in brief interludes as segments of the congregation made their way to the front of the church for special prayers; and finally at the end of the service as the leaders and the congregation exited the church.

Each week three or four of the choir's ten lead singers would meet to determine the songs they wanted to sing for the coming Sunday service. Together, in consultation with the choir master, the lead singers would discuss what the theme of that week's service was about and which songs related to that message. Then they would consider which songs were suited to which singers' voices. For these reasons, the recordings were particularly important for the choir's lead singers. One of the lead singers told me that if he was designated to sing on a coming Sunday he would then spend hours during the week listening to the recording of the song—usually at night after he returned home from work and while his wife and children watched television. He would shut himself in his room, read the passages from the Bible that were related to the message of the song, and listen to the recording over and over, eventually singing along with it. That way he was sure to put himself in the correct frame of mind to sing the song that Sunday. He would also refine his approach to the song during choir rehearsals.

The choir rehearsed at least twice a week during most of the year. On Tuesdays, the full choir was expected to attend if they planned to sing during the service on Sunday. On Thursdays, the practice was for instrumentalists and lead singers to refine their arrangements and to make sure that the musical program for that Sunday's service was planned out. In addition to these regular weekly rehearsals, in the first part of each year a core group of musicians—lead singers, instrumentalists, and composers—would meet frequently to plan, rehearse, and produce the songs for the Choir Day festival that took place each April. In the weeks leading up to Choir Day the musicians involved would rehearse nearly every night, and would stage weekly dress rehearsals in the month before the festival that would begin after people left work on a Friday evening and run until dawn on Saturday morning. The production of a new album similarly required additional time and effort, and many choir members made space in their busy work and family schedules to ensure that the endeavor would be a success.

Starting at 4:30 p.m. each Tuesday choir members would begin to arrive for rehearsal, though many often would not get there until much later than the official 5:00 p.m. starting time, delayed by Lagos's notorious traffic jams and crowded public transportation as they made their way to the church after work. As people arrived they would make their way to the choir stall, and sit with other choir members who performed similar roles to themselves: lead singers together in the front row behind the microphones, instrumentalists together on the right, hymn heralds in the center directly in front of the choir master's seat, and choir executives and elders to the left. Each group in the choir would discuss together any issues, concerns, or requirements they faced that week: dividing up songs, negotiating keys and tempos, or discussing plans for decorating the choir stall or the need for instruments to be better organized when they were stored between rehearsals.

Around 5:15 p.m. the conductor would step to the front of the choir stall, and knock lightly on a music stand to get everyone's attention. The conversations and the sound of people warming up their voices or their instruments would die down and the conductor would review the list of hymns to be sung at that Sunday's service. He or she would then ask the musicians to begin the opening hymn for that week. Most rehearsals were perfunctory sessions, as the choir ran through the songs for that Sunday's service quickly to ensure that everyone knew what songs were to be sung, what tempos were to be used, and to ensure that everyone paid attention to musical details. As one of the guitar players, who had been a member of the choir for over twenty years explained to me, "We don't need to rehearse too much because we have been together for so long." A trumpet player added that it was important for members of the Youth Fellowship Choir—in other words for younger members of the church—to be more disciplined about their practice, so that they could learn, improve, and at the same time become "strong in the Holy Spirit." He went on to say, "When we are strong in the Holy Spirit, like we are now, it helps to prevent major problems in the choir from occurring. This is why the rehearsal isn't really compulsory for us anymore. The Holy Spirit brings us together."

However, even given the perfunctory nature of the choir's rehearsals, choir members were urged to cultivate an ethical orientation toward their musical practice, an ethic characterized by discipline, training, and hard work. The choir master would often lecture the choir about the importance of both "discipline" and "training." Choir members who did not bring their church uniform to wear during practice were fined. At rehearsals, or during special prayer meetings for members of the choir, and before or after worship services, one of the officers of the choir would stress that choir members should not be late for service, that they must work hard at mastering their instruments or singing parts, and that they should be exemplary members of the church.

Each rehearsal ended with announcements and prayers. Some of these announcements concerned choir members' participation in events that were to be held in the church during the week such as a wedding or naming ceremony for which musicians were needed. Other announcements concerned the disciplinary practices of the choir. For example, at the end of one rehearsal there was an announcement made by the head coordinator of singers of a spiritual message that had been received following the previous Thursday's rehearsal: "There should be no disagreement in the choir. We all need to be working harder and we must be honest. Those who are lazy will reap what they sow. We must learn the message of forgiveness: we should forgive each other." The head coordinator then narrated a story of a woman who came to the church in search of healing. According to the head coordinator, the woman was sick and after consultation with Prophet G. O. Fakeye, the leader of the Ayọ ni o Church, was told to forgive her husband. However, she refused to forgive him and died the next day. The head coordinator emphasized the lesson to be learned from this story by noting: "We should be humble: make room for those behind you too, even if you're the best singer you should give way to others too."

At times the choir was lectured on the need to pay more attention to their musical practice and not get carried away by their emotions while singing together. For example, during one rehearsal the conductor stopped the choir while they were rehearsing a hymn and said, "Even when you are feeling joy because the music is so powerful, you have to pay attention to how you are singing." He then gave a brief lesson on how to read the dynamic markings printed in the hymnal, and urged the choir members to be sure to follow them while they were singing. Many people around me took notes in their hymnbook about what the dynamic markings meant and circled them. In this way, a particular musical technique of volume control was linked to the need to make one's emotions match the message of a given song. Such practices reinforced the linkages made between music, melody, and message in performance. Despite the fact that choir rehearsals often seemed to be perfunctory, they were defining moments in which the labor of immediacy was cultivated, articulated, and disciplined. It was during these events that choir members perfected the necessary embodied and emotional dispositions required of their musical practice, so that the spiritual goals of the congregation could be accomplished.

Take Control

In order to bring out how the labor of immediacy shapes the potential recontextualization of the songs from the recordings by performing them live during church worship it is worth examining a specific rehearsal in detail. One Tuesday in October 2003 the choir rehearsed a song titled "Take Control," which one of the lead singers was going to sing that Sunday. There was a great deal of anticipation among the choir members because they had not sung this song for a long time. This was due in part to the fact that the vocalist who had sung the song on the recording was no longer attending the church. The choir watched as the lead singer went over his notes on the appropriate musical key and tempo with the conductor, the organist, and the head of the instrumental section.

"Take Control" was the title track for the group's album of the same name, which was recorded and released by the Ayọ̀ ni o Church choir in late 1993. It was one of only a handful of recorded songs that the choir sang in English, rather than in Yoruba. "Take Control" featured the 12/8 wọ́rọ́ dance rhythm, which implies that the message of the song concerns social and political criticism (Dosunmu 2005). The lyrics were simple and repetitive, and called on God to come down and "Take Control" of the troubled situation the world found itself in:

LEAD: Jesus (Jesus) / Lord divine (Divine) / Descend today, and take control (Take control)

CHORUS: Take control / Take control / Take control, my Redeemer / Take control

VERSE 1: Children are hungry / Parents are helpless / We multiply in sin / Violence day and night, miracle maker

CHORUS: [Repeat]

VERSE 2: In thy gracious mercy / Accept my life today / Bless all my efforts / With success and joy, son of Mary

CHORUS: [Repeat]

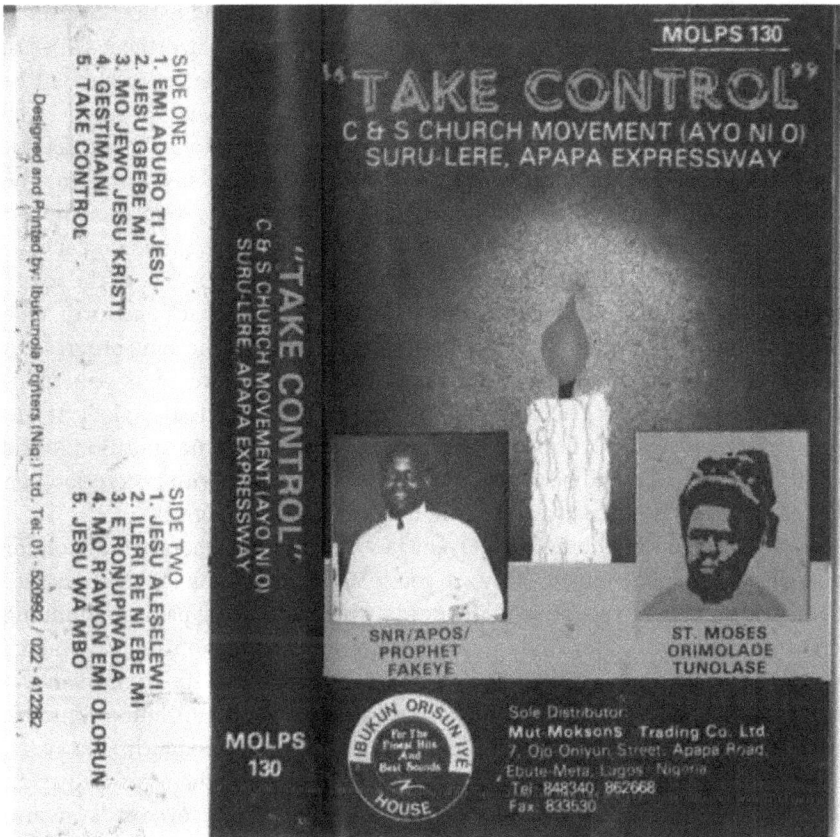

Album cover for *Take Control*

That the album had originally been released in 1993 was significant to how many members of the choir anticipated performing the song. In June 1993, Nigeria held democratic elections following a period of military rulers and political instability. M. K. O. Abiola, an extremely wealthy businessman with influential international ties won the election by an overwhelming margin in what had been deemed the most fair and transparent elections held in Nigeria to that date. However, his victory was short-lived when military ruler Ibrahim Babangida annulled the election results. The political crisis that resulted from Babangida's annulment of the elections led to Sani Abacha seizing power with the assistance of the Nigerian army in November of that year. Thus, "Take Control" had originally been released in a context of political and economic uncertainty in Nigeria. As such, for many church members the recording of "Take Control" was a soundtrack for those tumultuous events, and the song's message, which asked God to take control of the chaos on earth in order to overcome uncertainty, provided them with the assurance that their religious practices could make a difference in shaping the future of Nigeria.[5]

That evening the drum section set a good pace for the song's characteristically danceable rhythm and the other instrumentalists quickly joined in. The three Ms for this song appeared to come together easily to the group, even though they had not performed it for some time. People began to smile and nod at each other as they realized that the singer had mastered the performance of the song's melody. As they began to sing the chorus, the group swayed back and forth. One of the women in the choir-at-large became very excited as the song progressed. She began vigorously jumping up and down, and then bent over to move her hips rhythmically to the fast-paced rhythm. Others turned their heads to look at her. Finally, Mrs. Oyenuga, an older woman who occupied a senior position in the choir hierarchy who had been watching the woman dance with a stern look on her face, raised her voice to ask the conductor to stop the song.

When the music stopped Mrs. Oyenuga scolded the members of the choir for enjoying the song too much. "Why are you so happy about this song?" she asked. She urged them to pay attention to the words, which were about pain and suffering on earth, and the need for God to "take control" of our situation and have mercy on the world. She warned that the music should not distract the choir members from the message of the song, saying: "The music is very beautiful, but we must use it in respect of the message and not allow ourselves to enjoy it too much." Before she sat down, she urged each member of the choir to listen to the recording again before church that Sunday to make sure they knew the music. However, it was also necessary that they consider what the message of the song would mean when we sang it on that particular Sunday. "Think about what is going on in our world and why we need God to take control right now," she said, "When we sing in church this Sunday the congregation must understand the meaning and message of the song."

The musicians began the tune again, and everyone sang soberly as they ran through the song. They rehearsed the other songs for that Sunday, and then ended, as usual, with a brief prayer. As everyone rushed away in order to get home quickly so they could eat dinner and get to bed at a reasonable hour, I paused to ask my friend Remi, who had been standing next to me during choir practice, what she thought was important to pay attention to when the choir sang the song in church that Sunday. She replied, "You should understand this message better than other songs because it is in English. What do you want God to take control of in your life?" Apologizing that she did not want to delay getting home any longer, she ran off, waving at me as she did so.

It is possible to understand the disciplining of emotion and bodily practice that the senior choir member argued was necessary to recontextualize the song

"Take Control" at that moment in relation to events that had taken place in Nigeria earlier that year. In April 2003, presidential elections took place and Olusegun Obasanjo, the incumbent candidate, was reelected. However, the election process itself had been deemed widely suspect by both internal and external observers and most opposition parties had refused to recognize the result. This political process was viewed cynically by most church members, many of whom had not even bothered to vote in the elections. Although things had more or less settled down by October, when the choir rehearsed "Take Control" the potential instability of an election year mirrored that in which the song was originally recorded. Even though an uneasy political stability had been achieved via national elections in 2003, local and state elections were scheduled for the spring of 2004.

Furthermore, life for many Nigerians had not necessarily improved since democratic transition in 1999 and many still struggled to find meaningful employment and to make ends meet for their families. In 2003, the Nigerian government began to implement a series of economic reforms aimed at raising the country's standard of living. These reforms included privatization of major utilities such as communications and electricity, the drawing up of new trade agreements, consolidating the banking sector, and remaking Nigeria's civil service. Many of these initiatives were in their infancy; yet their impact had been felt by many church members. Earlier that year an attempt to remove the subsidy on the sale of petroleum in Nigerian domestic markets was met with general transportation strikes, which shut down Lagos for days at a time. In addition, the government had banned the importation of a number of consumer goods, such as used cars and textiles, that members of the middle class saw as symbols of economic success. Many church members employed in the banking industry or related fields were worried about their future employment outlook. These transformations may indeed have been what Mrs. Oyenuga had in mind that day when she stopped rehearsal and urged the members of the choir to "think about what is going on in our world and why we need God to take control right now."

However, these structural transformations of Nigeria's political economy were understood on a much more personal level. "What do you want God to take control of in *your* life?" Remi asked me by way of explaining the meaning of the song. Making use of the message embedded in "Take Control" in 2003 was thus not as simple as hitting the play button on a tape recorder. Nor was it possible to "just sing" the song. Rather, the recontextualization of "Take Control" required a particular form of labor, one that required choir members to enact appropriate modes of emotionality. Properly singing the song also entailed a disciplined ethical self such as the one produced through choir practice. This location of larger social, political, and economic transformations onto individual persons via the labor of immediacy drew together aesthetic, economic, and moral modes of value and practice.

Creativity and the Limits of Repetition

The modes of value and practice emphasized during choir rehearsals were also crucial factors in the composition of new songs by members of the choir. Here again, the recordings played an important role in the creative process, serving as inspiration and example. To meet the expectations of the group, new songs had to bring together musical, lyrical, and affective elements to produce a composition that was recognizable and new at the same time. Rehearsals were a space within which new ideas could be tried out, evaluated, and worked on as a song was developed. The deliberation over new compositions in the choir brings out the limits of recontextualization and iterability as the labor of immediacy was brought to bear on the composition process.

Most of the new songs sung by the Ayọ̀ ni o Church choir during worship were composed in anticipation of the annual Choir Day. Choir Day was a daylong performance of drama, music, and dance organized around a chosen Biblical passage that typically took place on the Saturday following the choir's celebration of their anniversary thanksgiving service during Sunday worship.[6] On Choir Day the space of the church was transformed into an auditorium, as participants set up a stage in the back of the church and turned the rows of pews and chairs so that they faced away from the altar. The Choir Day performance featured a multi-act dramatic play, interwoven with intricate song and dance numbers, extravagant costumes, detailed props, and a number of special audio-visual effects including images projected on a video screen behind the performers.

Preparations for Choir Day involved choosing a theme for the event, typically one that reflected a message that the organizers thought would be important for church members to reflect on in that particular year. For example, in 2003 the theme for Choir Day was "In His Steps," which emphasized the need for members of the church to follow the example set by Jesus.[7] All involved in the production—musicians, composers, choreographers, set and costume designers, directors—tried to emphasize this message in their contribution. The new songs created for the Choir Day performance also formed the basis for the choir's new album, and were written with the intention of being recorded.

For these reasons composers worked hard before the festival writing songs connected to the theme. In doing so, they would first research the theme, through consulting appropriate Bible passages or hymns connected to the topic. Just as the lead singer would spend hours to prepare himself to sing a given song during Sunday worship, locking himself in his room, reading the Bible, and listening to recordings repeatedly, so would composers enter into their research into the theme so that they would be would be able to bring together the three Ms appropriately and effectively in their composition. At the same time composers would pray fervently that God should inspire them to compose a new song. It was understood that the interaction between these two acts—meditative research on the album's theme and deep prayer—would lead to the ability of the composer to hear a new song.

The agency of the composer in the creative process was understood to be of a particular kind. It was not due to the talent or genius of a given individual, rather it was due to their hard work, to the labor of immediacy they devoted to the compositional process that allowed them to develop the gift that God had given them. Furthermore, new songs were often understood to be spiritual compositions given to the composer by God in their dreams, much like the song recorded on the choir's first album that was given to Korode in a dream vision. Most of the composers that I interviewed explained that a new song would come to them while they were sleeping or in a spiritual trance. As one composer explained to me, she would often wake up in the morning with the fragment of a melody echoing in her head, or occasionally a phrase repeating in her thoughts that would not stop until she wrote it down. Once she started writing, the words would just flow and she would quickly have the basis of a new song soon after waking in the morning.

Once a composer had been inspired to write a new song, he or she would bring the new composition to a rehearsal to be presented to the choir. Most often, composers presented new songs at the Thursday rehearsals, so that the instrumentalists and lead singers could develop the song even further. Often the composer would only have a brief melodic phrase, or a chorus, and the group would develop the song by adding additional lyrics, expanding the melody, or composing verses to alternate with the chorus. Together the group also worked to determine the song's rhythm and tempo, as well as deciding what instruments would be best suited to the song's message. For these reasons, songs were not understood to be the product of individual composers, but rather of the group's efforts. Choir members were often reluctant to name an individual composer for any given song when I would ask, but they would occasionally identify the person who had the original inspirational experience that lead to the song's composition.

As this discussion suggests, the practice of composition itself involved processes of entextualization and recontextualization. Fragments of song heard in a given individual's dreams were repeated and transformed through their repetition during rehearsals. While something of the original visionary experience of the composer was brought along with each repetition, the final product, the song that became fixed through the act of recording, was often very different from what the composer originally heard in their dream. It is here that an understanding of how recording technologies transformed the disciplinary musical practices of choir members becomes apparent.

The following example of a composer presenting a new song to the choir brings out the limits of this iterability. At the beginning of choir rehearsal one Tuesday in March 2003 one of the composers distributed photocopies with the lyrics to a new song printed on it. Standing at the front of the choir stall, she used the microphone to sing each line of the song. The choir repeated each line until they had correctly reproduced the melody, after which she moved on to the next line of the song. Slowly the singers worked through the lyrics on the sheet, as the composer stopped the group frequently and restarted the line as she attempted to get them to sing it as she had heard it in her dream. Once the group was able to perform each line to her satisfaction, the choir attempted to sing all of the lines together.

Finally, the singers sang the all the way through. When it was finished, they began it again so that the instrumentalists could join in. The organ first provided a harmonic basis for the song, shouting the chord changes over his shoulder so that the guitarists could join in by playing arpeggios over the basic progression. The man at the jazz drum set began a highlife rhythm, and then pushed the tempo a bit faster. Finally, the work of the composer had produced something that was recognizable as a song. Some of the singers stood up and began to dance, holding the photocopied lyrics in front of them so they could still sing along.

This moment of musical breakthrough was interrupted by one of the trumpet players, who loudly blasted the melody we had been singing into the microphone that was used by the horn players. The sound of his trumpet overpowered that of the singers, and many turned around to look at him indignantly, wondering why he had broken the flow of the song. His reason was soon made clear as he continued with the melody, and a few of the lead singers smiled and nodded in recognition as they began singing the well-known lyrics of an entirely different song that featured the melody they had been singing. As it turned out, the melody of the song that the choir had spent the first part of rehearsal learning was one that appeared on the choir's 1981 recording, *T'Oluwa Nile*.

With this realization, the song ended in chaos, as the conductor tried to rein in the musicians, the drummers extended their playing with a flourish, and various members of the choir started exclaiming loudly about what had happened. "She didn't remember it correctly!" one person shouted. Others playfully teased the composer by dancing while singing the song that the choir had inadvertently copied.

Visibly frustrated, the composer stood in front of the choir with her hands over her ears trying to recreate the melody she heard in her dream. But it was clearly impossible, at least at that moment. The conductor told her to take her seat so that we could continue on with the rest of the rehearsal. He also said that she should pray that night to see if the Holy Spirit would return to her so that she could hear the song again and teach it to us at a later date. Later, one of the lead singers, himself a composer, told me that they saved the lyrics, so that a different melody might be written for them at a future date if desired.

After rehearsal had ended that evening I spoke with another one of the lead singers about what had happened as we carpooled home together. She noted that what I had witnessed had happened before, and that it was a problem. As she explained to me, repeated listening to the recordings could often make melodies stick in your head. This was especially true if there was a similarity between the messages of the two songs. She thought it was likely that the composer had not written the song down carefully enough, and had not made a deliberate enough attempt to memorize the melody that had come to her in the vision. She also noted that this was why the choir had begun to teach solfege to all of the members of the Youth Fellowship Choir—so that they would be able to not only write down the lyrics of the songs when they heard them, but so that they could also easily notate the melodies in order to accurately teach them to the choir. As she explained to me, it was through such disciplinary practices that the choir members would learn to be better musicians and to discipline their musical talents as part of their Christian worship.

The Labor of Immediacy

Here I have considered the kinds of religious experiences and ethical orientations produced through the use of musical recordings by members of the Ayọ̀ ni o choir. As this discussion has shown, electronic sound media, and the forms of circulation they enabled, served to extend the reach and power of the church into the everyday lives of church members, and allowed them to achieve certain desirable religious modes of experience. However, the use of electronic sound media in religious practice did not diminish the role that live performance served in worship, nor did it invite complacency on the part of church musicians.

In order to understand precisely how electronic media such as sound recordings were used by choir members to produce affective and effective spiritual experiences, I have focused on the labor of immediacy that served as the foundation of their musical practices. For members of the choir, listening to recordings served as a disciplinary practice in which they trained themselves in exactly how to cultivate a particular feeling, one that drew on aesthetic values central to producing that feeling, and then disciplined themselves in order to reproduce it while singing. The lectures and warnings made by the choirmaster and other leaders in the choir emphasized that choir members should not take their musical labors for granted. Thus the recordings served as a means to emphasize renewed commitment and rigor to musical and religious practice.

In his study of the hiplife genre of popular music in Ghana, Jesse Shipley (2009) argues that hiplife reconfigures the relationship that young Ghanaians have to modes of production, consumption, and speaking characteristic of privatization in Ghana. These reconfigurations alter the conceptions of life, survival, and existence in an increasingly market-oriented world, and circulate these conceptions in musical forms that speak to how young Ghanaians imagine freedom, success, and possibility. A similar process occurs in the case I describe here, as middle-class Nigerian Christians sought to reperform previously recorded music live during Christian worship. In doing so they took prior aesthetic and affective musical forms—such as the song "Take Control"—and reproduced them in the contemporary moments. Their recontextualization of these songs was indeed a reconfiguration of values, even though the performance often sounded as identical to the song on the recording as possible. Rather, the transformation occurred at the level of the individual, as choir members disciplined their emotions and behaviors so that their performance spoke to a different context. The disciplinary practices necessary to achieve a successful performance was also one that allowed choir members to see past uncertainty in the present and to envision success, happiness, and well-being in the future.

Electronic recordings allow songs to be recontextualized by choir members as they sing to themselves in their daily devotions, as they listen to them as a form of ethical entertainment, and as they train themselves to hear and appropriately reproduce aesthetic values and affective reactions to those values. Each of these recontextualizations entailed a necessary transformation, but a great deal of work went into erasing those transformations so that the performance of a previously recorded song could be successful in achieving the spiritual goals of the congregation. As the example of the rehearsal of "Take Control" makes clear, this involved not just reproducing the song on the recording exactly, but making sure you do it correctly, which entailed locating the song in the context in which it will be sung. In addition, the iterability enabled by the availability of the recordings also necessitated additional disciplinary practices that reinforced the acceptable limits of repetition, as the example of the failed new composition suggests. Such recontexualizations and their erasures were made possible by the labor of immediacy undertaken during choir rehearsals, as well as in everyday practices of listening and repetition. This labor of immediacy thus worked to produce a certain kind of religious subject, as well as an ethical self.

Notes

1. For an overview of this, see Meyer (2011). Matthew Engelke's (2007) discussion of the "problem of presence" exemplified in the Friday Masowe Apostolics of Zimbabwe's rejection of scripture is also insightful in this regard.

2. Entextualiztion and contextualization are semiotic processes through which a fragment of ongoing discourse is lifted from its original context and then re-inserted in a new context. Entextualization refers to the process whereby discourse is objectified and transformed into a text-artifact that allows discourse to be extracted from a context. Contextualization is the process by which this text-artifact is returned to discourse, which itself allows for the generation of new text-artifacts (Bauman and Briggs 1990; Silverstein and Urban 1996). In the case considered in this chapter, entextualization is the process by which sung discourse becomes identifiable and recognizable as a "song" that can then be reproduced in a new context. Following

Eisenlohr, I am particularly interested in how electronic recording media enables and transforms this ongoing dialectical process of entextualization, contextualization, and recontextualization.

3. Quote taken from pamphlet commemorating the choir's twenty-fifth anniversary in 1998.

4. During the time of my research (2002–2004), most music available for sale was in cassette form. The average Nigerian music consumer made use of cassette technology, both at home and in the car, and relatively few people had access to compact disc players. Video CD (VCD) technology was used to play music videos at home, and the few music compact discs that were available could also be played on VCD players through the television's audio. By 2008, the compact disc and cassette seemed to share equal space in kiosks and more people owned CD players. In 2010, the compact disc was the clear winner at music stalls, but many listeners had begun using their cell phones to exchange gospel music tracks as digital files.

5. The links between the original performance of "Take Control" by the choir, the events of 1993, and the future of Nigeria are apparent in the promotional video that the choir created to go with the song. In the video images of political protests, Nigerian soldiers, explosions, and hungry crying babies are intercut with video clips of the choir singing and dancing to the song. Significantly, the members of the choir do not wear their white prayer gowns in the video, instead they wear clothing that represents the native dress of Nigeria's main ethnic groups—Yoruba, Hausa, Igbo, Calibar, and. Thus they stand for the entire population of Nigeria—not just for members of the church—all raising their hands toward heaven as they sing the chorus of the song asking God to come and "Take Control"

6. The church congregation is divided into a number of smaller groups, known as ẹgbẹ́, each of which celebrates its anniversary with a thanksgiving service that is part of a given Sunday worship service. The choir's thanksgiving service typically takes place on the third Sunday in April and the Choir Day would occur on the Saturday following this thanksgiving service.

7. This is a well-known Christian sentiment that is not limited to the Cherubim and Seraphim, or even to Christians in Nigeria. In the United States this idea is often referred to with the phrase "What would Jesus do," and Christians are urged to ask this question before the take any action. The elaboration of this message by the Ayọ̀ ni o Choir in 2003 expanded the message of following Christ's example to urge church members to also follow the example of Cherubim and Seraphim elders in their Christian practice.

5   Straight to Heaven

Thanks to their spiritual creaturehood, the angels provide mortals with the
ideal mode of worship replicating the standard of the seraphim—burning
in love to God and zeal for His glory against sin.

—S. F. Korode, *Cherubim and Seraphim Legacies*

On a sunday in July 2003, the sermon at the Ayọ ni o Church was delivered by
Most Senior Apostle Pastor G. O. Ogunleye, the church's general secretary. Pastor Ogunleye was known among church members for his lively preaching and
contagious spirit. The topic of the sermon was the importance of the white prayer
gown that church members wore for worship. Noting that there were many outside of the church critical of distinctly Cherubim and Seraphim practices such as
wearing the white garment, Pastor Ogunleye argued that the clothing worn by the
congregation was a crucial part of how they served God. He explained that their
apparel was similar to that of the angels in heaven, and that whoever wore the
church uniform was beautiful before the eyes of God. For this reason, the uniform
was powerful because it made whoever wore it appear as an angel worshipping
God in heaven and thus better able to receive God's attention and blessings.

Pastor Ogunleye's discussion of the meaning of the church uniform was interrupted as an elderly prophetess who was seated in the front of the church stood
up and made her way into the open space before the church altar. The pastor
paused briefly, and then gestured to a churchwarden to find a microphone so the
woman could address the congregation. As the warden held the microphone in
front of her mouth, the woman began to sing:

> About our uniform
> They say our cloth is dazzling white
> And overflowing on the ground
> Whether you like it or not
> You will wear white cloth
> Jesus, have mercy upon us
> Deliver us from the hands of the enemy.

Her voice was low-pitched, strong, and confident. The melody of the song was
simple, almost chant-like. I was surprised that no one joined her as she sang, as

was typical when church members introduced impromptu songs into the service. Usually, when someone spontaneously began to sing during the service, the church organist and other members of the choir recognized the song and would begin to add harmonic and rhythmic accompaniment for the singer. Indeed, most songs sung in this way during church services were taken from the church hymnal or from one of the choir's recordings and thus familiar to the congregation. Such familiarity was crucial to the ability for everyone in the church to sing the same song and thus achieve a musical togetherness that was understood to be linked to moral and social unity through religious practice. However, as the woman sang her song everyone sat in silence, their eyes wide as they listened to her voice. Around the church people who had been leaning on the pew in front of them and resting their heads on their arms sat up straight and craned their necks to see who was singing. The woman's song arrested the attention of the congregation, and even though they were musically unfamiliar with it, it nevertheless managed to strike a chord with them, drawing them back toward participation in the church service.

When she finished singing, the congregation erupted with applause and shouts of delight. As she made her way back to her seat, the pastor attempted to resume his remarks. However, before he could begin speaking one of the lead singers from the choir began another song with lyrics that referenced the church uniform:

> In flowing robes of spotless white
> See every one arrayed
> Dwelling in everlasting light
> And Joys that never fade
> Singing Glory Glory Glory

This well-known hymn prompted the entire congregation to begin singing and swaying together. Their performance imitated the lyrics of the song as the church was filled with people wearing white robes and singing about glory together. Catalyzed by these two songs, the church prophets, prophetesses, and members of the choir began to spontaneously offer a series of songs and Bible verses that all described the Cherubim and Seraphim as angels dancing and singing before God's throne in heaven. As one song or recitation ended, another would begin from someone else in the church. The sermon that day ended with Prophet S. F. Korode, the church's choir master, going into a spiritual trance and delivering a message from God directly to the congregation.

In order to understand the chain of events that happened in church that day, as the straightforward lecture style of the sermon was transformed through music and dance into spirit-filled worship that ended with the intervention of the Holy Spirit into the space of the church, this chapter discusses the relationships between Cherubim and Seraphim cosmological conceptions and the forms of media—

song, costume, bodily comportment, and physical and architectural space among others—that enabled church members to bring this cosmology to life and activated its power in this world. Members of the Cherubim and Seraphim Church drew on angelic symbolism and mimicry to produce a direct connection between paradise and the church, to collapse the space between "the world" and "heaven." In this movement between heaven and earth, religious texts and sacred forms of dress were combined with music and dance to re-enact a vision of angels worshipping before the throne of God. Thus music, dance, incense, costume, lighting, and other media were manipulated in order to produce multiple, simultaneous affects that activated sensory domains—sound, sight, smell, and touch. These sensory affects became materially linked—through things like white robes, candles, incense, lighting, the interior space of church, and most crucially through singing and bodily comportment—to the efficacy of church members' actions in navigating the realities of contemporary Nigeria.

As was already discussed, early members of the Cherubim and Seraphim churches developed a set of Christian doctrines and practices that was both grounded in their reading of the Bible and inspired by spiritual visions experienced by individuals who would go on to found the church. These visions, in which church members were visited by angelic spirits and taken to heaven, led to the establishment of distinctive worship practices, most notably forms of angelic mimicry in terms of dress, bodily comportment, and musical practice. Indeed, as the sermon discussed above makes clear, church members wore white robes, they moved their bodies together in a way that resembled weightless flight, and they sang together as a choir, just as the angels are described in the Bible and in countless hymns and songs.

The various media forms used in Cherubim and Seraphim worship practices accomplished two things. First, they were an aesthetic means through which church members were made as religious subjects. Church members wore their distinctive costume, and sang and danced together in a space that was marked as separate through a variety of bodily practices—such as removing one's shoes before entering the church building and organizing the bodies of church members in the space in such a way that the hierarchy of the church was iconically reproduced. These practices constituted a mode of bodily and sensory discipline that induced a certain sense of the self and its relationship to the world. Second, these bodily and sensory disciplines were embedded in ritualized and aestheticized mimetic practices that produced links between church members, angels in heaven, and each other. These aesthetic formations and embodied practices were central to the making of religious community. Furthermore, this shared aesthetic style reassured church members of the continuity of their ethical values.

Church members made use of angelic and heavenly mimicry in order to mediate relationships between heaven and earth, God and human, past and present, here and there, and similarity and difference. In what follows I discuss the cosmological and material conceptions that were brought together in Cherubim and Seraphim worship in order to demonstrate how these ideas and objects that were crucial to the correct performance of church ritual only became efficacious when they were sung and danced together. I analyze Cherubim and Seraphim conceptions of sound, space, and the body and explain how these were actively made in the world through musical practices of singing and dancing during church worship. These worship practices, correctly performed, were understood by church members to be effective in achieving God's intervention in their lives.

It was through these ritual worship practices that cosmological conceptions were made real, tangible, and available to church members as they remade themselves in line with church doctrine to better navigate the contemporary reality of Nigeria. These ritualized actions were constructed by church members as a particularly powerful way of responding to and acting on their political and economic circumstances. In other words, Cherubim and Seraphim worship practices in the early parts of the twenty-first century were both understood as continuous with the history of the church as well as capable of responding to changing social circumstances. Through church worship, members of the Ayọ̀ ni o Church recreated a vision of society based on principles that were assumed to embody "Yoruba values." These values, which emphasized hard work and respect for one's position in a social hierarchy, were seen as especially relevant in the context of political transition and economic transformation that has characterized the experience of Nigerians since 2001.

The Earth Is a Marketplace, Heaven Is Home

Embedded in Cherubim and Seraphim worship practices was a particular conception of the relationship between God and humans, and the cosmological domains in which the two were located. The church was conceived of as creating a link between heaven (ọ̀run) and earth (ayé).[1] Cherubim and Seraphim worship, and especially the performance of music within the church, linked earth to heaven and allowed church members to bridge these domains through their worship practices in order to make tangible, divinely sanctioned changes to their lives.

Although most members of Cherubim and Seraphim churches were careful to distinguish their Christian beliefs and practice from indigenous Yoruba religious thought, many drew on proverbs and other ideas about the world and about life that came from what was described as àṣà Yorùbá (Yoruba culture). Key among these was the conceptualization of the relationship between heaven and the earth as distinct parts of a larger whole, with the possibility of movement between the two through religious practice. In addition, many church members conceived of the purpose of life on earth as a journey toward one's ultimate spiritual home in heaven. These ideas were built on the Yoruba conceptualization of the cosmos as divided into two: ọrun and ayé, with spiritual entities residing in the former, while humans resided in the latter (Adogame 2000:6; Idowu 1962).[2] The name of the Yoruba high god, Ọlọ̀run, which is also the Yoruba name most commonly used to refer to the Christian God, literally means that he is the owner of heaven (*oní+ ọ̀run*).[3] For church members heaven was also populated by angelic beings, who sit before the throne of God and worship him at all times through song and dance.

The relationship between heaven and earth is often expressed in the proverb "Ayé lọjà, ọrun ni ílé" (the earth is a marketplace, heaven is home), a proverb frequently drawn on by Christian evangelists and pastors. In an article discussing Yoruba conceptions of home, Lawuyi and Olupona (1988) unpack some of the metaphorical meanings inherent in this proverb. They are particularly interested in the connections between death and the marketplace and life and the home (1988, 2). Drawing on Yoruba proverbs and myths, they elaborate some of the metaphoric and symbolic meanings behind the proverb by explaining Yoruba understandings of *ilé* (home) and *ọjà* (market). They describe ilé as follows:

> The data we have [from proverbs] conveys the idea that a home guarantees security, sets up standards of morality, and is instrumental to the construction of self-identity. And in terms of its social prescriptions to residents and the methods of its socialization process, the house in Yorubaland must confer a specific identity distinctive in terms of kinship relationships which stipulate the recognition of and caring for one's kin.

By contrast, ọjà is a place of fragmentation and possibility, where relationships of various kinds are transacted. Lawuyi and Olupona summarize the differences between the two as follows "in the home, relationships are fairly strictly regulated; authority is hierarchical from father to children. In the market relationships are not as clearly regulated; you can sell at any price, and authority is horizontally structured in a negotiation for equal benefits" (1988, 9–11).

In the market, identities are multiple and subject to transaction, but in the home they are pre-defined, given and absolute.[4] This is connected to the Yoruba concept of *orí* (destiny), which is believed to be predetermined; given to a person in heaven by Ọlọ̀run, it resides in one's head (also *orí*). The purpose of life (*iyè*) is to achieve that destiny in the world by successfully negotiating between these two contradictory domains.[5] In doing so, life is conceived of as a journey toward one's final resting place in heaven; however through ritual practices—such as the practices of angelic mimicry involved in Cherubim and Seraphim worship— one attempts to replicate heaven in the context of one's life on earth. This enables a kind of iconicity between heaven and one's home on earth, and part of the moral practices of the Cherubim and Seraphim is to achieve through their worship a mediation between these two senses of home (see Olupona 2003; Renne 2009).

Following on this, the "home" in the proverb "the earth is a marketplace, heaven is home" can also be understood to be about correctly ordered social relationships. In other words, home is a place where the proper means of respect are used and followed. Cherubim and Seraphim worship practices enabled church members to put social relationships in order and to negotiate between conflicting and contradictory experiences of political and economic transformation and instability. Such an interpretation was indeed articulated by church members. Their commitment to Cherubim and Seraphim modes of practice was often explained not only through reference to the Bible as authority, but also as a reaffirmation of the importance of respect for elders and hierarchical forms of political organization that were central to understandings of what it meant to be properly Yoruba and thus a good person.

Mrs. Adeyemi was a senior member of the Ayọ ni o Church choir and the director of a nursery school located in a middle-class suburb of Lagos. She invited me to her home one day because, as she put it, she wanted to make sure that I understood what was distinctive about the Cherubim and Seraphim. She explained to me: "We Yorubas truly have culture." When pressed to explain what she meant by that she replied:

> You know, us Yorubas, we have honoristic values. That is we defer a lot to anyone who is older then us. So we have the honoristic value. We always give respect, it is a highly respectful culture. That is the Yoruba culture. The young one is not supposed to look the adult in the eye, is not supposed to sit down while the adult is standing, and you are supposed to *kùnle* [kneel down]. We don't have a single language. We have pronouns that are for young ones and pronouns that are for adults. And this all stems from our honoristic culture.

Here the idea of home was constituted by relationships in order, described as an "honoristic culture" that was central to what it means to be Yoruba, to truly "have culture." Reproducing this culture of respect was necessary to protect oneself from the insecurities and uncertainties of the market. Indeed, Mrs. Adeyemi explained to me that it was a lesson that she ensured her own children learned, as well as the children who were enrolled in her nursery school. As we talked, her older daughter came home and, upon entering the room, knelt to greet us. Mrs. Adeyemi told me approvingly that her daughter had just earned admission to the University of Lagos, where she wanted to follow in her father's footsteps by studying architecture. She attributed her daughter's academic and professional success to her good behavior. Thus knowing one's place in society, and following the rules, recreated a moral order that enabled one to be happy, prosperous, and successful.

These ideas about Yoruba culture are embedded in Cherubim and Seraphim Christian practices. As Mrs. Adeyemi explained:

This also you can see reflected in our own religion when we accepted Christianity. You find out that when the Yoruba man is talking, he uses the pluralistic pronoun when he's going to refer to God. And we do not believe that we are all equal in terms of age grade in the church. And that is why you still find out that like in some other denominations where you just call yourselves brothers and sisters, in the Cherubim and Seraphim Church we defer to anyone who is older than us. And also when you are higher in rank than someone, you defer to an individual if such an individual is older than you. So that is part of Yoruba culture that has gone into it.

Here she made a case against the more recent trend in Pentecostal churches to try to equalize relations among church members by referring to everyone as "brother" or "sister." The Protestant idea that anyone can know God in the same way if one reads one's Bible and prays to God for guidance was often articulated by members of Cherubim and Seraphim churches; however, this attitude was complicated by the profusion of titles and ranks found within the Cherubim and Seraphim Church organization. The church was organized into a complex array of hierarchical titles based on one's spiritual abilities as well as one's length of time in the church. These included religious specialists—such as choir members, prayerists, and prophets—as well as titles that mark one's progressive seniority; for example a male church member could progress from apostle, to senior apostle, to most senior apostle. However, as Mrs. Adeyemi noted, age still served to constrain one's rank, as "you defer to an individual if such an individual is older than you."

Part of the appeal of Cherubim and Seraphim Christianity for many church members was that the church reinforced idealized orderings of society based on principles of Yoruba social hierarchy, ideals that were derived from the emergence of Yoruba cultural nationalism during the colonial period (see Ayandele 1967, Ajayi 1965). The reason Cherubim and Seraphim forms of Christian worship appealed to church members was the promise that if the social hierarchy was kept in order, one was certain to be successful in achieving one's destiny in the world. Cherubim and Seraphim worship affirmed an ideal of social relationships that involved the wealthy gaining support from his or her followers only through doing favors in turn. Indeed, the Cherubim and Seraphim negotiated between opposing conceptions of practices of patron-clientage: it was understood as a problem when those not worthy of respect attempted to purchase it and thus produced corruption; but it was seen as a potential solution for the political and economic instability that characterized the Nigerian postcolony when it operated according to legitimate and moral directions of respect.

In their worship practices the Cherubim and Seraphim performed a proper moral way of ordering society, reproducing these ontological categories and articulating the moral relationships between them, in order to (re)make a Yoruba sense of home in the world. Cherubim and Seraphim worship itself, with its emphasis on gender and age hierarchy, liturgical roles, and ordered progression of song and dance, all reinforced these social values and principles through sensory and embodied forms of religious practice. This was apparent in the event that I described at the beginning of this chapter, when the older prophetess interrupted the pastor's sermon to deliver a song that, while not recognizable to the congregation, nevertheless demanded their attention due to her senior age and position. As I learned later in a conversation with some members of the choir about what happened during the sermon that day, one of the things that they found compelling about the song is that they were sure that it was old; that it perhaps dated back to the founding of the church and thus conveyed the wisdom of their elders. This feeling that they were hearing a song that conveyed the authoritative voice of Cherubim and Seraphim tradition from the past was what drew the space of the church closer to heaven through the chain of singing, dancing, and Bible recitation that followed, and furthermore inspired the Holy Spirit to deliver a special message to the congregation.

Ilé Àdúrà: Creating Sacred Space in the World

The space of the church itself was organized and used in a way that reinforced and maximized the ideas about social hierarchy and the feeling of home discussed in the previous section. Most Cherubim and Seraphim churches in Nigeria meet in a building that is specifically designated for worship, usually referred to as *ilé àdúrà* (house of prayer).[6] The size of the church ranged from a small room accommodating perhaps fifteen to twenty churchgoers, to a cavernous "cathedral" able to seat hundreds of people for Sunday worship service. The Ayò ni o Church in Lagos was the largest Cherubim and Seraphim Church building that I visited during my time in Nigeria (many Nigerians insisted that it was in fact the largest Cherubim and Seraphim Church in the world). The main church seats 1,000–1,500 churchgoers, with separate worship spaces for the Youth Fellowship (church members between the ages of eighteen and thirty) and the children's fellowship. Canopies and benches set up outside of the House of Prayer enabled additional churchgoers to participate in the services through the use of loudspeakers. Because the church did not keep official attendance records, it is impossible to know precisely how many people attend worship services each Sunday. However, I would estimate based on head counts the course of my research, that on an average Sunday between 3,000 and 5,000 people attended church services on the Ayò ni o campus.

All Cherubim and Seraphim churches, large and small, organized space within their place of worship similarly. Pews were laid out in rows, with a special space near the front of the church for the choir. There were usually multiple entrances, with the main entrance located opposite the altar area with a wide center aisle leading toward the front of the church. These entrances were usually blocked off with a rope or chain at particular points of the service, especially during

Worshippers exiting the Main Church, 2010

Outside of the Youth Chapel, 2010

congregational prayers when no one was allowed to enter or leave the church build-ing. In all churches, seating was segregated by gender, and organized in the order of the church hierarchy.[7] Most churches also had an open space near the front of the church for dancing or special prayers, but in smaller churches this space was cre-ated by pushing aside pews or chairs as needed.

The focal point of the church was an arch surrounding a small alcove, with the words "MÍMỌ́ MÍMỌ́ MÍMỌ́ OLÚWA, ỌLÓRUN, OLÓDÙMARÈ" (Holy Holy Holy, Lord God Almighty) written on it. These are the words that the angels flying around the throne of God in heaven sing. Depictions of angels in flight were typically painted on the wall around the arch. The space inside the alcove was called the "Ibi Mímọ́ Jù Lọ," the "Most Holy Place" or "Holy of Holies." Inside the alcove was an altar with candelabra, illustrations of Jesus, representations of angels, and a photograph of Moses Orimolade, one of the founders of the Cherubim and Seraphim churches.

The altar was the locus point through which God's power entered the church. During Sunday worship a designated worship leader stood facing the altar through-out the entire service. The worship leader did not have a distinct speaking role in the service, though he participated in praying and singing, and he ensured that God's power entered into the church. I was told that the worship leader prepared himself to perform this activity correctly by fasting and praying for a week before he was to lead the service. Because of the physical and spiritual strength required of the worship leader a different person performed this role each Sunday.

To the left of the altar as one faced it was a large chair reserved for the leader of the church; when he sat there he was understood to be seated at the right hand of God. Chairs reserved for other important male elders, particularly those who delivered the sermon or led congregational prayers on a given Sunday, line the sides of the alcove. When services were not in session a curtain was drawn across the arch concealing the altar. The arch-framed alcove containing the altar was an architectural feature of every Cherubim and Seraphim church I visited, no matter the size of the congregation, and the same construction is also described by Peel (1968) in his study of Cherubim and Seraphim churches in the early 1960s.

Everyone was required to remove their shoes before entering the church. Menstruating women or women who had recently given birth were not allowed to enter the church; instead they worshipped outside, often under special cano-pies set up to accommodate them. Women were also required to cover their heads while in the church, whether they wore the white prayer gown or not. Women were also restricted from entering the frontmost area of the church, and were es-pecially forbidden from entering the Holy of Holies.[8]

Church services typically began with a procession that entered through the door in the rear of the church and proceeded down the center aisle toward the altar. The procession, a practice derived from similar practices in Anglican mission churches, included a number of choir members, several church elders, prophets and prophetesses, those who would be reading lessons or leading prayers during the service, as well as the "fathers of the church," the most senior men in the church. The procession was led by a churchwarden carrying incense and another carrying a tall brass cross. The cross was brought in through the front door, carried into the altar, and then brought out again and through the church at least one more time during the service. At times, people came up to the open area in the front of the church to receive prayers or to leave their contribution. Through such movements there was a continual distribution of a sense of sacredness, an attempt to make sure that everyone in the church had some sort of contact with God's power as the space between heaven and earth were collapsed through ritual.

Musical performance was central to this mediation and circulation of spiritual power. As one prophetess explained in a lecture on the meaning of the choir in the church: "the key role of the choir is to draw the congregation into the presence of the Lord." The location of the choir near the front of the church was significant in terms of the spatiality of sacredness expressed in the layout of the church. Fitting the choir's status as the means through which communication between heaven and earth, God and the churchgoers, was initiated, the choir was located in the front of the church near the altar. Further, seating in the choir was oriented so that choir members mediated between the altar and the congregation. In contrast to the forward-facing rows of seats in the majority of the church's space the choir faced the side of the church. Thus the spatial location and orientation of the choir expressed its central role as the motor which was driving the church closer toward heaven, using song to open up the channel of communication between church members and God via the medium of song.

Because of the size of the Ayọ ni o Church, electronic amplification was necessary so that the congregation could hear all parts of the service. The use of amplification also enabled the sounds of worship to spill outside of the confines of the church itself. Indeed, speakers were placed on the exterior of the church building, as well as in other locations in the church compound, so that the services could be broadcast while they are in session. Large stacks of amplifiers divided the church into three sections, and microphones were a regular part of the way the service was conducted. This also placed limitations on who was actually able to speak and be heard by the congregation. The largest number of microphones were used by the choir, with a row of them placed at the front of the choir stall for the lead singers to use, in addition to one used by the hymn herald, who called out each line of the hymn as it is being sung. Additional microphones were used to amplify acoustic instruments, particularly the trumpets and talking drums. There were also microphones located in and just outside of the Holy of Holies, which were used by the officiates of the service to read the Biblical passages for the day, lead congregational prayers, make church announcements, and to deliver the sermons.

The spatial organization of the church replicated the ideal scene of angels worshipping before the throne of God in heaven as well as visually and spatially reinforced the importance of church hierarchy. The use of amplification in the church furthered these ideals. With the space of worship organized according to these ideal principles, cosmological principles were made real through the ritual performance of music. The correctly organized space of the church made the angelic mimesis of the congregation's worship practices a method for achieving the desired ends of ritual: health, prosperity, and happiness.

Aṣọ funfun: Making the Body Sacred

One of the most distinctive aspects of Cherubim and Seraphim churches was their wearing of the white prayer gown. This uniform was often referred to by those who did not belong to such churches as a "white garment" and churches who required such sartorial practices were referred to as "white garment churches." The wearing of special robes during church worship was characteristic of most Alàdúrà churches in Nigeria. The Cherubim and Seraphim churches, the Church of the Lord, Alàdúrà, and the Celestial Church of Christ all required their members to wear a floor-length white cassock with long sleeves, usually tied at the waist with a sash. Women also covered their heads with a white cap. Earrings and necklaces were not worn with this uniform, although a wristwatch was permitted. In addition, church members did not wear shoes inside the worship space, though they were not forbidden from wearing shoes while wearing the prayer gown outside of the church.[9]

Wearing the white garment was central to religious worship for Cherubim and Seraphim Church members. Usually the Bible was cited as precedent for wearing the uniform for worship services. In a pamphlet concerning Cherubim and Seraphim worship practices, Korode wrote that "the Bible is replete with many references to the symbols and spiritual utility of the robes of believers and saints both in the Old and New Testaments" (1995, 45). He then supported this statement with three pages of examples taken from the Bible. However, as Renne suggests, "the use of cloth as a means of expressing connections between earthly and spiritual realms, between descendants and ancestors, and between members of particular religious groups has a long history in southwestern Nigeria" (2004, 131). Òrìṣànlá, the most senior of the òrìṣà, is also called Ọbàtálá ("King in white clothing") and, as Idowu writes, "immaculate whiteness is often associated with him—this symbolizes 'holiness' and purity" (1962, 73), echoing Korode's earlier statement about the Cherubim and Seraphim replicating the ideal standard of worship in holiness and purity.[10] Finally, Yoruba funerary practice calls for wrapping the deceased in white cloth: "The importance of wrapping the deceased in cloth is expressed in the adage 'the corpse of the elder should not be thrown away; it is white cloth that I

A churchwarden and his son in their church uniforms, 2010

wore from heaven to the world'" (Drewal 1992, 40).[11] As this proverb suggests, wearing white cloth for religious worship connected heaven and earth and served as a medium through which humans moved between the two realms at birth and death.

The connection of the white cloth, heaven, and funerary traditions is a prominent theme in Cherubim and Seraphim worship. Indeed, the song that interrupted the sermon described at the beginning of this chapter makes this connection explicit. The prophetess sang, "About our uniform, they say our cloth is dazzling white and overflowing on the ground." The specific reference to the "dazzling white" and "overflowing" cloth points to the fullness and whiteness of the cloth the angels in heaven wear. The song goes on to state, "Whether you like it or not you will wear white cloth," referring to the Yoruba practice of burying their dead in white. In a conversation about the meaning of this song, one church member explained to me that this was a reminder that ultimately everyone will be judged in the eyes of God, suggesting that it was better to accept God while living, rather than die without salvation. Thus the church uniform iconically linked the bodies of church members to angels in heaven at the same time as it drew on the symbolism of the white cloth as representing the transition from life to death, and from earth to heaven.

A woman wearing her church uniform with a sash indicating her ẹgbẹ́ membership, 2010

Church members also explained that it was particularly important to wear the prayer gown for church worship services because it represented that everyone was equal before God. They stressed that this was the central meaning behind wearing the uniform, because in contrast to other churches where everybody wore their best clothes and tried to outdo each other sartorially, in the Cherubim and Seraphim Church everyone appeared to be one before the Lord. As an elder in the choir put it, "the uniform reinforces that spiritual strength does not depend on material wealth."

The uniform also served to focus the congregation's attention on the worship service, rather than paying attention to what other people in the church were wearing. As Mr. Babatunde, a senior member of the choir and the owner of an import-export business, explained:

> Then we have the uniform, which will make us equal before God. Because if you allow people in this church to wear any attire they like, you will see that some people will put on a sort of garment that will be so huge that instead of a chair to occupy five people, the garment is taking up two seats, and you will deprive other people of the chance of sitting down. Or you'll be hearing the sort of shoes that will be making too much noise while you are praying: "pa-ko, pa-ko" [imitating noisy shoes]. You will see some women they put some cap, this hat, funny things.

> But our own is uniform. And once its uniform we believe that you are closer, nearer to God. Because before God uniformity means a common place for everybody.

Furthermore, as the pastor noted in the sermon discussed at the beginning of the chapter, the church uniform was also an aesthetic means through which spiritual power was concentrated and transferred to the body of the church member. As the pastor argued, the white garment was both beautiful and powerful; in other words its aesthetic qualities were linked to its spiritual efficacy. Many church members reported to me that they regularly changed into their uniforms before praying at home because this would ensure that God would hear their prayers. This significance was also brought home to me one afternoon after church when I wished to find a place to change out of the uniform into my street clothes because I had borrowed a friend's car and was going to drive myself home that day. A woman in the choir asked me why I could not just drive home wearing the uniform, and when I explained that I was worried about being stopped by police who might be more likely to notice and harass a white woman wearing the distinctive white garment, she responded that if I kept the uniform on while driving the police would not even notice me at all because God would protect me. It would be as though I was invisible because God would look out for me. Another choir member, overhearing our conversation, begged me to keep my uniform on, because he said that it would protect me from getting into an accident on the way home.

Finally, the white garment served as a reminder to the wearer of the moral beliefs and practices required to be a Christian. In his pamphlet *Cherubim and Seraphim Legacies*, Korode wrote: "The white garment is merely an object symbol requiring the wearer to replicate the whiteness in the purity of his mind and conduct," stressing that "the souls of believers, their attitudes, behavior and conduct must reflect the purity, holiness and beauty of the robes they wear" (Korode 1995, 47–48). In other words, the uniform did not just iconically transform humans into angels; one did not become moral or even a member of the church community through merely putting the white cloth on. Rather, the efficacy of the white garment—its ability to make material transformations through the intervention of the Holy Spirit in the lives of individual church members at the same time as it remade community according to the ethical and moral ideals embedded in "Yoruba culture"—required a transformation of self such that the person wearing the uniform was ethically remade. This self-transformation was best accomplished by participation in church worship while wearing the white garment.

Singing and Dancing in Cherubim and Seraphim Worship

Wearing the prayer gown during church worship collapsed the distance between heaven and earth and enabled communication with the divine. The space of the church was organized to maximize this iconic representation of heaven, and furthermore reflected cosmological conceptions of the relationships between heaven and earth and God and humans. These elements all contributed to the perceived efficacy of Cherubim and Seraphim worship; its ability to attract the attention of God who as the Holy Spirit descends into the space of the church, possesses the body of church members, and delivers messages to the congregation.

However, merely wearing the prayer gown or praying in the space of the church was not sufficient to produce these desired connections between heaven and earth, between humans and God, and among members of the congregation. Music, especially singing, was an important means through which these relationships were mediated. Church members saw musical performance in the context of worship as the way in which the orientations and behaviors of church members were calibrated with Cherubim and Seraphim values so that their "souls . . . attitudes, behavior, and conduct" (Korode 1995, 47–48) were brought into line with those of the angels in heaven. Music, performed correctly, also had the capacity to effect material changes in the world. The visible or audible presence of the Holy Spirit in the bodies of church members was most likely to appear during musical portions of church worship. All of these elements came together in the example discussed at the beginning of the chapter: the white garment, the performance of church hierarchy, and the performative use of music and dance to activate spiritual power and make real the divine.

Singing together during church worship was a bodily practice, one that created a link between church members and angels, working to reproduce the former as appropriate worshippers of God. The understanding of music as required by God in order to draw down his power as well as producing the congregation as a unified group was itself understood as a practice of angelic mimicry: "using the Bible as authority, members believe that 'Cherubim and Seraphim are the names given to the angels around the throne of God in heaven singing praises unto Him continually day and night'" (Omoyajowo 1982, 114). This mimetic practice was deliberately cultivated to allow the Cherubim and Seraphim to appeal directly to God through a medium that was both recognizable and desirable. As Korode explained to me in an interview:

> The seraphim have no other responsibility than declaration of God's holiness in their regular chant: "Holy, Holy, Holy, Lord God Almighty." And it's a kind of one shouting to the other, reminding each other to remember to keep the Lord holy. That's what you will read in Isaiah 6:1–8. And it's on account of that that you discover that wherever you encounter the Seraphim, they are involved in singing. They are involved in praising the Lord, they are involved in declaring the glory of God or the holiness of God.

> God wants to celebrate his holiness and glory more than he wants to celebrate his power. Because that's what actually makes God feel God. When it comes to a sheer show of power, it's looking at the other side of God. Yes, he's mighty in everything, but he enjoys his holiness and his purity. When you adore him with praises it's like pushing the heart of God himself.

As this quote suggests, singing was seen as efficacious because it mimics what the angels in heaven do, it praises God in the way he wants to be praised, and in doing so "pushes the heart of God himself." This allowed humans to access what Korode calls "the other side of God" in which beauty and the ability to accomplish things in the world were linked. Much like the understanding of the white garment articulated by Pastor Ogunleye in the sermon discussed at the beginning of the chapter, singing and dancing transformed church members into angels who were thus deserving and capable of receiving God's attention.

Furthermore, singing and dancing were also central means through which a link between an individual church member, the church as a congregation, and God was created. Church members connected wearing the white garment to the remaking of the self in line with Christian ethical ideals. By singing and dancing while wearing the white garment they put this into practice and actively transformed themselves. Singing and dancing made the white garment actually do its work by making it efficacious. As Korode went on in our conversation:

> The Seraphim are "redeemed men," baptized in the blood of the Lord Jesus Christ, singing the song of redemption. So each time we get into the singing

mood, we are actually charged and challenged. You will discover that behavior of people in songs will differ from their behavior in any other form of church worship or expression, because at that point there is a kind of unity. You are all together. When it's prayer, you can find people praying for so many different things. But when it's a song that you are raising together, it goes on in a chant, a collective chorus that rises to high heavens.

Here Korode noted that singing together produced a unity among worshippers that was unobtainable through other practices. It is this song that "rises to high heavens" and "pushes on the heart of God."

In addition, dancing is an embodied behavior that allows the body of the church member to receive God's power, in the form of blessings, healing, or deliverance from evil. As Prophet G. O. Fakeye, the leader of the Ayọ ni o Church noted in another sermon, delivered in September 2003:

Let me tell you about some things that are important to this sect: dancing, clapping, and stomping. David danced. This is the importance of praise worship. This is the importance of dancing for God: exercising your body from head to toe will help all ailments to disappear. Church members should use the time when the choir is singing to praise God by dancing: don't do any other thing. Adore God with body and soul and mind so that Satan can disappear.

For these reasons music and dance were crucial elements in creating the "right kind of worship" for the Cherubim and Seraphim. Singing and dancing opened up a space of communication between heaven and the world and enabled the circulation of spiritual power in the space of the church to occur. In addition, singing and dancing transformed the bodies of church members into angels before God's throne in heaven. In doing so, it allowed a bit of the order of heaven to enter and reform the uncertainty of the market of the world.

Mediating Heaven and Earth

With these elements of Cherubim and Seraphim belief and practice now unpacked, it is possible to return to the event with which this chapter opened in order to understand how the sermon was transformed that day from a one-sided lecture into a spirit-filled, charismatic performance that ended with the transmission of a special message from God to the congregation. As I have shown in this chapter, cosmological conceptions of social order, the architectural space of the church, the clothed and gesturing body, and the performance of song and dance, all work together to produce the efficacy of worship for the Cherubim and Seraphim.

The song that set off the chain of events leading to the descent of the Holy Spirit into the church was peculiar. Unknown to the majority of the congregation, yet understood by many to be "old" and thus offering a glimpse of the church's past, it lyrically described the power of the church uniform, the "dazzling white" cloth that is "overflowing on the ground." The song also linked that cloth to the ability of the human body dressed in white to mediate between heaven and earth, between home and the market. "Whether you like it or not, you will wear the white cloth," the song noted, pointing to the Yoruba practice of dressing corpses in white for burial. While this line served as a reminder of God's judgment, at the same time it also pointed to the potential of the white garment to enable church members to transgress these cosmological boundaries, to reach heaven through church worship, and to penetrate God's heart.

Just as the white garment alone was not able to accomplish this transformation, the woman's song could not work to transform human bodies and earthly space into angels in heaven without the sequence of songs and Bible readings that followed it. I viewed a videotape of the sermon discussed here with Gbenga, one of the lead guitarists from the choir and a primary school teacher, who at that time was a prophet-in-training. He explained what had happened in church that day: "What sparked it off is the dazzling white talk about heaven and it suddenly brings everybody's focus to heaven. Thinking about God, that is the ultimate. So that's why all these references are coming." It was these well-known songs and passages, which reiterated the message of the pastor's sermon and the woman's song, which animated the congregation and drew them to their feet to sing and dance together. It was this feeling of closeness to God and to each other that caused people around the church that day to enter into spiritual trances and to begin shouting, shaking, and speaking in tongues.

As I also learned from Gbenga, part of the significance of the hymns sung during the sermon was that they were those typically sung during wake keeping services for deceased members of the church. In other words, church members were inspired to sing hymns used to usher a deceased person's soul from this world into heaven. They sang these songs at the same time as they recreated heaven through the organization of space in the church and the transformation of their human bodies into angelic entities through mimetic practices of dressing, singing, swaying, and dancing. Thus, the gap between church members and God, between heaven and earth, was closed. Church members activated that "other side of God's power" by reminding him of his glory and holiness in their songs that imitated those of the seraphim around God's throne in heaven. It was this that caused the message to be delivered to the congregation, a message that contained specific lessons and warnings that church members could apply to their lives outside of the church and use to navigate the uncertainties of Nigeria—to evade the attention of traffic police on their way home from work, to enhance their ability to procure fuel to run generators at home in case the electricity failed, or to ensure financial success in a business world characterized by corrupt practices.

As I viewed the video tape of the sermon with Gbenga in order to transcribe the order of songs and Bible passages from that day, he smiled, paused, and put down the pen he was using to take notes and watched intently as the choir sang the following lyrics:

> Father before thy throne of light
> The guardian angels bend
> And ever in Thy presence bright
> Their psalms adoring blend
> And casting down each golden crown
> Beside the crystal sea
> With voice and lyres in happy choir
> Hymn glory God to Thee

At this point he turned to me and said of the congregation on the video: "They just want to transfer straight to heaven at this point."

Notes

1. Adogame suggests that members of the Celestial Church of Christ (CCC) "believed that God sent down this 'heavenly' church to the world thus also making CCC a 'heavenly' place on earth. A bridge was therefore built connecting *ọrun* and *ayé*" (2000, 8).

2. There are many accounts of Yoruba cosmology, and there are as many arguments over the validity of those accounts. I am not concerned here with determining what was "really" believed by Yorubas before the introduction of Islam and Christianity. Rather, I am interested here in representing what is believed by most Yorubas to be indigenous views of the cosmos and religious understandings, recognizing that these views may or may not be "invented traditions."

3. Other names for the Yoruba high god/supreme deity that are used by Yoruba Christians are Olodumare/Edumare, and Oluwa.

4. This is a sociohistorical construction of Yoruba ideas of home and senses of order, an ideal vision of Yoruba society created in the face of colonization see Oyewumni 1997; Peel 2000; Waterman 1997).

5. This understanding of the relationship between earth and heaven has been shaped by the introduction of Islam and Christianity. Peel observes that Christian missionaries were often frustrated in their attempts to teach Judeo-Christian concepts of heaven and hell to early Yoruba converts: "The missionaries repeatedly challenged the notions of replication and return which ran through these [traditional Yoruba] images of the afterlife. For them heaven was a place of moral redress, even status reversal, and assuredly there was no return from it" (2000, 175). Further, he suggests that at the time of Christian conversion certain Yoruba groups had a conception of hell with the notion of judgment after death, most likely introduced through earlier Muslim influence in certain Yoruba regions. However, fear of punishment in hell does not seem to be a significant religious motivation for Yoruba Christians. During the time of my research I found church members to be more concerned with redressing and defeating Satan's workings on earth, as befits a Cherubim and Seraphim conceptualization of spiritual power (see Harris 2006) and the belief that the purpose of religious worship is to make changes in the world (see also Meyer 1999).

6. Churches without an established premises for worship may meet in a leader's house, or sometimes on a beach or other open air place.

7. The exception to this is the choir, where men and women usually sit together, and are organized according to their role in the choir (instrumentalist, lead singer, etc.).

8. Only men are allowed in the Holy of Holies and this space is further restricted to men who are most senior in the church hierarchy. I attended one Cherubim and Seraphim Church that had a woman as a leader; in that church a special seating area had been constructed for her outside of the Holy of Holies yet positioned so that she was seated at the right hand of God.

9. By contrast, members of the Celestial Church of Christ were not allowed to wear shoes while wearing their white church uniform, even when outside of the church premises.

10. Òrìṣàńlá/Ọbàtálá is the supreme òrìṣà, but he is still subject to Olódùmarè, the supreme deity. Idowu describes him as "the image or symbol of Olódùmarè on earth" (1962, 71). The names Òrìṣàńlá or Ọbàtálá are not used to refer to the Christian God.

11. See also Apter (1992) for a discussion of aṣọ àlà, the white cloth of death and ritual purity in Yoruba òrìṣà worship.

6   In His Steps

The journey through life is an eventful one and the Christian journey is full of trials and temptations. However, the hope that one day the experiences will eventually lead to a glorious end is enough to encourage Christians to endure whatever hardship is faced. Romans 8:18 says, "For I consider that the suffering of this present time is not worthy to be compared with the glory which shall be revealed in us."

No crown without a cross is a popular saying and every Christian who wishes to wear a cross at the last day must be prepared to bear their cross while on earth. . . .

Our message this year therefore is:
  There is no crown without a cross.
  The Christian journey through life is full of trials and temptations.
  The crown is only reserved for those who can endure to the end.
  Walking in His Steps is a pre-requisite to entering His rest.

These words were printed in the program for the annual festival of songs performed by the Cherubim and Seraphim Ayọ̀ ni o Church choir on April 26, 2003. It introduced the theme for that year's event and the message that the performers hoped to convey through their musical and dramatic offerings. The event was a spectacle of singing, dancing, and dramatic performances that included elaborate costumes, sets, and special effects. Typically, the choir debuted a selection of new songs and these songs would then be released on the group's new album.

Each year the organizers and performers attempted to go beyond what had been done the year before. Members of both the Main Church choir and the youth choir prepared for months—composing new songs, writing dramatic scenes, designing costumes, creating scenery and lighting designs, choreographing dance sequences, and then rehearsing everything until it was seamless. For many their participation in this event had entailed devoting hours of their time after work or on weekends, giving up time spent with family or other leisure activities. In the weeks before the event participants had conducted endless hours of rehearsals, including two dress rehearsals that ran from dusk until dawn. I had attended an all-night rehearsal three days prior to the event, staying up all night in the church as the performers ran through the timing of each element of the performance. Just before dawn, many of the performers had stretched out on the floor or on a bench in the church to sleep for an hour or two before jumping up and running off bleary-eyed to get ready to head to work that day. Participation in Choir Day required dedication and sacrifice, but most people I spoke with seemed exhilarated by the anticipation of performing in front of an audience on the appointed day.

In 2003, the theme of the festival was "In His Steps." A committee had chosen the theme eight months earlier. That year's festival also marked the thirtieth anniversary of the church choir, and the organizers took this milestone to heart—noting that not only did it represent a significant accomplishment for the choir, but also that the age of the choir was the age at which Jesus started his ministry. As they saw it, the choir as a group had reached a kind of spiritual maturity; they were now ready to "forge ahead" by following Christ's example in their spiritual mission. For this reason the festival's theme had a dual meaning as it referred both to the Christian message that they hoped to portray through the festival performance, but also the group's aspirations for itself as a spiritual and evangelical arm of the church.

To stage the festival the organizers worked with hundreds of church members—songwriters and dramatists, actors and singers, tailors and carpenters—in carrying out their vision. In deliberations about the production the organizers were insistent that the performance had to make the theme real for the audience and to transmit it in a way in which the message the performance would convey would be clear. The goal was for the audience to both see themselves in the performance and then to use the lessons taught through the drama to transform their lives. At the same time, the musical performances should reinforce the message of the drama, and allow people to understand it on an emotional and embodied level. "Music makes the message sweeter," many church members noted, explaining why spoken forms of exegesis such as sermons were only partly successful at teaching Christian lessons to church members. Music was crucial due to its ability to make sure that the lessons learned became part of lived experience. For this reason the choir festival intertwined dramatic and musical performances in an attempt to reinforce the lesson of the event.

The "In His Steps" theme emphasized that one should emulate the life of Jesus in order to achieve one's goals in life as a Christian, the corresponding lesson advised, "there is no crown without a cross." According to this logic one's life would be full of trials and temptations (the cross) that one had to endure in order to achieve one's final rest with God in heaven (the crown). The organizers and the performers hoped that through viewing the performance people would come to understand their lives and to shape their actions in relation to this Christian narrative of struggle and salvation. Through a dramatic recreation of what they saw as typical scenes of daily life in Lagos, the performers worked to shape how people

Cover of program for Choir Day, 2003

came to understand their life choices, as well as their pasts, presents and futures. In order to navigate these issues—the choices and decisions that one makes on a daily basis—a particular moral and ethical stance was required. Specifically, this stance demanded that one that emulate Jesus and walk "in his steps" in order to survive the journey through life's trials and temptations. Such a trajectory was required in order to achieve well-being (*àláàfíà*) in one's day-to-day life, as well as final salvation in heaven at the end of one's life. At the same time the church was positioned as the answer to troubles and tribulations, to doubts and frustrations that one encountered along this journey of walking "in Jesus's steps."

The Ayọ̀ ni o Church choir's performance featured three dramatic acts that alternated with singing and dancing. The songs performed by the choir included a variety of musical styles referencing forms of popular culture as well as music identified with specific Yoruba communities or social contexts. For example, the opening musical set included the juju-influenced song "Ad'eda, As'eda," which drew on the still-influential Yoruba popular music style performed frequently by groups at parties (Waterman 1990). The music set at the conclusion of the first act of the drama featured *wákà* rhythmic and melodic styles, which originally had been associated with Muslim communities in Lagos, but had been adapted by the choir as a marker of Yoruba music and dance.[1] Finally, the musical interlude between acts two and three contained an Afrobeat song performed by one of the lead singers who was dressed in tight trousers and a shirt that was open to his navel, a costume that resembled those worn by the musician Femi Kuti during his nightclub performances.[2] Although these musical performances only occasionally referred deliberately to the narrative of the drama, the lyrics of the songs helped to reinforce the lessons that the choir intended to deliver through the dramatic production.

The choir festival was in some ways a harkening back to earlier modes of Christian performance. Dramatic forms emerging out of independent and Africanist churches, known as "native air" performances, served as an important means through which Christian forms of music, dance, and drama created new religious publics in Lagos in the middle of the twentieth century (Barber 2003). Although the Choir Day performance was based in this historical tradition of Yoruba Christian performance, the spectacle of the performance and the melodramatic nature of the drama owed much to contemporary dramatic forms. Starting in the late 1980s, the nature of public religiosity in Lagos was transformed through the dramatic rise of new forms of Christianity, namely the rapid growth of neo-Pentecostal churches (Marshall 2009; Ojo 2006; Ukah 2008). Live Christian dramatic productions gave way to the video-film and the rise of the Nollywood film industry (Haynes 2000, 2010; Meyer 2015). Both the shift in religiosity as well as in the entertainment industry had much to do with both the collapse of Nigeria's oil boom economy beginning in the 1980s and the introduction of aus-

Singing and dancing during Choir Day, 2003

terity measures that made life difficult for average Nigerians.[3] The favored form of entertainment for many middle-class Yorubas became video films, inexpensively made and able to be viewed at home, featuring dramatic tales of loss and redemption through becoming born-again as a Christian (Haynes 2000; Ukah 2003).

Like many popular forms in Lagos, especially Nollywood films but also television soap operas, the drama performed by the choir drew on aspects characteristic of melodrama in order to make its point. The scenes portrayed were based in everyday life, yet also promised that a underneath the mundane events of daily activities lay a struggle between good and evil; this struggle was one that could be revealed to show the true meaning and purpose of life and action (Meyer 2004, 2015; Pype 2012). The performers and organizers accomplished this through their dramatization of these issues and concerns. Their deliberate choices of costumes, props, mannerisms, and language use helped to recreate a recognizable sense of reality on the stage. In viewing the play, church members were invited to imagine their own lives and experiences through such a frame. Moreover, the production offered a church-centered vision of the world, one in which the specter of apocalypse lay beneath daily life. Thus one needed to be vigilant and ready for the judgment that event entailed. For this reason the performers dramatized ethical forms of decision-making and action, demonstrating through their performance that Cherubim and Seraphim Christianity provided the means through which one acquired certainty that one's actions were correct and learned to restrain one's behavior according to a moral code that ensured one was able to achieve happiness and success in life.

Act One: The Valley of Decision

I arrived at the church compound early on the morning of the performance and made my way to the Choir Hall where I found a flurry of preparation and activity. When I said that I wanted to help I was sent to the main church hall to help set up chairs. I discovered that the space had been transformed into a theater: the benches that typically faced the altar in the front of the church were turned around to face a temporary stage erected in the back of the church. The stage was surrounded by tall stacks of amplifiers and stage lighting hung from the ceiling above it. Stacks of white plastic chairs stood near the stage, and I helped others to neatly arrange them in rows closest to the stage for the special guests.

As people began to arrive for the day's activities, about twenty people from the choir formed a procession. Singing hymns, accompanied by snare drum, trumpet, and tambourine, they marched around the church compound, and made their way to the flagpoles near the front gate. There, a prayer for the success of the event was offered, and a flag that served as the choir's herald was raised beside the three national flags that typically flew outside the church's main entrance: the Nigerian flag, the British flag, and the American flag. Once this prayer was over, it signaled that the event was about to begin, and members of the youth choir served as ushers, escorting special guests to their seats in the hall and gesturing to those who had just arrived to find a seat in the benches. Others distributed programs to people in the audience. As people claimed their seats and conversed with their friends and family, technicians completed their sound checks and lighting tests.

An elaborate opening ceremony followed a script that was similar to many other Yoruba parties and special events. These included a late start even though the timing of the event was meticulously noted in the program; a burst of activity as the hosts made sure that everything was in place; and then finally the master of ceremonies took the microphone to welcome everyone and to introduce the special guests. As each of the invited guests was introduced, he or she would stand up and a member of the youth choir would escort them to the special seating section in the front of the hall. In this way the structure of the event resembled more ceremonial events that people participated in regularly outside of the church: conferences and workshops, celebrations including birthday parties and civic anniversaries, business openings and the launching of political campaigns.[4] This structure served to further distinguish the performance from worship practices that typically took place in the space of the church, connecting the performance

Choir performs during flag raising at Choir Day, 2003

that was about to happen to forms of entertainment and more secular modes of celebration.

Members of the youth choir marched onto the stage to sing the opening song. This was followed by a short speech from the master of ceremonies who welcomed the audience and introduced the chairman of the event. In his remarks, the chairman told the audience that what they were about to experience that day was not merely an instance of "entertainment"; rather, it was "a spiritual thing" that promised to transform the viewers. He acknowledged the members of the organizing committee and thanked them for their hard work. This portion of the program concluded with an opening prayer. Finally, the stage was cleared for the drama to begin.

A group of five travelers, a mix of men and women led by a young man, appeared at stage left, and stopped to discuss their situation. The travelers had set off on a journey in search of the palace of the good king. This destination was described by the group's leader as a place of peace and joy, where they would be together with their loved ones and could live a life free of troubles. They discussed the next stage of their journey: crossing "the city" in search of the path to their destination. As the group moved toward the center of the stage, they met a man

Flag raising at Choir Day, 2003

who asked them where they were going. When told their destination, he promised them that he knew the way through the city and would help them find their path. However, as the travelers moved across the stage and encountered a number of people in the city, they became convinced that this man who claimed to be helping them was really an agent of the devil trying to prevent them from reaching their journey's end. It was through their encounters with other people in the city that they came to recognize this misdirection.

The travelers first came across a large family of seven children, with their mother. The children were hungry and begged their mother for food so they could eat breakfast. To the amusement of the audience, the smallest child kept saying that he wanted to eat "yam and egg" in a bright, confident voice. However, the mother told the children that there was no money for eggs, and no food in the house at all. As the children began crying, their father rode toward them across the stage on a bicycle. He was visibly drunk. One of the pilgrims helped him off of his bike, explained that his family was hungry, and asked if he had money to buy food for them.

The father first looked at his children with love and pity, and reached into his pockets for his wallet. The stranger who had offered to lead the group walked behind the father and whispered something in his ear, which made him stuff his wallet back into his pocket. The father glared at the children, told them that there was no money to buy food, and climbed back on his bicycle. As he was about to ride away, he overheard two women in the group of travelers discussing the situation. They noted that it was a shame that the man did not provide for his family. The man hesitated, approached the leader of the travelers, and asked where they were going. The leader of the group of pilgrims explained their destination—they were seeking the palace of the good king, but that only those who did not drink during the day but instead worked to provide for their family would be allowed to enter. "Won't you reconsider?" the leader asked the father. The father looked at his children one more time, and then removed money from his wallet and gave it to his wife. "Go and buy food to feed our family," he said, and the children thronged around him and hugged his legs. The father asked the travelers if he could join them on their journey, so that he would learn to follow the correct path and be a better provider for his family.

As this drama was unfolding on one side of the stage, the stranger had drawn away two of the young women from the group of pilgrims. The audience's attention was drawn to their conversation. The agent said that he knew a place where they could relax and enjoy some dancing. The young women were swayed by his message, and the stranger led them away from the pilgrims to the other side of the stage. Green, red, and blue-tinted lights lit this section of the stage, suggesting a nightclub atmosphere. Young men holding cigarettes and glasses of what

A pilgrim during the Choir Day drama, 2003

appeared to be beer leaned against a bar at the back of the stage. Men and women danced together suggestively to a slow rhythm and blues song.

The rest of the group of pilgrims left the scene of the family to watch as two of their members joined in the dancing. One pointed out another young woman in the nightclub who was being plied with drinks by an older man wearing an *agbádá*, a voluminous men's robe often made of luxurious cloth. The agbádá here symbolized the man's wealth, seniority, and power. The man told the young woman not to worry about her exams, that it did not matter if she passed. He also offered her money to "help with her feeding." "I just want to take care of you, my dear," the man said in a lecherous tone of voice.

The group of pilgrims began discussing her situation; in their opinion, the man was taking advantage of the girl. She needed to face her studies and not allow herself to be used by this older man. As they were about to intervene, the stranger waved his hands and the volume of the music increased. The pilgrims began dancing as though they were in a trance. The leader of the group, however, was able to resist the sound of the music and began moving from person to person, shaking them, and trying to get them to stop their dancing. When no one responded, he knelt down in the center of the dance floor, and began to loudly sing a hymn. One by one the other travelers were pulled out of their trance, and joined him in his singing. As the sound of the hymn became louder than the dance music, the devil's agent ran off of the stage with his hands over his ears. The young woman turned to look at the old man and told him that she was not interested in him, and that she had to go home to study for her exam. She thanked the travelers for their help and asked if she too could join them on their journey. The travelers agreed and moved on off the stage.

Living in the Valley of Indecision

As evidenced by the reactions of the audience, the scenes portrayed in this act, with their comedy and their pathos, appealed to those present. The pilgrims' interactions with various residents of the city resembled, on the one hand, plot lines from numerous television and video dramas; on the other hand, they represented encounters that church members were familiar with from their daily lives. One of the scriptwriters explained to me that he had drawn from issues that he had experienced in his own life in writing the different scenes in the valley of indecision. The actor who played the father in the first act—who was himself a father of four children—told me that the intention of the drama was to remind audience members of what they go through on a daily basis in Lagos and to reassure them that even through they struggle and often encounter difficulties in their life, their reward after all of that struggle was with God at the end. In line with the message of the festival, the scriptwriters, actors, and director all wanted to show to church members that in such situations they were supposed to follow the example of

Jesus and do what was necessary instead of giving in to the devil's temptation even if it meant sacrificing pleasure or comfort in the immediate moment.

The types of interactions portrayed in the scenes were intended to speak across gender, age-based, class, and occupational divides in the church. The membership of the Ayọ̀ ni o Church was made up of a mix of highly educated and successful members of Lagos's middle and upper classes—executives from financial and insurance industries, lawyers, owners of middle-sized businesses such as printing presses or industrial laundries—with those who worked a bit lower down on the economic scale: office clerks, school teachers, and small entrepreneurs. The church also attracted members who worked in more menial occupations, as petty traders, bus drivers, touts, or in construction. A number of people were unemployed. Two-thirds of the members were women. Nearly all had finished their primary education, and a majority of them some secondary education. Postsecondary education and training was emphasized as well: many had completed some university education or occupational training. Nearly half of them were born in Lagos, the rest were migrants from other parts of Yoruba-land and were socially and geographically mobile.

Many members of the church viewed the scenes depicted in the drama as emblematic of their own experiences of struggle and temptation. Indeed, in discussion with church members of their own biographies and their decisions for joining the church, they often narrated their life history similarly. For them their lives were characterized by hardship, but they saw joining the church and membership in the church as a way of overcoming such adversity. As such they made the church a part of their everyday lives. Participation in the church served to help them structure their decisions and choices in life.

Tobi

Many church members whom I interviewed described their lives before joining the church as one characterized by struggle. Tobi, a man in his mid-thirties, was one of the lead singers in the choir. He explained that he had grown up in a polygamous household, where his parents had "stopped loving each other" when he was five years old. His mother left him in his father's house to be raised by his stepmothers, who often beat him or refused to feed him. At the age of thirteen he left his father's house and began staying with different relatives, moving from house to house until they became unable to care for him in addition to their own families. Tobi, who had grown up attending a small Cherubim and Seraphim Church, started sleeping in different churches whose members would offer him charity.

It was in the church that Tobi also started singing. He learned to play the drums used during church services and would sing and play after worship had ended at a number of churches near where he was living in the hopes that people would give him pocket change so that he could buy food. He later became an official member of one of the church choirs and that was where he claimed that he really learned how to sing—he learned a bit about music theory and how to harmonize his voice with others. He especially enjoyed singing at revival services because he saw how the spirit would move people through music so that they would go into a spiritual trance. He claimed that this was how he knew he had been chosen by God, since God allowed his voice to move others closer to spirit.

Tobi managed to complete secondary school, but he failed his college entrance exams and was unable to complete any higher education. This limited his opportunities for employment. He spent a lot of time in his young adulthood participating in various schemes to apply for a travel visa so he could go to the United States. He desperately wanted to get out of Nigeria because he felt that his opportunities were limited there. The life of struggle in Lagos was too hard, and did not seem to offer any way of improving oneself. He had tried to get a travel visa by performing with a church choir, but when he went to apply for the visa he learned that his name was removed from the interview list because he was accused of impregnating another member of the choir. He offered to marry the woman in question but was instead forced out of the church in disgrace.

After that incident, Tobi moved to two more churches before joining the Ayọ ni o Church. He waited two years until he was invited to join the choir. Once he was a part of the group, he explained to me, his life was transformed. Some of the senior members of the choir looked out for him, helped him find steady employment so that he was not dependent on church charity, and helped him find a decent place to live. He also made friends with the other singers in the choir and could turn to them in times of emotional or material distress. He was grateful to the church and to the choir for helping him organize his life.

In 2004, he married a woman he met through the church. They had two children in the course of their first two years of marriage. When we talked about how his life had changed since he had joined the church he recalled how he had been beaten and treated badly by his own father, and abandoned by his mother. Because of this experience, Tobi claimed, he tried especially hard to be a good father and husband: "They are my closest and best friends," he said. "I love them and I would never treat them badly."

When Tobi described the progression of his life, he said that now he knows what God's plan was. It was never to leave Nigeria, but it was for him to "face [his] life" here. It was through his dedication to God, and through fellowship in the church, that he was able to start his family, to find steady work that he loved at a printing company, and to find friendship and meaningful activity by singing with the church choir. Although he still expressed a desire to travel to the United States, he said that he was happy with his life. He said, "I thank God."

Iya Bunmi

Iya Bunmi was another member of the choir whose life outside of the church was characterized by hard work and sacrifice. When I met her she was in her late fifties and was attending the Cherubim and Seraphim Theological Institute located in the church compound studying to be a pastor. She explained to me that while she had had little opportunity for education early in her life, she had received a calling to serve God and the church. She was eager to expand her knowledge and to share it with others because she owed so much to her faith and to the church for her success in life.

Iya Bunmi had eight children, ranging in ages between fifteen and thirty. All but two of them still lived with her. She also cared for two grandchildren; one of her daughters had children from an early marriage that did not last. The daughter's husband had left her, and when the daughter remarried Iya Bunmi took in the grandchildren to care for them as though they were her own children. When I asked about her own husband, Iya Bunmi told me that he had not been around for years; he had left when the children were small. She raised them herself.

To care for her family, Iya Bunmi worked as a petty trader. She would go to the large markets at Mile 2 in Lagos to buy small household items such as candles, matches, and packets of soap and detergent. She sold them out of a kiosk in front of the building where she rented a small one-bedroom apartment. She paid rent to the building owner each week so she could have the kiosk there. Now that Iya Bunmi was training to be a pastor, one of her daughters ran the kiosk under her direction. Iya Bunmi also ran a small Bible study group in the sitting room of her apartment two evenings each week. She carried phone charge cards in her purse everywhere she went in case there was any opportunity to make a sale.

When I asked about her early life she began with a story of hearing G. O. Fakeye, the leader of the Ayọ ni o Church, delivering a sermon on the radio. She decided to attend the Ayọ ni o Church because she found that his prayers were powerful—she knew that if she attended his church that her life would improve. She was in her thirties then, and was struggling to feed and provide for her children because their father had left. She was often forced to go to the family of her children's father to ask them for funds to pay school fees or to purchase groceries in especially hard times. After joining the church, she occasionally depended on other members to help make ends meet. She was able to set up her kiosk with a loan from a member of the church ẹgbẹ (a small group of church members organized around similar spiritual interests) that she belonged to, the Esther Band. When she paid that back, she joined a micro-credit group where each member of the group contributed a certain amount to create a larger pot, which then rotated to a different member each month. That was how she was able to restock her kiosk when the supplies ran out.

Iya Bunmi came to the church compound nearly every day. The church was the center of her life. After checking to make sure that her daughter was in the kiosk she would make her way by bus to the church for early morning services, to attend pastor training classes, for choir practice, or special prayer sessions. There was always something to do in the compound, and during the times in-between meetings, classes, or prayer sessions Iya Bunmi could be found in the kiosk on the church compound talking and laughing with other women there. She also worked with Prophet Atansuyi, the director of the theological institute, helping him around the compound, carrying his papers, and organizing his office.

When I asked Iya Bunmi what singing in the choir meant to her, she explained that she knew that joining the choir had made a significant difference in her life. When she sang in the church, she explained, she could "feel God's presence." That was how she knew that no matter how hard things were in her life that she would make it through. According to her, she always prioritized choir practice because she knew how important it was for everyone who attended church services to be able to have God in their lives as well.

Both Tobi and Iya Bunmi faced numerous difficulties in their lives. They relied on the church materially, pragmatically, and emotionally. It was through their connection to the church that they were able to overcome the temptations that beset them in what constituted their valleys of indecision. The choir in particular served as an important social, emotional, and material hub through which they were encouraged to stay on the correct path and to make good decisions in their lives—to be a good Christian. Aspects of their lives, and of the lives of others, were mirrored on the stage at the choir festival that afternoon in order to show how the struggle of daily life necessitated a religious response. One had to learn to embody ethical values that were central to Cherubim and Seraphim Christianity including hard work, respect for hierarchy, and the need for those who were better off than others to provide assistance. However, finding the right church in which to learn and live these values was not straightforward given the complexities of life in Lagos. It was to this very different kind of indecision that characterized life for many in Lagos that the drama turned in the second act.

Act Two: Odysseys of Life

The stage had been cleared and prepared for the next act of the drama. The pilgrims entered on the left, and stopped to assess their situation. They discussed how they had a long way to go to reach their destination. They wondered aloud if there was any church that could help them with their quest. In this act the pilgrims moved across the stage from left to right, encountering representatives of different Christian denominations and churches in Lagos who came forward to offer their assistance to the pilgrims. Using costumes and props, actors depicted different types of Christianity found in Lagos: a priest from the Catholic Church representing the so-called orthodox mission-derived churches, a prophet from the Celestial Church of Christ representing Aladura churches, and a two pastors representing different Pentecostal churches. As the pilgrims encountered each representative they told him or her of their intention to reach the palace of the good king and listened as the religious leader attempted to convince them of the power and ability of their methods of worshipping God for reaching their destination.

The interactions between the pilgrims and the religious representatives were portrayed in ways that stereotyped assumptions about different Christian denominations as well as the peculiarities of well-known pastors and church leaders. The actors imitated, and sometimes mocked, worship practices peculiar to other denominations. The audience frequently laughed as they recognized the religious personalities and idiosyncrasies that characterized each church portrayed. The use of humor in this scene conveyed a message about the proliferation of choices that Christians faced in Lagos: the absurdity that so many churches competed for members rather than joining together to achieve God's purpose in the world.

The depiction of Lagos's Christian marketplace in the Choir Day drama reproduced stereotypes and concerns about how certain churches were hiding traditional practices under a Christian shell. The interaction between the pilgrims and the prophet from the Celestial Church of Christ was especially notable in this regard. A man wearing a dingy white garment with his feet bare greeted the pilgrims. He carried a Bible and a large metal staff—a sign that he was a prophet—and was accompanied by a woman also wearing white who carried a tambourine. The prophet began to sing loudly as the woman shook the tambourine and banged on its membrane. She danced in a circle around the prophet. One of the pilgrims stopped to watch the duo. The prophet and the woman began to circle the pilgrim with their dance, and then asked him to kneel. He did as they asked and the prophet began to pray while the woman clapped her hands vigorously and began shaking uncontrollably. The prophet's prayer became incoherent, and he began shouting. His cries were not in imitation of the sounds of glossolalia as typically heard as evidence of the presence of the Holy Spirit in the church, but instead the prophet said nonsensical yet discernible words in a variety of languages: English, Yoruba, Igbo, Hausa, and a little bit of French.

When the prophet stopped shouting, the woman kneeled down next to the pilgrim, and in an exaggerated stage whisper spoke into the pilgrim's ear that he was supposed to go and bathe in the river with black soap, to rub a leaf all over his body, and to bring certain items—a chicken, some yam flour, and some palm oil—and throw them in the river. The man responded to each of these orders with incredulity, "You want me to do what? And then what?!" He quickly rose to his feet and ran back to the group of pilgrims as the audience laughed at the exaggerated performance and the scandalous requests of the Celestial Church representatives. The actors in this scene imitated a church that was often compared to Cherubim and Seraphim churches by outsiders, but was seen by church members as potentially engaging in practices that were not properly Christian. Through their exaggerated performance they suggested that Celestial Church practices were similar to indigenous religious practices.

The Celestial prophet and his assistant demonstrated the falsity of their practices though their exaggerated movements and obviously fake glossolalia. Their requests—to bathe in the river with black soap and to make certain sacrificial offerings—were very obviously borrowed from indigenous religious practices. Through both depiction and rejection of this religious formation, the creators of the drama emphasized that the Ayọ̀ ni o Church was truly Christian.

Another memorable interaction was with a representative from the Mountain of Fire and Miracles Ministry, a large Pentecostal megachurch in Lagos renowned for faith healing and deliverance. A male pastor wearing an expensive looking, shiny black suit with a bright yellow shirt and red tie approached the group and asked if they needed his assistance. When they explained the purpose of their journey, the man assured them that he could help, and offered to pray over them. One of the pilgrims agreed to see if he could help her, and she knelt in front of him.

The pastor began praying loudly in English, with an exaggerated—and often humorously incorrect—American accent. He called down the Holy Spirit, he asked that the pilgrim be covered with the blood of Jesus, and repeated each phrase multiple times. Occasionally he would tap the woman on her shoulder or her back to emphasize his prayer and each time she would startle, open her eyes, and give the pastor a dirty look, but then close her eyes again and fold her hands in front of her. Finally he stood to the side of the kneeling woman, crouched down, and began shouting "FIRE! FIRE! FIRE! Fire in the body!" She recoiled in fright and began to shuffle away from him on her knees, but he moved to her other side and repeated his refrain. At the end of his prayer, the pastor slapped the woman's forehead with the palm of his hand, causing her to fall over backward. She jumped up in fright and ran back to her fellow pilgrims. Throughout this sequence the audience laughed uproariously, some imitating the pastor's refrain of "Fire in the body." This portrayal of a charismatic Pentecostal leader as a charlatan was humorous and recognizable to the audience, but also called into question the authenticity of exaggerated performances of healing and deliverance staged by Pentecostal pastors (see Ukah 2011).

As the pilgrims reached the other side of the stage, they stopped to lament their lack of success. Each representative of a different church had been found wanting. They were unable to find a person or a place where their problems would be solved and where they would feel at home with God. They expressed their frustration and insecurity at being able to find a source of salvation in the city. The leader also lamented that there seemed to be a number of churches and religious leaders offering their services to Christians in search of guidance and support, but that none of them were genuine. None were able to help them reach their destination in heaven.

Where Do You Fellowship?

The pilgrims' experience of confusion as they searched for comfort and guidance in organized religion depicted a scene that many in the church lamented: there were so many different churches and Christian leaders in Lagos, but it was often difficult to tell whether they were genuine. Most church members had a keen awareness that not all churches were the same, and that certain Christian practices or church leaders were better than others. In Bible study sessions and theological lectures the situation was often described as a religious "marketplace" where "churches competed for souls." At the same time, church members endured criticisms of their own Christian practices made by others outside of the church. Thus a kind of skepticism or critical attitude toward other Christian leaders or congregations existed, as each particular group asserted the righteousness of their own group in relation to that of others.

Indeed, the number of different churches in Lagos and different kinds of Christianity reaching out to religious seekers was overwhelming. Did one attend a mission-derived denomination—a Methodist fellowship or a large Anglican cathedral? Or did one turn to one of the Aladura churches, such as the Cherubim and Seraphim churches? Even within the Cherubim and Seraphim denomination there were options: the Holy Order of Cherubim and Seraphim, the Sacred and Eternal, the Cherubim and Seraphim Church Movement. And within a given denomination there may be hundreds of individual physical churches with a congregation and some sort of worship space, each with a charismatic leader and its own distinctive worship practices designed to appeal to a soul in search of salvation. Some church leaders were reputed to be able to heal illness or to ensure fertility and prosperity, adding to their appeal to Christians to begin attending their particular branch.

Adding to this confusion was the explosion of Pentecostalism in southwest Nigeria, beginning in the 1990s and continuing up until the current moment. Neo-Pentecostal churches claimed that they were more modern than orthodox or Aladura churches, and thus more capable of dealing with contemporary issues and troubles that people faced. Their pastors wore Western-style suits and dresses, and spoke in American-accented English (Marshall 2007; Meyer 2007; Ukah 2008). Pentecostals also used mass media effectively, both advertising their spiritual abilities and denouncing other forms of Christianity as holding people back from success and happiness due to their use of forms of religious practice too reliant on human religious authorities, that is priests and prophets who act as surrogates between an individual and God, but also on their suspected use of

African religious ideas and practices—potentially demonic, certainly harmful in the assessment of many Christians. Pentecostal leaders urged people to read their Bibles, talk to God, become born again, and leave behind such unnecessary objects and figures who just stood in the way of your individual relationship with God.

Of course, even choosing a Pentecostal church was complicated by many factors, beginning with the sheer number of pastors and congregations from which to choose. The larger neo-Pentecostal denominations in Lagos included the Redeemed Christian Church of God, the Mountain of Fire and Miracles, and Deeper Life, but these were joined by hundreds of other churches. All of these churches used the radio or television or an entertaining film to advertise its ability to, though fellowship, lead you toward communion with God. Some sought to reform adherents' behavior through avoiding certain activities—no short skirts or makeup for young women, no alcohol, no associating with friends who were not members of the church. Others offered elaborate and effervescent worship sessions and massive revivals where, through singing, dancing, and sweating, one came to physically feel the presence of God.

Islam and indigenous religion rounded out the profusion of religious choices available to seekers in Lagos. The choices and decisions that people made concerning religion as they moved through their life was seen as crucial to being healthy, happy, and successful. Further, the necessity of religion in one's life was emphasized in popular culture, particularly in Nollywood films where the protagonist usually suffered through a series of struggles—brought on either by his own selfishness or bad choices or through the bad intentions of others against him—before making his life right again through finding God and being saved.

Various ways of evaluating whether a particular church "worked" and was efficacious for its members in their search for health, wealth, and happiness existed. Stories and testimonies of those who had found what they were looking for in a certain congregation or with a specific pastor circulated widely. For example, a friend in Ibadan insisted that I visit his particular Cherubim and Seraphim branch by describing how the leader there had healed a relative who suffered from epilepsy: "After the prophet prayed over him and fasted for 30 days the seizures stopped," he assured me. Other evidence that a particular church worked could be deduced through examining who attended a particular branch, both in terms of individual members, known to a person, as well as the kinds of people who attended. One friend, who was not a member of the Ayọ ni o Church, reported that a recent convert at her church had made his decision to attend by counting the number of luxury cars in the parking lot during the Sunday worship service.

As the Choir Day drama emphasized, these evaluations and decisions had to be made in a context where different people were telling you different things, placing demands on your attention and shaping your interests in and requirements for your church. For some, attending the flashiest, loudest, and biggest church was enough. For others it was about having a direct connection with a charismatic leader able to listen to your troubles and help you put them into the context of God's kingdom. Alternately, stories about corrupt pastors who stole from the offering basket or had affairs with the wives of church members served as a caution against particular churches.

The majority of the members of the Ayọ̀ ni o Church had been born into Christian households and were the children of Christian parents. A little over half were members since birth of one of the Cherubim and Seraphim denominations, though not necessarily one that was a part of the Cherubim and Seraphim Movement. However, most of the members—especially those who worshipped in the Main Church—had joined the church in the 1980s, leaving their previous congregations to worship at the Ayọ̀ ni o Church in Surulere.

As we saw in the story of Iya Bunmi, who, when I asked her to tell me about her early life, began with when she first heard Fakeye on the radio, for many church members their decision to join the church marked a significant moment of transition in their lives. For some, it was a matter of peer pressure. One senior member of the choir explained to me that he noticed that many of the friends with whom he used to play football on the weekends were no longer available. When he asked one of them what they were doing instead, he was told that they were attending a new church: the Ayọ̀ ni o Church. He joined them the next weekend, and from there he just continued attending.

Bàbá Dami

Bàbá Dami ran a successful industrial laundry business. He joined the church in 1985 following a personal and professional crisis. His business had grown so rapidly that he had been able to build a factory so that he could bid on large contracts. One day he had a large order come in so he had people working around the clock in the factory to fill it. That night, armed robbers came and stole most of the cash on hand, computers and other equipment, along with two of the company's delivery trucks. Bàbá Dami wondered what he had done wrong so that what should have been his greatest financial success had resulted in a massive loss. When he learned that one of his tenants—who rented an apartment in a building he owned—was the thief, he worried that someone so close to him could have betrayed him. He went to the Ayọ̀ ni o Church seeking help in turning his fortune around. They prayed with him, and told him that he needed to come to church regularly, and to be sure to sing and pray fervently, in order to put his life on "the right track." He explained to me that at first he took their advice half-heartedly, wondering how singing and praying would be able to help him recover from his financial losses. But eventually he observed that their prayers were effective as his business began to recover and the police were able to return the two stolen trucks to him. After that, he and his wife attended church regularly.

Rotimi

Others had more complicated religious backgrounds. Rotimi, who was responsible for maintaining and setting up the electronic sound equipment for the choir, had been born and raised as a Muslim. When he was ten years old he began attending a school affiliated with the Methodist church and converted to Christianity. After he finished school he stopped going to church. He explained to me that one day he saw a man dropping off his white church uniform to be cleaned by a local laundry person. Rotimi said that he had looked down on the person with the white garment because, like many others, he was suspicious that the churches whose members wore them were like a cult. However, he began a conversation with the man at the laundry. The man invited him to attend his child's naming ceremony at the Ayọ ni o Church.

After this chance meeting with a member of the Ayọ ni o Church, Rotimi began attending worship services occasionally but not on a regular basis. That changed when he attended an end-of-year prayer vigil to ensure security and prosperity in the New Year. He had initially decided not to go, but then at the last minute, he changed his mind. Just before midnight he took his Bible and began walking toward the church, thinking that he would just go and pray with them for a short time and then leave when the opportunity arose. However, when he arrived, the church security closed the gates and the prayer leader said that no one should leave the church until the next morning. Rotimi's life was transformed by his experience during the all-night prayers. "I felt God's presence during that vigil," he described to me. After that experience he began attending the church regularly and he quickly became an official church member.

Deborah

The increasing visibility of Pentecostal churches in the 2000s, and their appealing promise of prosperity and a direct relationship with God, caused many people to leave the Ayọ ni o Church. This was especially true of younger members, those whose parents had joined the church in the 1970s and 1980s and who were born into the church. In the mid-1990s the Ayọ ni o Church leadership created the Youth Fellowship in response to this initial loss of young members—a space in which young people could worship together and have a leadership stake in how the church was run. The Youth Fellowship was vibrant, lively, and very active during the time of my research. They organized their own revivals and outreach programs that supplemented those offered by the main church.

However, not all efforts to keep members were successful. At the age of twenty-eight, Deborah was the youngest member of the Main Church choir. She had been a member of the Youth Fellowship but had received a spiritual directive that she should join the Main Church before she was officially eligible to do so.

Her father was an elder in the church, and sat in the front near the altar. When I joined the choir Deborah was assigned to help me learn the songs and how to play the tambourine and shaker with the choir. She had a clear singing voice and she prayed enthusiastically during the special prayer sessions in the church. Because of the closeness of our age, we were often paired together for special prayers.

Deborah's dream was to own a clothing boutique on Victoria Island, an upper-class neighborhood of Lagos. She had traveled to Dubai twice to bring back fashionable clothes and shoes to sell. For now, because she did not have her own shop, she carried her wares to offices and homes to sell directly to her customers. This work was more difficult than she would have liked. Because she did not have a car she had to rely on taxis and public transportation. She lived at home with her parents, who were eager for her to find a husband. While she was anxious to get married and start a family, she wanted to make sure that her trading career was established first.

When I returned to the church in 2007 after a three-year absence, Deborah was no longer in the choir. When I asked the other members of the choir about her, I was told simply, "She has left us." I located a phone number for her and arranged to meet her at a fast food restaurant to catch up. She arrived, carrying her bags full of dresses and shoes, and told me that she was now a member of the Redeemed Christian Church of God, a neo-Pentecostal church. She had left the Ayọ̀ ni o Church because she was frustrated with her lack of progress in life. A friend who had just gotten married had invited her to attend a revival at her branch of the Redeemed Church and Deborah had joined her. She told me that her life had been stalled due to her membership in the Ayọ̀ ni o Church, and that she felt as though she had been able to achieve a new connection with God through the Redeemed Church. She was sure that her change in church membership was making a difference in her life.

The Ayọ̀ ni o Church had to continually adapt in order to prevent the loss of additional members to other churches. When I returned to visit the church in the summer of 2010, I found that an additional fellowship, the Disciples of Christ Ministry, had been added to the groups that worshipped in the Ayọ̀ ni o Compound. The Disciples of Christ fellowship was started by a group of former leaders in the Youth Chapel who were too old to continue to fellowship there, but felt out of place and a distinct lack of agency in the Main Church whose upper administration was dominated by senior church members, most over the age of sixty. These young adults between the ages of twenty and forty were allowed to create a temporary home for themselves in Orimolade Hall, a space in the Ayọ̀ ni o compound that had been used previously for meetings and smaller services such as naming ceremonies. Although some elders may have perceived the unwillingness of this group of young men and women to be subject to their authority in the main church as a challenge, it had been accepted by most as a further means of preventing the loss of young church members to Pentecostal churches.

The organizers of the group noted that they saw these changes as necessary to keep young church members engaged in their Christian practice. The Disciples of Christ described their mode of worship as more modern, more emotional, and more passionate than what they said they experienced in the Main Church.

The stories of Bàbá Dami, Rotimi, and Deborah all depict some of the ways in which individuals in Lagos negotiated the terrain of religious possibility in Lagos. Choosing to attend a church was often based on a specific event in one's life, sometimes dramatic as in the case of Bàbá Dami's setbacks. In other cases the decision to attend a particular church was based on personal connections and individual feelings of transcendence during worship, as in the case of Rotimi. However, the religious marketplace, depicted in a humorous fashion during act two of the choir drama, offered numerous possibilities for seekers who sought a variety of means of ensuring their happiness and success in life. Deborah's decision to leave the church to join a neo-Pentecostal congregation was enabled by the array of choices available to her as well as the ideas and arguments about what made one church better than another that circulated in Lagos through various forms of media: radio, television, printed materials, and so on.

The second act of the Choir Day drama concluded with two songs—"Those that wait on the Lord" and "Teach me Lord to be vigilant and abide with you"— both of which featured lyrics commenting on the actions depicted in the dramatic scene that had preceded it. These songs were musically more somber than the celebratory songs performed between acts one and two. Both were ballads, and featured slower tempos and less complicated rhythms. This musical style helped enhance the lessons of both the drama as well as the lyrics of the songs, which urged those seeking heaven to be steadfast and true to their purpose in life. While the production emphasized vigilance and faith in the Lord as necessary to find a fellowship that would help them to achieve salvation in heaven, the stories of church members and the institutional changes made within the church speak to the earth-bound requirements of church members searching for happiness and success in this world.

Act Three: Revelation

When the last song of the interlude between acts two and three ended, there was a short pause as the stage was reset. The master of ceremonies came to the front of a stage with a microphone and started bantering with the audience: "Are you enjoying yourself?" "Aren't they wonderful?" He also acknowledged any additional special guests in the audience who had arrived after the performance had started. Once the set was ready he told the crowd to enjoy the final act, which was "truly spectacular." He then stepped aside to allow the action to resume.

The pilgrims entered from the left, and sat toward the front of the stage. They talked to each other and repeated their frustrations with their journey. They had come so far but still had not found the palace of the good king. One member said that perhaps they should go back to their lives; perhaps the place they were seeking did not exist. Some of the pilgrims moved away from the leader and made plans to go back to their homes so they could rest. The leader encouraged them to stay. He reminded them of the ultimate goal of their journey, to find salvation and respite at the palace of the good king.

As the group discussed the possibility of ending their journey before reaching their destination, an old man approached the pilgrims. He asked them what they were seeking. One member of the group described their journey, and said that they were giving up on it because there was no hope. The old man expressed surprise that they would quit before their journey was finished. He asked questions of the different members of the group concerning their intentions at the beginning of the journey and the decisions they had made in their lives.

For example, he asked one of the young men in the group what had led him to go on the journey. The young pilgrim explained that he had graduated from the university at the top of his class, but he had been unable to find employment. Out of all the applications he sent out, only one place had offered him employment; moreover, the position he was offered did not suit him because the salary was too low and the work too menial for someone with his skills. The old man told him that the job would have changed his life because the company had gone on to enjoy great success. The starting position would have led to an opportunity even greater than the one he imagined for himself if he had just humbled himself and worked hard to prove his worth. The young man, like each of the pilgrims that he spoke with, came to a new understanding of his troubles that had led him to begin his journey. It was clear that many of the pilgrims had contributed to their own problems. The lesson offered by the old man for each pilgrim was that they needed to look within themselves to discern the nature of their difficulties, rather than seeking a solution outside of themselves.

The old man said that he had one more revelation for the group. He gestured toward a white screen that had been hung at the back of the stage. As he did the stage lights dimmed and apocalyptic scenes appeared on the screen: scenes of warfare, of children crying, of people suffering from hunger. These scenes were followed by an animation of the second coming of Christ, made up of stock images of horses, angels, and a depiction of the descent of Jesus from heaven. Loud sound effects featuring thunder claps boomed from the speakers. Mist from a fog machine filled the air. This depiction borrowed heavily from images described in the Book of Revelations in the Bible, showing the second coming of Christ and the election of the worthy.

As the projection ended, the old man told the group that he hoped they knew what to do now. "To get to the palace of the good king you must walk in His steps," he said. As the old man walked off the stage, the leader of the pilgrims got on his knees, picked up his Bible, held it between his hands in front of him, and began to pray out loud. The rest of the group imitated his actions. They did not pray in unison, but prayed loudly and extemporaneously.

The overhead lights in the church were turned up so that the entire room was full of light. Behind the pilgrims, the white screen was raised to reveal a stairway leading to a platform. On each step of the stairs stood a woman wearing the white church uniform. The women standing on the stairs began to sing a hymn. At first they sang quietly, but as the pilgrims' prayers became more fervent, the volume of the singing increased. Only ten women were visible on the stairs, their voices were joined by the sounds of an organ as well as what sounded like a large choir, singing off stage. The pilgrims, distracted by the singing, stopped praying and turned to look at the stairs. As they did so, the women held out their arms in a gesture of welcome.

Drawn by the singing, the pilgrims stood up and moved toward the center of the stage. They turned to look at the staircase. Prophet Korode, the charismatic leader of the Ayò ni o Church choir, stepped forward. He was wearing a uniform made of white satin cloth, lit from the front and the back with spotlights that made his uniform appear even whiter. He smiled broadly and held his arms open in welcome as he sang. The pilgrims all stared up at him. As they did the singers lowered their voices and Korode spoke to them through a microphone. He welcomed them and said that he knew that they had traveled far but that they had finally shown themselves to be worthy of paradise. As his speech concluded the refrain of the hymn started again and everyone joined in singing the hymn.

The pilgrims turned to face the audience. They were also singing and smiling, and they held their arms out in a gesture of welcome. Members of the choir who had been singing backstage filed onto the stage and lined up in front of the platform. A group of women brought a church uniform to each of the pilgrims and helped them to put them on. Now everyone on the stage was dressed in white. They smiled and sang as they too gestured toward the audience. The pilgrims were wanderers no longer; they were now part of this group. Through singing together and wearing the white church uniform they were transformed into angels worshipping God in heaven. They had found their home.

At Home in the World

The three acts of the choir day drama, punctuated with songs, provided a narrative within which church members could understand their own lives and the lives of their family, friends, and other church members, in relation to a Christian narrative of suffering and redemption. The performers dramatized the point of church worship: the journey from struggle to salvation, the role of revelation in the lives of church members, and the cosmological differences between heaven and earth, home and the marketplace. The marketplace as depicted in this play was characterized by two things: on the one hand, the daily struggle to take care of oneself and to provide for one's family; on the other, the proliferation of churches and pastors in Lagos's crowded Christian marketplace. Both were worldly concerns that had to be addressed correctly, as moral discernment was acquired through disciplined practices of singing and praying. Furthermore, the production asserted that in the face of temptation one prays and sings to remain steadfast and certain in one's orientation to the world.

The trajectories of individuals, such as Tobi or Deborah, as they moved into or out of the church, demonstrate how people came to understand their lives through their connection to the church. Their life stories were understood as characterized by struggle and redemption, and their decision to join the church was a major life event, a turning point in their journey that allowed for real transformation. Similarly, as we saw in the case of Deborah, leaving the church was also understood as such a transformative moment. This possibility is one that the dramatic production allowed for in their depiction of the religious choices facing people in Lagos, but that was curtailed by their argument that Cherubim and Seraphim Christianity was the correct path toward salvation. Deborah's decision to leave the church was a deviation from this narrative but one that was also made possible through it as she was convinced that her path to happiness led her in a different direction.

Given the emphasis in the drama on Cherubim and Seraphim Christianity as representing the right path, it is fitting that in the final act, when the pilgrims finally reach the palace of the good king—heaven—they find that it is full of music. As they recognize both the difficult choices and hard work entailed in the Christian journey, as well as the assurance of salvation at the end of that journey, the travelers were transformed from pilgrims to angels. This was symbolized both by their being clothed in the white cloth of the church uniform and by their joining the choir in singing songs praising god. Thus, as described in earlier chapters, angelic mimicry was linked to the achievement of a good life through Christian practice.

What is particularly interesting about the Choir Day performance is that these Christian messages were articulated not through worship itself, but here in an in-between form that mimicked entertainment but was supposed to be seen as having a spiritual purpose. Recall the remarks of the chairman at the beginning of the performance: the choir festival was, in his words, "a spiritual thing." This was a way of bringing the church out into the lives of members, but also of bringing their lives into the church as they dramatically staged typical events and struggles that people encountered in their daily lives.

This was the point of the choir festival—to extend the orientations and practices of the church outside of worship itself. Church members should come to see themselves represented in the scenes depicted and understand the right way to act. At the same time the music performed served to further push the messages of the church into the daily lives of church members. The songs sung during choir day, and recorded by the choir mediated the relationships between church members' lives in the church and their everyday lives without.

Notes

1. Wákà is a style of musical chanting and drumming that is usually associated with Yoruba Muslim communities. Songs in the wákà style were usually sung by women during Ramadan. Musical styles associated with Yoruba Muslim communities have been recently appropriated by Yoruba gospel musicians and with the addition of Christian lyrics made a part of Christian popular cultures (see Brennan 2015).

2. Femi Kuti is the son of Fẹla Anikulapo-Kuti, the musician credited with the development of the Afrobeat style of Nigerian popular music in the 1970s. Femi Kuti performs regularly at the New Africa Shrine, a nightclub in Lagos modeled on Fẹla's original Afrika Shrine nightclub.

3. For more on the shift toward Pentecostalism in Nigeria since the 1980s, see Marshall (2009); see Gifford (2004) on similar shifts in Ghana.

4. See Drewal (1992) and Trager (2001) for further discussion and analysis of how this Yoruba ceremonial form is a way of reinforcing a nationalist vision Yoruba community in the face of distinctions and divisions that exist within the community.

7   Living in the Spirit

> I say then: Walk in the Spirit, and you shall not fulfill the lust of the flesh. For
> the flesh lusts against the Spirit, and the Spirit against the flesh; and these
> are contrary to one another, so that you do not do the things that you wish.
> —Galatians 5:16–17

THE CONGREGATION WAS stuffed into the rows of benches in the church, everybody touching someone else, as the amplified sound of the choir filled the air.
Waves of music bounced around the church—organ, electric guitars, drums, and
voices joining together in a fast-paced upbeat rhythm. The entire congregation
was standing, a sea of white cloth. Everyone joined in the singing. It was loud. If
I listened carefully I could make out distinct voices of the people standing beside
me, but when I closed my eyes everything merged into a coherent wall of sound.
People were dancing in the aisles of the church, in between the pews, bobbing
their knees and swinging their arms to and fro. Sweat was dripping from everyone's faces from a combination of heat and exertion.

There was a short break in the singing, and then the drums kicked in—the
interlocking rhythms of the talking drums floating on top of the fast-moving
groove of the conga and jazz kit. People raised their arms toward the sky, some
throwing their heads back and shouting "hallelujah!" I felt the seat of the pew
behind me press against the back of my legs; suddenly the bench lurched forward
and then away, far to the back. A man who was not wearing the white church uniform was shaking violently. Before his Bible fell from his hands the person sitting
next to him took it. He bent forward, doubling at the waist and then up again, his
shoulders vibrating up and down around his ears. He shook his head back and
forth and began to mumble what sounded like words but had no discernable
meaning. He was no longer singing along with the choir. This was evidence that
the spirit had entered him: he was ẹlẹ́míì, in a spiritual trance.

Someone pressed the Bible into the possessed man's hands and removed the
man's glasses to prevent them from flying off of his face as the man's head began to
move violently back and forth. One of the church prophets approached the possessed man and placed his hand over the man's quivering hands clasped around
the bible. The prophet held his curved, metal staff in the air and pointed it toward
the man's head. He began to mutter an inaudible prayer. The music continued, and

the other congregants in the row returned to singing and dancing with the music, only glancing at the possessed man occasionally as he was tended to by the prophet and his assistant. The assistant scribbled frantically into a notebook as the prophet spoke directly in the man's ear, pausing occasionally to listen as the spirit spoke. Eventually the trance was broken and the man slumped forward and then sat down on the bench exhausted. He wiped his forehead with a handkerchief and pressed his fingers to his eyes as he listened to the prophet speak in his ear about what happened.

Participation in singing and dancing enables church members to transform their physical, spiritual and moral selves through the experience of being ẹlẹ́míì. Sound plays a critical role in the occurrence of such religious experiences for members of the Cherubim and Seraphim churches. Through an emphasis on how sound is crucial to embodied religious experiences, I discuss how such moments of being ẹlẹ́míì are prompted via singing by sensory engagement and enhanced by practices such as fasting and sleep deprivation in the context of focused prayer sessions. These practices of physical discipline are understood as necessary to strengthen one's spiritual self.

The body is of special importance to this discussion as bodies for the Cherubim and Seraphim enable and play host to divine interaction. Angela Zito (2011) discusses how religious worlds are created by bodies at the same time as they are represented by bodies, arguing that analysts should understand the role of the body in religious ritual as both *site* and *sign*. Indeed, body symbolism is central to Cherubim and Seraphim worship practices. Church members clothe their bodies in white cloth, and they sing and dance together in imitation of angels worshipping before the throne of God in heaven. The body is also a site for disciplinary practices and ethical self-making. Following Zito I investigate "the situation of the lived body itself as a location for various practices, performances, and disciplines that shape and subjectify the self" (2011, 21). Indeed, part of what is involved in the performance of worship practices that are able to have a direct, material effect on church members' lives is the making of a certain kind of self.

Church members cultivate the ability to act as a medium for the divine, whether through being ẹlẹ́míì, speaking in tongues, or receiving direct messages from God through the medium of the church prophets. This self is made through cultivating bodily disciplines and modes of being. These disciplinary practices include praying, fasting, clothing the body, and stylized ways of moving the body. Part of this bodily discipline also involves cultivating one's senses so that they all are oriented toward the purpose of worship: drawing the human spirit up and the Holy Spirit down, and in this way transcending the division between heaven and earth.

For church members embodied practices such as being ẹlẹ́míì ideally produce a transformation of the self via engagement with Holy Spirit. Church members' engagement with Holy Spirit is facilitated by training the senses and through learned body techniques. Sound, and music in particular, plays a crucial role in shaping sensorial and embodied responses to worship.

On the Holy Spirit

My first glimpse of the presence of the Holy Spirit in church worship was during a visit one Sunday toward the beginning of my research. Because I was new to the church, I was seated in the back with other visitors and special guests. One of the prophetesses entered into a spiritual trance and delivered a message to the congregation while speaking in tongues. The trance occurred as the choir sang a hymn that was indicated in that day's church program as one specifically dedicated to "Appreciation and Thanksgiving." The hymn's lyrics offered thanks and praise to God. Its tempo was a slow and measured 4/4 beat, lightly marked with the bass kick drum in the jazz kit and the tambourine. The church organ was the dominant instrumental sound and voices were brought to the front of the musical mix, especially the high-pitched soprano voice singing lead. As they sang, church members raised their arms in the air, closed their eyes, and swayed back and forth slowly to the music.

As the hymn progressed, shouts and whoops could be heard from across the church. This was a sonic indication of the presence of the Holy Spirit in the worship space. This was followed by the sound of a woman speaking in tongues, amplified through the sound system. From my position in the back of the church I could not see the prophetess in her trance but I heard her through a microphone held in front of her mouth by a churchwarden. Another man with his own microphone translated the spirit's message for the congregation to hear. As she began to speak the singing stopped, the organ and drums quietly vamped, and then faded out. Most of the congregation was transfixed, listening to the voices that alternated between the glossolalia of the woman speaking in tongues, and the translation of the Holy Spirit's message provided by the interpreter. Others who were in their own trances shook quietly, occasionally calling out before dropping their heads on their chests. As the trance ended, the interpreter offered a prayer of thanks to God, and then the congregation continued on to the Bible readings and lessons that constituted the next part of the service.

This trance and message had occurred at a particular moment in the order of the service—during the hymn of appreciation and thanksgiving. This hymn was sung near the beginning of the service, and followed a series of prayers that open worship for the day. These prayers took place in a certain order, one that was delineated in the church program and repeated every Sunday. First, church members confessed their sins and asked for forgiveness. This was done through congregational prayer, as everyone in the church simultaneously spoke out loud their individual confession and asked God for forgiveness. The cacophony of congregational confessions was followed by a series of prayers led by the worship leader who also asked for forgiveness on behalf of the congregation and for sanctification and dedication of the place of worship, along with the hearts and the homes of worshippers. Finally, the worship leader made a special prayer request for the manifestation of the Holy Spirit in their lives and hearts. This prayer was immediately followed by the congregation's recitation in unison of the Lord's Prayer. After the worship leader offered a final statement intended to "seal" the prayers, thereby sending them to heaven, a churchwarden stood in the open space before the altar and with a microphone led the congregation in repeating "hallelujah," "hosanna," and "ìyè" (life), three times each.[1] As they chanted hallelujah and hosanna they held their arms above their heads and spread their hands wide. During the chanting of ìyè, they still held their arms open, but brought their hands to their heads, with some moving their hands down to cross over their hearts. The chant concluded with the phrase, "Iyìn ni Olúwa Ológo!" ("Praise God!").

These sounds, prayers, and gestures were crucial practices that drew the attention of the Holy Spirit into the church and invited the spirit into the bodies of the church members. Within the context of church worship then, church members first readied themselves to be open to the Holy Spirit by confessing their sins and asking for forgiveness. The worship leader, who had prepared his body by praying and fasting for the week before the service, then uttered a prayer that prepared the space of the church and called on the Holy Spirit to descend. In contrast to the cacophony of the group prayers in which church members gave their confessions out loud but not in unison, the chanting of the Lord's Prayer all together represented a transformation of the congregation, as they were united sonically together toward the entry of the spirit into the church. The call-and-response chanting of hallelujah, hosanna, and ìyè with their accompanying gestures—a verbal and physical act of praising God—furthered this sanctification and transformation of self as church members' arms opened their bodies toward God in heaven, and then drew the spirit down into their heads and hearts. Thus, it was not a coincidence that it was immediately following these prayers, in which bodies and spaces of worship were ritually prepared for the entrance of the spirit, that the prophetess entered into her trance on the day I visited the church.

The ritual practices of self-transformation that enabled church members to become ẹlẹ́mìí, and the central role of the Holy Spirit in such practices, were reinforced through a variety of lectures and Bible study sessions in which church members participated. For example, all who wish to join the church were made to attend a series of "New Entrants" classes in order to understand the theological underpinnings of church practices. These classes were required in order to become a full member of the church. Classes were led by senior pastors and conducted in a mixture of English and Yoruba. Participants were urged to take notes on the lectures to make sure they integrated their newly learned knowledge into their spiritual practices, so that they "didn't just go through the motions." A number of senior pastors that I spoke with over the course of my research lamented that the majority of current church members had not attended the new entrants lectures, because they had belonged to the church before the practice was instituted, and therefore were in church to enjoy themselves and "have a good time" without paying attention to the work and discipline necessary to worship and pray properly.

When I attended the lectures, an entire session was devoted to the Holy Spirit and the gifts of the spirit.[2] At that lecture, the pastor leading the session provided a definition of the Holy Spirit as follows: "The Holy Spirit is the third person in the Trinity. It is associated with the work of creation—it gives the Christian person a new life, it is the source of knowledge, and it guides and helps the church in all ages. The Holy Spirit makes salvation a real experience to individuals." In this way, the pastor emphasized the links between the Holy Spirit, the individual church member, and the body of the church as a whole.

Furthermore, as the pastor noted, the Holy Spirit was central to the self-transformation that was necessary to become a full member of the church. This "new life" provided by the spirit entailed an ethical transformation. For example during the lecture new entrants were told that the Holy Spirit was the means through which knowledge of God could be gained, as well as how God would come to know them. Therefore, church members needed to behave appropriately; as he warned, "it is possible to make the Holy Spirit sad. You can insult Him with your bad conduct." To avoid insulting the Holy Spirit, and ultimately God, one had to open oneself to the Holy Spirit. As he explained, "The work of the Holy Spirit is to transform our character. When our character is transformed, then our lives will conform with Christ." Following this comment, the pastor then cited Galatians 5:22–23 in English ("If we live in the Spirit, let us also walk in the Spirit") and repeated each of the characteristics delineated in that Bible verse in Yoruba: "But the fruit of the Spirit is love (*ife*), joy (*ayọ̀*), peace (*àlàáfíà*), patience (*sùúrù*), kindness (*inú rere*), goodness (*iṣòóre*), faithfulness (*igbàgbọ́*), gentleness (*iwa tútù*), self-control (*ikóra ẹni ní ìjanu*); against such things there is no law."

The overall message conveyed in this lesson was that individual bodies and behaviors needed to be transformed through proper religious practices to bring a person to Christ and thus the church as a whole. As part of how church members experienced God, the Holy Spirit was a crucial and necessary interlocutor through which the process of transformation and rebirth into the church could occur. One of the key mediums through which the Holy Spirit worked to cultivate good character and reanimate the body toward sanctified spiritual practices was through disciplining the body and the emotions via sounded embodied practices such as prayer and musical performance.

Learning the Spirit

While church members experienced the Holy Spirit through a number of bodily practices, not every instance of a church member becoming ẹlẹ́míì involved the presence of the Holy Spirit. Soon after the event described at the beginning of this chapter, I met with the prophet who had ministered to the man in a trance and asked him to help me understand what I had seen. How was I to understand the violent movements of the man, as his upper body shook uncontrollably, and his head slumped down on his chest? What was the man saying when he was ẹlẹ́míì and how did the prophet understand what was said? What caused the trance? Did the man know it was going to happen?

The prophet smiled as I asked my questions, and reassured me that he could explain everything. "It is a miracle," he said. However, the prophet added, "What you saw was not the Holy Spirit." Registering my surprise and confusion, he went on to clarify that the man was possessed by a demonic spirit. Therefore, instead of transcribing a message from God as I had assumed he was doing, the prophet was discerning the nature of the spirit and what it wanted so that it would leave the man. The prophet told me I should have known this because the music was not right for the Holy Spirit. The music that the congregation was singing at that time was too fast, too frenzied. The prophet explained that the music was designed to move people to dance, and through moving their body to exercise their spirit. The drums and guitars activated the participants and helped lead them closer to God. "Certainly, people will go into trance," he explained, "But you cannot always trust that it will be the Holy Spirit. Don't believe what you see. You have to evaluate the person and the spirit—that is how you know it is the real thing."

So that I could better understand what enabled a person to become ẹlẹ́míì and to learn more about practices of discernment that allowed church members to identify what kind of spirit was present, the prophet suggested that I attend a class offered by the church's theological institute for people training to be pastors. On a Thursday afternoon I entered the small classroom where the class was to be held, and sat on a bench behind a long desk. The woman sitting beside me was both learning to be a pastor and training to be a prophetess which, she explained, required a different set of classes. She told me that she wanted to learn how to increase her prophetic gifts, so she had been reading about the examples of the prophets in the Bible. "God called me," she said. She explained that she hoped to be able to work full-time as a prophet and pastor, to devote her life to Christ. Until then she would continue to work as a cashier at a grocery store in a middle class suburb of Lagos. She also sold phone charge cards and reaching for her handbag, asked if I needed credits for my phone. Before I could answer the pastor leading the class entered and we stopped talking, took out our notebooks and pens, and looked at him attentively.

The pastor began by talking about how God endowed every person with a spiritual gift. He explained, "God gives each of us spiritual gifts. For some it is to speak, some to hear and interpret, others have the gift of healing and miracles." He listed the nine gifts from God that were received via the Holy Spirit and explained, "to have these gifts you must be holy. It is a free gift—God can send it to anyone. But you must prepare yourself to accept it." Because the people in the class were training to be pastors, they were told that they needed to have the gift of the word. The members of the class were advised to pray and ask God to endow him or herself with that gift.

According to the pastor, a great deal of physical and spiritual discipline was required to receive one of God's gifts. Echoing the lesson taught at the new entrants lecture about the relationship between behavior, character, and the work of the Holy Spirit in transforming the self, he explained that "only the anointing of the Holy Spirit will make you strong enough to resist the temptations in life." To achieve this anointing it was necessary to subdue the body. By way of example he explained that in order to be the worship leader for Sunday service a person must have two gifts, that of the word and that of faith. To enhance these gifts, the worship leader avoided fatty foods, sweets, and drinks other than water for one week before leading the service, did not have sex for one week, and could not be near anyone who was sick. During the last three days he undertook "white fasting" to make him holy. This involved abstaining from morning and afternoon meals, and only eating fruits and vegetables with white rice or *gàárí* (a flour made from ground, dried cassava) at night.

To explain the need for such discipline and the work that it did for each person, the pastor outlined a theory of the relationship between body and spirit. According to him, there were three levels to each individual person. The first level was that of the physical self or the outer body (*ara*). Then, he explained, there was the soul or inner body (*inù*). The soul was made up of the will (decision making), the mind (intellect, knowledge of good and evil), and emotions (which he identified as love or hatred, which could be expressed for good or evil). He further explained that there was a struggle between the body and the soul, because as he put it, "the soul is subject to the eyes, mouth, and ears." In other words a person's ability to develop a sound mind, to make proper decisions, and to control their emotions was subject to physical experience and sensory input—all of which are fallible given what the pastor described as the sinful nature of the world and the human propensity to sin. Thus, the senses and bodily experiences were often unreliable and could not be trusted to properly shape the aspects of one's soul necessary for receiving and utilizing God's gifts.

However, the third level of the self—what the pastor called the "inner inner" (*inù inù*)—could shift this relationship between body and soul. According to the pastor the inner inner represented a person's spirit: it was the seat of consciousness, of intuition, and of communion with others, both human and spirits. It was through the spirit that humans received divine revelation, inspiration, and connection with God and with other people. Most of the time the soul and outer body controlled the inner inner. The pastor explained that this was why it was important to discipline both the body and soul. One means of achieving this discipline was fasting. As the pastor explained, "Fasting weakens the physical body, to allow the spirit of God to enter and penetrate to the inner inner." Cultivating physical weakness of this type was key to developing spiritual strength because once the Holy Spirit entered the inner inner, it could take control and govern the outer layers, thereby reversing the directionality of one's bodily and sensory engagement with God and the world. "This is why we call for the enabling power of the Holy Spirit to take control," explained the pastor.

As the pastor's discussion made clear, church members sought to cultivate a form of subjectivity open to outside forces, particularly to that of the Holy Spirit. The penetration of the Holy Spirit gave strength to the inner inner, allowing it to overtake the flesh, so that one's character could be developed in accordance with Christian ethics. Church members trained themselves to be transgressed by the Holy Spirit via their senses so that their inner inner could be transformed. Unlike the self proposed in Western psychoanalytic accounts, in which a primal interiority must be defended against hostile external forces in order to be a functioning, ethical member of society (see Keane 2007; Sahlins 2002), the self that the church sought to make through its worship practices was to be open to external entities who would enter and transform the person for the better (Luhrmann 2012). Furthermore, such openness to external forces for church members did not imply a loss of individual self nor was it understood as a form of alienation. Instead such weakness leads to empowerment, the self is made stronger through openness and submission to the Holy Spirit.

According to church members, when one was successful in achieving the proper control over one's body, and had submitted fully to the Holy Spirit, material changes would become apparent in one's life. This was seen as evidence that one had achieved a communion with God via disciplinary practices and that one's self had been remade according to the ethical ideals and moral standards of the church. For example, Mrs. Ola, who worked as an accountant for a large international consulting service, explained to me that she came to the church because she had been suffering from fibroids in her uterus that were very painful. The doctors wanted her to have surgery, but she was fearful of complications from the procedure. She met with Prophet G. O. Fakeye, the leader of the church, for special healing prayers and he convinced her that she needed to join the church and submit to a discipline of fasting and praying. After she had been with the church for three months, the fibroids began to shrink on their own. Mrs. Ola attributed this to the intervention of the Holy Spirit into her life. She had allowed the Holy Spirit to take control and through this she was healed. However, she also noted one needed to be ever vigilant of following these practices and not taking this transformation for granted. It required constant attention to bodily comportment and emotional attention through fasting, praying, and participation in church worship. She explained to me that this was why she often led the Bible study classes before Sunday worship services; this was how she cultivated the gifts that the Holy Spirit had given her.

Sonic Cues

In the theory of self described by the pastor in the training session, the body was identified as the central instrument through which the spirit entered and transformed the life of a person. Being visibly ẹlẹ́míì was seen as key evidence of the Holy Spirit's presence in the body of church members, but not everyone was able to achieve this state. In the training session, the pastor explained that everyone was given the gift of certain spiritual capacities from God, but not everyone received the same gifts. However, in order to cultivate one's gifts one needed to be open to the spirit so they were urged to engage in certain bodily disciplines and activities to ensure that the spirit could penetrate to one's inner inner. Practices such as fasting and praying were key to orienting the body toward the Holy Spirit, and ensuring that the spirit would make material changes in the lives of an ethically shaped church member. As the pastor put it, "when we fast and pray together we usher prosperity into our lives. Any time you fast you must witness prosperity." Fasting took up a great deal of the pastor's lecture on bodily disciplines, but he also emphasized that other practices were crucial to the making of an ethical and efficacious Christian self. These practices included praying, singing, and dancing. It was in these practices that sound became a key medium through which the physical body was transgressed, weakened, and ultimately transformed through a spiritual strengthening of the self.

Prayer was a central medium through which church members understood their religious practices to be efficacious. Early members of Cherubim and Seraphim churches—especially Moses Orimolade, the charismatic founder of the church—were renowned for their ability to achieve healing and prosperity via prayer. Praying also required certain modes of bodily comportment. Most prayers were uttered out loud in Yoruba and during church services worshippers all spoke—or sometimes even shouted—their prayers at the same time, resulting in a loud vibrating noise in which individual voices were not discernible even though all were speaking their own personal requests and offerings of thanks. The practice of improvised, spoken prayer was most common; indeed, with the exception of the Lord's Prayer and a few other formulae, very few group prayers were chanted in unison. Bodily movements such as snapping one's fingers, clapping hands, and stomping feet were key components of the act of praying. Furthermore, these practices were also carried over when church members prayed at home.

In the new entrants lecture this method of prayer was emphasized as particularly powerful because it "gave life to prayer" in contrast to prayers that were uttered by rote which were described as "dull" and "dead." The life of prayer was understood to be due to the work of the individual's spirit, which itself was activated by one's emotions. The pastor leading the new entrants' session on prayer described their method as being characterized by "zeal," and urged them to pray with their hearts. Referring to the greeting of "Ayọ̀ ni o" (It is joy), common among church members, and from which the branch's nickname was derived, he explained, "We greet each other because it is that joy that we all feel when we are in the church. That joy is the Holy Spirit." Prophet S. F. Korode, the choirmaster, in his pamphlet about Cherubim and Seraphim legacies, described their form of prayer as being "alive and aflame, having direct emphasis on emotions and feelings" (1995, 35). Thus prayer was understood as an embodied practice that activated one's spirit via the emotions, and that further connected one's individual spirit to God in order to receive forgiveness, blessings, and results.

Prayer itself was also connected to other bodily disciplines, such as fasting, which had the power to make it even more efficacious. Other practices, such as engaging in prayer vigils also entailed controlling the instincts of the body for spiritual purposes. Traditionally, the church had held prayer vigils each Friday night, in which church members stayed in church from 10 p.m. until dawn the next day in order to pray together. During this time, the church door would be locked and no one would be able to leave or enter. The prayer vigil consisted of a series of directed prayers, led by an elder of the church who had been designated a prayer warrior. Everyone present would pray fervently all night, alternating between singing and dancing and extemporaneous group prayers. Citing issues of safety, the Ayọ̀ ni o Church had changed this practice before I began my research, instead holding a prayer warrior service on Saturday afternoons. However, church members were urged to hold their own all-night prayer vigils, either with family members or alone, in order to increase their communion with God and to ensure that their prayers would be heard. Many of the church's egbẹ́ (smaller groupings of church members organized around similar spiritual interests) would also hold vigils, particularly if there was an important event being celebrated by a member of the group such as the marriage of a family member or a naming ceremony. Many told me that participation in such vigils had marked key events in their lives, such as promotions at work or conceiving a child, or had helped them to overcome a serious illness or other problem that had afflicted them.

Singing and dancing were also bodily practices in which body, emotions and spirit were linked in order for prayer to achieve its desired effects. According to the pastor at the theological institute, singing and praying went together. "Music elevates," he explained, "it allows the spirit to go up to heaven. Music is an arouser of spirit." The pastor here was talking about how the spirit of each member of the congregation present during the service was woken and lifted up toward heaven through their participation in congregational song. In addition, via dance, the exercising of the body and the stimulation of the senses allowed one's spirit to be raised and thus prepared for the Holy Spirit to enter into the body.

But singing and dancing were not just aimed at activating the spirit of the worshipper. The pastor went on: "The Holy Spirit too is elevated by music. To invoke the Holy Spirit you use music. Then the Spirit will be radiating." Thus the activation of bodies and emotions via participation in music also activated the Holy Spirit. This was what enabled the lifted spirit of the individual worshipper to be linked to the equally lifted Holy Spirit; their body could then be penetrated so their inner inner could be taken over by the Holy Spirit.

The ability to be open to the spirit and to have the spirit enter one was not automatic, but had to be learned. As the pastor described, "It takes a long time before you can express it correctly. You must undergo fasting, perform a night vigil, experience quiet time. Then you will become attuned, and you can lock on with Christ. That is how you prepare yourself to let the spirit take control." Thus the bodily practices described here were understood to be interconnected. As Mrs. Oyenuga, a senior member of the choir explained to me, "music appeals to soul and spirit, the body reacts to it. The mind is constantly working when you are singing and dancing. Music can give you a peaceful state of mind." Note here again the conception of the self as having three parts: body, soul, spirit. Mrs. Oyenuga identified music as being able to assist in the reversal of the process of perception, from outside in, to inside out. It was this coordination of body, emotions, and spirit that allowed one to achieve the proper state of being, an ethical self capable of receiving God's gifts.

I stayed after class at the theological institute on the day the pastor discussed these bodily practices in order to ask about the example I discussed at the beginning of this chapter: when the prophet had told me that I should have known that the man was not possessed by the Holy Spirit because of the style of the music. He repeated the prophet's assertion that the Holy Spirit required a certain kind of music. "The music must be a type that will lift your spirit," he explained. He continued:

> There are special types of songs for specific occasions. Songs for different purposes. When the choir wants to play music the rhythm they play must go in line with the occasion. There are songs that make you jump up with happiness and joy, that make you dance. In contrast, the song that precedes the descent of the Holy Spirit must be solemn. It is the quiet, solemn song that carries you to the spirit.

He went on to explain that it was most frequently during the faster songs, particularly the ones featuring extended sections of drum and percussion, when other spirits might enter into the body of a person who was not adequately prepared. This was why praying correctly, fasting, and engaging in other disciplinary practices was so important. "Everybody wants to jump up and dance when they hear the music, but you also need to be spiritually strong to experience the Holy Spirit. This is when you know it is real because the person can be ẹlẹ́mìí during the quietest moments. That is the ultimate."

The choir was often instructed that they especially needed to undertake extra disciplinary practices of fasting and praying so that they would have the proper attitude toward singing in church. As Mrs. Aderemi explained during choir rehearsal one evening, "It is not a matter of entertainment. You can feel happy when you are singing and dancing but it is something else to have the joy that leads one to the Holy Spirit." She advised choir members to be sure to pray before they came to church on Sunday so that they would have the right attitude to participate in worship.

These lessons were brought to life during church worship later on in my research. On this Sunday I was sitting with the choir. We had been there since 8:30 a.m., singing hymns and praise and worship songs for the first hour and a half of the service. The service began with a series of fast-paced choruses, in a call and response style. Without a break in the music the choir transitioned to a song with a slower tempo, in the style that choir members use the word "ballad" to refer to. The talking drum and complicated guitar lines faded away, and the sound of the organ took over. The shimmery sounds of cymbals filled the air. The choir swayed back and forth slowly. A female lead singer took the microphone and sang the opening words of the well-known chorus "Oṣuba re re o" ("You Are Worthy, Oh Lord"). The lyrics of this song talk about worshipping God: "He is the king who we cannot see, yet we see the works of his hands in the world." Members of the congregation raised their hands in the air with their palms open and waved them slowly. No one was dancing anymore, though some swayed slowly from side to side. Some turned their heads up toward the ceiling while others hung their heads on their chests and shook them back and forth slightly. Nearly everyone's eyes were closed. The rich sound of the organ and lead voice filled the room as the singer sang the second verse. The singer's performance featured a lot of vibrato, which was enhanced by the inclusion of reverb and echo effects through the soundboard.

From the back of the church shrieks could be heard. People began to go into trance. The shoulders of a woman standing in front of me began to vibrate up and down, and she bent forward at the waist as the spirit moved through her. I looked across the aisle and noticed that the prophet who I had initially asked about the spirit was in a trance. While his feet were firmly planted on the ground, his body from the waist up was vibrating as though something was bubbling up from within him. As he vibrated, he rotated back and forth at the waist. He hugged his Bible firmly to his chest, his prophet staff held in his right hand. A churchwarden brought a microphone from the stand in front of the church to the prophet and held it to his mouth. The sounds of the prophet's voice entered the sonic mix. He was speaking in tongues. The lead singer stopped singing. The organist together with the drum player and the bassist repeated the chord progression of the song quietly, providing a musical texture underneath the prophet's voice. As the prophet's glossolalia continued, another prophet stood beside him and into a second microphone translated the message for the congregation. This was the Holy Spirit, in the space of the church and in the sanctified and prepared body of the prophet, transmitting spiritual messages for the benefit of the church members.

Cautionary Tales

Practices of self-transformation enabled a person to become ẹlẹ́míì, so that the Holy Spirit possessed the person visibly and perhaps audibly, though shaking and speaking in tongues. Because being open to the Holy Spirit, and especially being ẹlẹ́míì, required a great deal of discipline one needed to learn how to engage in these practices correctly. For this reason, learning was crucial and church members were urged to identify their gifts and then attend classes and Bible study sessions in order to learn better how to use their gifts of the spirit. Otherwise one risked being open to other, potentially dangerous spirits, and further to an unmaking of the self that had been achieved through earlier work.

These issues were central at another event I attended on June 3, 2003; a lecture on the topic of "Effective Preaching for Soul Winning" delivered to members of the Daniel Band during their anniversary week. The Daniel Band was a subgrouping of church members who were prophets and prophetesses. The lecture, given by Prophet Korode, was also open to church members who were not yet prophets, but who felt that they had a calling to become a prophet. During the question-and-answer period a young woman stood up and explained that she had been fasting and praying as told, but that she still had not had the experience of ẹlẹ́míì. She wanted to know how she could go into trance.

Korode repeated the woman's question, and then said that a number of people had come to him with similar questions. He knew that there was a desire for people to have this experience. "It is a powerful thing," he said. However, he went on to explain that while baptism in the Holy Spirit is important, it is incorrect to grant too much power to ẹlẹ́míì. Korode then read from 1 Corinthians 12:4–7, "Now there are diversities of gifts, but the same Spirit. And there are differences of administrations, but the same Lord. And there are diversities of operations, but it is the same God which worketh all in all. But the manifestation of the Spirit is given to every man to profit withal." Korode continued, paraphrasing the verses that followed these, which outlined the various gifts—the word of wisdom, the word of knowledge, faith, healing, and so on—concluding with verse 11, "But all these worketh that one and the selfsame Spirit, dividing to every man severally as he will."

Korode then translated the meaning of the passage: "This means that *faith* is also a gift from the Holy Spirit. It is not just ẹlẹ́míì!" He went on to urge the attendees not to emphasize or over-cultivate their desire to be ẹlẹ́míì because faith, knowledge, and wisdom were also necessary. For this reason, he explained, education was key. "Education is a way to combat ungodly behavior. You will learn to reject parts that are not of the Lord." He then warned those in attendance not to drop out of school, or to leave their occupation because they felt they were called by God to become a pastor because God may want them to contribute in other ways: "You need to have the education God wants you to have, it is necessary to finish."

This idea that there are multiple gifts from God, that they are distributed by God according to his plan, and that one should be sure to learn the proper ways to use these gifts, was repeated often throughout my time with the church. For example, during one long choir rehearsal the choir worked for a long time to perform a hymn correctly. The man who had been leading the rehearsal had frequently stopped the choir and scolded them for singing too loudly, or with too fast of a tempo. He urged them to have the correct mood while singing, so that the congregation would also be sure to have the appropriate feeling while they were singing the song. At the conclusion of the rehearsal, one of the women in the choir asked how they were to know when their singing had achieved the appropriate mood: "Can we only know that it works when people fall into a trance?" An older woman, who was an elder in the choir, replied first by saying that "We have done a good job when our songs heal, when we uplift."

Following this exchange, Korode stood and again repeated his admonition against too easily desiring the experience of being ẹlẹ́mìí. He reiterated his argument about the different gifts of the Holy Spirit, and the different roles that individual church members were given by the spirit. "Not everybody must speak in tongues. It is not compulsory!" he warned. He went on: "You must go beyond the learning of your parents. You cannot just accept what they tell you. You have to read the Bible and understand it yourself. Some people are even going into trance and speaking in tongues falsely. A demonic spirit may actually be speaking. Most rising churches actually have satanic origins, their songs are evil, devoted only to money and riches."

This chapter has examined the embodied and affective practices through which members of Cherubim and Seraphim churches become open to the Holy Spirit for the purpose of spiritual self-transformation. Being ẹlẹ́mìí, possessed by the Holy Spirit, is a key modality through which this transformation of the self is made visible and the work of the spirit in church members lives made palpable. Part of what is involved in the making of an efficacious worship practice is the making of a certain kind of self through cultivating bodily disciplines and modes of being. Church members develop such bodily practices in order to be the right kind of person who is able to participate effectively in the right kind of worship. Sound plays a key role, whether it is through the practice of extemporaneous prayer, through singing before and after prayers at home, or through extended periods of singing and dancing during church worship. Furthermore, there are certain styles of music that enable church members to achieve experiences where the body surrenders to the spirit and allows it to take control. It is in this way that church members learn to apply the lessons of Galatians: "This I say then: Walk in the Spirit, and ye shall not fulfill the lust of the flesh" (Galatians 5:16).

At the level of theorizing the self there are several provocations that emerge from this discussion. On an immediate level, this account of weakening the body in order to strengthen the self resonates with the broader scholarly critique of North Atlantic particularism that often masquerades as universal theories of self-making. In this case, as elsewhere—especially in the work of Hirschkind (2006) and Mahmood (2004) on Muslim self-fashioning—the Freudian architecture of a primal interiority surrounded by hostile exteriorities is dismantled. Following from Csordas's (1997) analysis of charismatic Catholics in the United States, the devout self in this case is less an achievement, a steady state and rather more a capacity that is not an ontological given so much as a historical process of submission (Foucault 2010).

By contrast, this is about a self that opens to outside forces of Holy Spirit. A self that is open to external entering and transformation. Church members train themselves to be transgressed by the spirit via senses and aesthetics. This is a material transgression, one that happens to and through the body—the medium in which the Holy Spirit is materialized. It is important to note that there is no corresponding loss of individual self, no violence done through the self through this process of submission as many North Atlantic theories of a sovereign self would have it. What we see in the case discussed here is empowerment through bodily weakness, openness, and submission.

Notes

1. "Hallelujah, Hallelujah, Hallelujah / Hosanna, Hosanna, Hosanna / Ìyè, Ìyè, Ìyè."
2. According to the pastor, the nine gifts of the spirit were: word of wisdom, word of knowledge, faith, healing, working of miracle, prophecy, discerning of spirit, speaking in tongues, and interpretation of tongues.

8   Show the Glory of God

This is the foundation of Truth that Jesus laid
Which the Baba Aladura follows
Let no one think that he derailed from it,
He stands on Christ the Rock

   —Cherubim and Seraphim Hymn #689

ON SUNDAY, SEPTEMBER 21, 2003, the Ẹgbẹ́ Fògo Ọlọ̀run Hàn (Show the Glory of God Band) at the Ayọ̀ ni o Church in Lagos celebrated its thirty-second anniversary. Commonly referred to by church members as "Fògo," the group's membership was made up of senior men from the congregation who understood themselves to be crucial to the maintenance of church tradition and to the reinforcement of the authority of the elders to lead the church. Fògo members maintained Cherubim and Seraphim standards of worship not as mere rule keepers or disciplinarians, but through their spiritually powerful performances that brought God's power down into the church and in doing so realigned reality so that it conformed to a Cherubim and Seraphim vision of an ethical society.

Fògo is a contraction of the Yoruba phrase "fi ogo hàn": to show glory, to make glory visible. Members of the church understood "glory" in this case to have a dual meaning. In one sense it referred to the practice of worshipping God by offering praises and thanksgiving to Him. It also referred to the specific quality of glory itself (*ogo*) that was understood to be an aspect of God's holiness. As the church program from the day of Fògo's anniversary celebration explained:

> GLORY depicts worship, adoration and praise of God. Fògo Band comprises people who are always glorifying God in their words, thoughts, and deeds due to His holiness. GREAT importance is attached to this Band in the Cherubim and Seraphim organization because we believe we are 'Ordered' to be glorifying God as part of our worship. We glorify God so that we can be delivered in the days of trouble.

Embedded in this statement is an articulation of the way in which church members conceptualized the purpose and efficacy of their worship practices: the congregation glorified God in their worship and in return received assistance from God—conceived of variously as deliverance, but also as protection, blessing, and salvation. In other words, worship was a form of ethical action that ensured one's well-being (*àlàáfíà*) in the world (see Lambek 2010).

Fògo's ritual practices were a way of making real, tangible, and perceptible church doctrine and cosmological precepts. As the members of the group described it, one of the most important things that members of Fògo did was emulate the angels worshipping God in heaven. The church program on the day of its anniversary stated: "The band of Show the Glory of God represents the Celestial Hosts of Heaven that are always praising God, day and night. Fògo members are always glorifying God in their words, thoughts and deeds." In other words, God's glory was demonstrated by members of the group through practices of angelic mimesis—including wearing the white prayer gown, and singing, and dancing appropriately.

In Fògo practices a connection was made between Cherubim and Seraphim worship and contemporary, material realities. For church members who were struggling to achieve the conditions whereby they could live a good life amid the hardships of contemporary Nigeria, the imperative to glorify God through worship promised "deliverance" from their troubles. The glorifying practices performed by Fògo during its anniversary celebration were the means through which the efficacy of Cherubim and Seraphim ritual practices was demonstrated. Tangible evidence of God's presence in response to worship was found in the visible possession of church members by the Holy Spirit during worship services and through the communication of "special messages" to the church prophets, which often took the form of warnings or advice to be heeded in order to achieve a certain end.

Understood as a charter for Cherubim and Seraphim worship, the Fògo ceremony reestablished and reaffirmed the relationship between God and the church. Cherubim and Seraphim worship practices as exemplified in the Fògo ceremony were also a way of (re)producing conditions of possibility and modes of sociality that placed Yoruba moral values at the center of socioeconomic organization. In the Fògo ceremony the various media involved in Cherubim and Seraphim worship—dress, space, body, movement, discipline, hymns, songs, recordings, and historical practice—worked together to make ritual efficacious. Sound, and music in particular, choreographed the specific movements through the ritual—the entrances of the Fògo members and of the Holy Spirit into the church, the transformation of the congregation into angels worshipping before the throne of God in heaven, and the connection of the congregation in the present to those who have come before them in the past. Shifts in musical style throughout the performance enabled changes in bodily performances of church members that both pointed to and enabled the transcendence of space, time, and community. In this way, the performance of the ritual articulated and embodied powerfully convincing forms of subjectivity and belonging, working to inscribe these into the bodies of church members through affecting performances of music and dance.

"Practicalizing" Worship

Most Senior Apostle Abiodun, a member of Fògo who was also an officer in the church's choir, Abiodun described the group's anniversary celebration as a "practicalizing" of Cherubim and Seraphim belief, staging it for the congregation so that they could see and learn what God wants them to do:

> Fògo is a band that is actually demonstrating to the world how the heavenly hosts worship God. Exactly how the heavenly hosts do it in heaven. That is what Fògo is just trying: to let us practice it. Let us see what we are doing. We are rehearsing what we are going to do with the Father Almighty. It is done according to the Bible. So when they say "Glory Glory Glory, all the angels singing," this is what we try to practicalize. So if you have that feeling, then you will have joy, being with the Lord. Then you know you are having a home; then you know you are going to have everlasting joy.

In this statement, spoken in English, not Yoruba, Abiodun used the term "practicalize" to explain the group's activity. When I provided him with a transcript of our interview, and asked if he meant to use the word "practice," he laughed, and went on to say that while he might have misspoken initially, that he thought that the term "practicalize" was appropriate since the Fògo ceremony was "both practice and practical. It is something that we must know how to do, because we will do it in God's kingdom to come. At the same time, it is useful to us. This is why it is required."

During the ceremony, the members of Fògo "practicalized" Cherubim and Seraphim Church doctrine, performing it so that the congregation would be able to live their lives according to ethical standards and guidelines of the community, which in turn produced the "feeling of joy" associated with "having a home." Abiodun explicitly connected the ways in which practicing the "right kind of worship" negotiated the space between heaven and earth, home and market, between this world (*ayé*)—the world inhabited by humans, and the other world (*òrun*)—the world inhabited by God. His commentary further articulated a specific theory of practice that stressed how angelic mimesis was able to draw down God's power and forged a connection between God and the church members. The relationship was understood as constituting a special covenant between God and the church, one that, if properly achieved, could change material circumstances for church members both individually and collectively.

The "practicalization" of Cherubim and Seraphim belief in the Fògo rite was also an act of historical mimesis. Members of the group saw themselves as historically linked through ritual practice to Moses Orimolade, the founder of the Cherubim and Seraphim churches. However, unlike the Holy Michael Day ritual described in chapter 2, in which the congregation performatively reenacted the history of the Cherubim and Seraphim movement, the Fògo celebration brought the practices of angels worshipping God in heaven to life in the world. According to many people I spoke with in the church, the specifics of Fògo ritual practice were revealed to the church's founders through a spiritual directive from God.

Abiodun explained how the Egbẹ́ Fògo in the Ayọ̀ ni o Church learned how to the perform the ritual correctly:

> When we had our own church [the Ayọ̀ ni o Church] established—which was thirty-three years ago, and the Cherubim and Seraphim is sixty-something—we had to go and study the Fògo anniversary rite. They invited the elders from another church to come and practice the rite with us. To teach us. It was not our own invention, rather it has been this way from time immemorial. From Moses Orimolade, who was taught by the angels himself. That's how they know how to perform the rite.

Note here the conception of the history of the ritual: it comes to current Cherubim and Seraphim members through the mediation of other church elders, who in turn learned it from Moses Orimolade, the saint-like founder of the church, to whom the practice was directly communicated by angels. This swelling of time also helps to produce the uniformity of the angelic mimesis of the ritual; they are recreating actions that have been done "from time immemorial."

Musical performance, which included singing and dancing, were crucial components of practices that opened up a connection between God and worshippers, creating a space of communication and circulation that transcended time and space. As I discuss in more detail below, the music performed during the ritual mainly consisted of hymns taken from the Cherubim and Seraphim hymnal. Some of the hymns performed during the Fògo ceremony were composed by early members of the Cherubim and Seraphim Church; however, the majority were taken from older Protestant hymnals and performed in a specific style. This also had the effect of making the ceremony appear as if it came "from time immemorial." In other words, part of the efficacy of the Fògo ceremony was derived from "singing the same songs" that were sung by early Yoruba Christians, and especially those sung by the founders of the Cherubim and Seraphim churches.

Cherubim and Seraphim Sociability: The Ẹgbẹ́ System

On each Sunday between April and September one or more of the spiritual groups at the Cherubim and Seraphim Ayọ̀ ni o Church known as *ẹgbé* celebrated its annual thanksgiving service. Ẹgbẹ́ is a Yoruba word used outside of the church to refer to organized clubs or associations, and is a common system of social organization in many Yoruba communities (Bascom 1969; Eades 1980; Fadipe 1970). The English word band is used interchangeably with the word ẹgbẹ́, in its most general sense to refer to a group of people who share a common interest or purpose (i.e., band of brothers) rather than to the more specific use of the word band to refer to a musical group. In Yoruba towns and cities there are numerous ẹgbẹ́ based on age, occupation, or for residents of a city who share a common place of origin.

The ẹgbẹ́ system at the Cherubim and Seraphim Ayọ̀ ni o Church divided the congregation into smaller, spiritually oriented groups that provided church members with personal connections to other members and opportunities to extend their religious practice beyond weekly Sunday worship. Ẹgbẹ́ were hierarchically organized with officers and officials, including a patron, a matron, a captain, a secretary, and a treasurer, among other roles, who coordinated the group's activities each year. An ẹgbẹ́'s activities included running a charity drive, sponsoring special prayer sessions, raising funds to support maintenance, renovation or construction of church facilities, and most important, planning and carrying out the group's thanksgiving and anniversary celebration each year.

There were eighty-three ẹgbẹ́ in the Ayọ̀ ni o Church during the time of my research. Most of them were gender specific, for either men or women. The few mixed gender groups in the church recognized specific spiritual skills developed or roles inhabited by church members. These included the Daniel Band for prophets and prophetesses, the Aládúrà Band for prayerists, the Emmanuel Band for children under ten years old, the Choir, and the Church Workers Band.

Many ẹgbẹ́ were added to the organizational system of the church in the late 1990s or early 2000s in order to accommodate the size of the congregation, to have small enough groups for the band system to work, and to allow for new modes of worship. For example, Ẹgbẹ́ Ina Olorun Tan, the Glowing Fire of God Band, was a women's group that started in the mid-1990s. Many of the women who organized the group were new members of the church at the time. They had struggled to find their place in the church hierarchy, which was dominated by the wives of church elders. Some of the more senior women in the church disapproved of the woman's exaggerated movements and exuberant singing during worship. In response, the church leadership created the Ẹgbẹ́ Ina Olorun Tan, which was coordinated by senior women but in which these more youthful women who were relatively new to the church were able to express themselves and also direct their religious activities toward their specific needs. The members of Ẹgbẹ́ Ina Olorun Tan saw it as their mission to make real through their fervent and energetic worship practices the action exemplified in using the metaphor of fire to conceptualize God's power. The group met regularly outside of Sunday services to pray and worship together, and to encourage each other in all matters of everyday life, from family to career-related concerns.

The ẹgbẹ́ system created relationships that were hierarchical and obligatory between church members. In doing so, they served as an exemplification of the church's emphasis on Yoruba values and modes of social organization. The importance of hierarchical relations and respect for elders were emphasized by the system, and the practices of particular ẹgbẹ́ reinforced the importance of hard work and of knowing one's place in relation to others. The ẹgbẹ́ system, which divided the large congregation of the Ayọ̀ ni o Church into smaller groups of men and women, created a mode of accountability and encouragement for individual church members. This relationship often went beyond the confines of religious worship. Membership in a particular ẹgbẹ́ provided a strong sense of solidarity and created relations of obligation toward one another. Members of ẹgbẹ́ assisted each other during times of hardship and difficulty. Church members often found employment or facilitated business deals through the relationships cultivated through ẹgbẹ́ membership.

These forms of organization and behavior together make up the ideal of "home" as articulated in a Yoruba proverb frequently summoned in Christian sermons and Bible studies sessions: "the earth is a marketplace, heaven is home." This proverb emphasized the security and moral foundation found in the home, in contrast to the fragmentation and chaos of the marketplace. Heaven and home were places where relationships between people were in proper order, and where everyone had the potential to achieve a good life, characterized by prosperity, health, and success. Members of Cherubim and Seraphim churches utilized a variety of media—music, gesture, movement, and costume, among others—in their ritual practices in order to reproduce heaven on earth. The performance of the annual anniversary and thanksgiving for each ẹgbẹ́ was a key site in which the connection between heaven and home was performatively reproduced for the members of the group. The anniversary served as a religious revival of sorts, in which the members of the celebrating ẹgbẹ́ were remade according to Cherubim and Seraphim moral values and social ideals, as well as with the specific spiritual directives and orientations of each group.

The Fògo anniversary was celebrated in late September, toward the end of the cycle of ẹgbẹ́ anniversary celebrations in the church, which culminated with the celebration of Holy Michael Day on September 29. Ẹgbẹ́ Fògo was one of the oldest of the Cherubim and Seraphim ẹgbẹ́, with the first started by Moses Orimolade in 1928. Membership in Fògo, like those of other church ẹgbẹ́, was decided by spiritual directive. Senior Apostle Abiodun explained to me how they take on new members:

> It is by spiritual vision. After Bible studies, the induction course and baptism, then they will write your name for spiritual direction, to know which band is best suited for you. [. . .] The band suited for you spiritually, they just put your name there. They will go and give the message that you have been asked to join the Fògo band. Give it to the captain of the band. Then you are absorbed. They may not know you. They may not know you before.

This selection by spiritual vision was a way of remaking individual identity and creating social linkages between church members, something that was especially relevant in a church as large as the Ayọ̀ ni o Church. Furthermore, the ẹgbẹ́ system itself created a social network of obligation among church members, one that recreated hierarchically organized social spaces in Lagos' urban setting. The seniority of Fògo members is thus particularly significant, for as male elders they were near the top of the social hierarchy that church members saw as crucial to the reproduction of Yoruba values and as central to morality.

The church program for the Fògo anniversary described the type of person who was a member: "It must be stressed here that anybody who is going to be a member of this Band must be a man of high integrity, must be truthful and great in worshiping God without any blemish in his character." It further specified that: "The moral codes of members have become excellence of character, kindness to all, uprightness in all our ways, transparent honesty in all our dealings, which are all good instruments of meaningful evangelization—the prime objective of Fògo Band today." Indeed, the membership of Fògo, senior men who for the most part were successful both in and out of the church, represented an ideal form of subjectivity for the leaders of the church, who asserted that this is what proper Cherubim and Seraphim worship should strive toward. This was the person that the leaders of the church were trying to produce through the Fògo ritual, and what seemed to be suggested was that worshipping in the correct way was necessary to produce yourself as a person who exemplified the ethical orientations described: honesty, kindness, excellence. The men who participated in Fògo—spiritually and materially wealthy, successful in business, leaders in their communities, and patriarchs of large families—exemplified how religious participation was linked to worldly success.

The life history of Most Senior Apostle Abiodun serves as a case in point. Abiodun joined the Cherubim and Seraphim Ayọ̀ ni o Church in Lagos in 1976. He was employed by a multinational shipping company at its branch in the Apapa port in Lagos, and when I met him in 2003 he was a senior executive at the company. Because of his successful career, he was not only able to build a house for his family in the Surulere neighborhood of Lagos, but he had also built a house in his hometown of Abeokuta, where he planned to move after retirement. Abiodun took pride in being able to provide for his family, which included sending one of his sons to the United States to continue his education. He credited his success to his membership in the church.

In our discussion, Abiodun frequently made connections between the trajectory of his career and his membership in the Ayọ̀ ni o Church, especially his work with the choir. He described one such moment to me in our conversation. Toward the start of his career he had decided to travel to Germany to pursue further training so that he could be promoted in the shipping industry. He was studying German at the Goethe Institute in Lagos, and had applied to a school in Germany where he could learn computer programming. At the same time that he was preparing to travel to pursue his education, he was also attending the Ayọ̀ ni o

Church regularly and had played an important role in the recording and commercial production of the choir's first album (discussed in chapter 3). When he informed his superiors at his place of employment of his intention to go to Germany, they told him that he could not leave his position at the company because he was a hard worker. Instead, they promoted him and sent him to the corporate headquarters in the Netherlands to undergo training. He became a computer operator, and was later promoted to manager of the computing division. As he described it, these two activities were related; he had been praying to God to help him find success in his work, but at the same time he was praying that God would also help him cope with being away from his family during his training. As he saw it, God found the better solution for him, which enabled him to travel briefly for training but also promoted him so that he could better provide for his family. This promotion also meant that he could continue his work with the choir.

According to Abiodun God made another intervention in his life five years later, when he was appointed Secretary of the choir. At that time he was the supervisor in his office at work, which entailed a great deal of time and effort, but he was eager to take on the duties involved in being an officer in the choir at church. He decided to pray to God that he should be able to buy a car so that he could move back and forth from his office to the church more easily. Later that year he was promoted from supervisor to manager in his office, jumping ahead in the career track at his place of employment. The manager position entailed new responsibilities, but it also came with a company car. Abiodun again attributed his promotion to God's work in his life. This action cemented his commitment to the church and especially to the choir. As he put it, "God was actually moving me upward. So I had the motivating factor, I got inspired with that, I was ready to work. I decided that anything church, anything choir, I am ready. Because of that encouragement from God."

Ten years later Abiodun was selected to join ẹgbẹ́ Fògo. Abiodun's life story, which combines hard work with a commitment to prayer and to the church, was typical of most members of Fògo. This was the ideal that was represented in the group's anniversary ritual, an exemplar for all members of the church to strive toward. In particular, the anniversary ceremony modeled an ideal form of worship, one that all church members should emulate, with the implicit argument that in doing so one could be as successful as the members of the group.

The Fògo Ceremony as Cherubim and Seraphim Practice

The Fògo ceremony provides a particularly rich understanding of the practices of the Cherubim and Seraphim Church because according to church leaders and many church members the performance of the Fògo ritual is a heightened example of their form of worship. The ceremony was a "totalized sensory experience" (Tambiah 1981, 153) that drew on multiple media in order to make religious beliefs tangible. In doing so, participation in the ritual potentially reshaped perceptions of the world. The Fògo ceremony can be understood as a rite of collective renewal that moved from entrance through action to exit in order to reestablish and reaffirm the relationship between God and the church (Turner 1967; Van Gennep 1960). In the following discussion I pay particular attention to the ways in which shifts in musical style both pointed to and enabled transitions through this process. Thus, the performance of the ritual articulated and embodied powerfully convincing forms of subjectivity and belonging, inscribing these modes of being into the bodies of church members through affecting performances of music and dance.

On the morning of September 21, 2003, when I arrived at the church for Sunday worship the interior had been decorated for the Fògo anniversary celebration. Arches of yellow balloons spanned the center aisle of the church in two places. Bunches of additional balloons tied with coordinating ribbon hung from the ceiling and dotted the walls along the side of the church. The Fògo banner, printed with the group's name and the dates of its anniversary hung in the front of the church, with yellow streamers and even more balloons surrounding it. In addition, a large light fixture that spelled out Fògo in yellow and white light bulbs hung from the ceiling.

As I took my place in the choir stall, I noticed that around the church crisp, white handkerchiefs were being distributed to members of the congregation. Two handkerchiefs were handed to me along with a copy of the church program for that day, and I stuffed the handkerchiefs into the pocket of my prayer gown, assuming that they were gifts for the congregation from Fògo to commemorate the celebration of its anniversary. It was common practice to distribute small gifts, such as handkerchiefs, pens, or notebooks that are printed with the name and date of the occasion being celebrated: birthdays, weddings, funerals, and in the church ẹgbẹ́ anniversaries. However, these particular handkerchiefs were actually part of the ceremony, used in the performance of the final celebratory dance.

Prelude: Fògo Annual Report & Anthem

The order of service was the same as any other Sunday, with a fixed liturgy of hymns, prayers, and Bible lessons. The celebration of the Fògo anniversary took place an hour or so into the service and began with the reading of Fògo's annual report, a business-like document that was read in English by Fògo's secretary. In a formal and businesslike speaking style, he greeted those in attendance, welcomed special guests who had been invited to attend the ceremony, and reviewed ẹgbẹ́ Fògo's accomplishments from the past year.

In this speech Fògo's leadership made two arguments that helped to contextualize the ceremony that was about to happen: the first was the characterization of current circumstances in Nigeria as being "harsh, unpredictable, and unreliable," which made people subject to "social and economic hardships." Second, the report suggested that there existed a spiritual means of overcoming the circumstances presented by "this historic period"; namely through the application of a ritual practice "from time immemorial." Indeed, the parting line of the report was "We enjoin you according to the words of the apostle Paul to the Corinthians, chapter 4, verse 13, that you should have the strength to face all conditions by the power that Christ has given us." The implication of these arguments was that the socioeconomic experience of contemporary Nigeria could be overcome through the "work" of the ritual that was about to take place.

Entrance

The air in the church was heavy and expectant, as the congregation waited for the anniversary celebration to begin. The ceiling fans in the front of the church had been turned off, and a woman standing next to me in the choir drew my attention toward them, noting that it was a signal that the ceremony was about to begin. A member of the choir announced the name and number of the Processional Hymn "K and S 72: Ọba awọn ẹni mimọ" (King of saints, to whom the number); an Anglican hymn written by the British evangelist John Ellerton in 1871 and translated from English to Yoruba. The organist sounded the song's opening line and the trumpets joined to play the melody. Two electric guitarists picked out arpeggios that outlined the hymn's harmonic progression. Minimal percussion instruments filled out the sonic texture: drum set, tambourine, clips and shaker provided a constant yet muted rhythmic accompaniment. The instrumentalists repeated the melody twice, and then the Hymn Herald called out the first line of the hymn and the chorus and the congregation began to sing in response to her call:

> King of Saints, to whom the number
> Of Thy starry host is known
> Many a name by man forgotten
> Lives forever round Thy throne.

The members of Ẹgbẹ́ Fògo marched into the church, making a path down the center aisle toward the altar. They moved slowly and carefully, taking steps on every other beat in rhythm with the hymn. Not only were the bodily movements of the members of the procession highly choreographed, but they also marched in a particular order, from junior to senior, and from the most peripheral to the most central participants in the ritual. Both movement and order were prescribed and controlled. The order of the procession as well as the mode of movement were printed in the program, which described the processional hymn as being "With Ceremonial Slow Marching and Occasional Ringing of Bell and all members of Fògo to lit Candles in their Hands [*sic*]). During the procession, Fògo performed for the congregation an idealized vision of an ordered society, one that followed proper forms of hierarchy and respect.

Ẹgbẹ́ Fògo members made up the majority of the procession. They wore a special version of the white prayer gown that featured long, pointed sleeves that nearly touched the floor when the men held their arms at their sides. Whispering in my ear, my neighbor explained to me that these sleeves represented "the wings of angels." A yellow ribbon medallion was pinned to each member's chest and on his head he wore a white pointed cap shaped like a bishop's miter with silver trim. The hat worn by the members of the group was particularly noticeable since in this Cherubim and Seraphim denomination men typically do not wear hats or cover their heads while inside the place of worship. All members of the procession carried a lit candle between their gloved hands, which were held in the iconic position one takes while praying: palms together and fingers pointing toward the ceiling.

At each repetition of the chorus the procession halted:

Holy Holy, Holy Holy, Holy Holy
Holy be thy name
To Thee all Honor and Glory
O Lord of Eternity

The lyrics of the chorus repeated the words "mímọ́ mímọ́" (holy holy) three times. With each repetition the members of the procession halted and bowed their heads on their chest. In this fashion they slowly inched their way toward the front of the church and formed two parallel lines extending outward from the altar. The hymn was repeated for nearly an hour as all members of the group entered the church and joined the formation.

The opening of the Fògo ceremony engaged one's senses completely, with the continuous sound of the choir emanating from the loudspeaker, the smell of incense wafting through the hot stillness of the air, and the visual focus on the procession of men holding lit candles. Ẹgbẹ́ Fògo members entered the church, and in the process were transformed from ordinary men into embodiments of angelic beings. Fògo members iconically represented angels in their style of dress, movement, and singing, and through their mimetic practice they directly connected the space of the church with heaven, and the bodies of church members with angels.

The second entrance during this part of the ceremony was that of the Holy Spirit. God's descent into the space of the church was also achieved through musical performance, which called down the Holy Spirit to manifest itself in the spaces of the church and the bodies of church members. Following a short formal prayer from the Captain of Ẹgbẹ́ Fògo, the organist began the opening phrases of the next hymn. The program refers to the hymn as "God's Throne Visionary Song (Orin Ijúbà Ọlọ́run)." The hymn herald called out the opening line of the hymn, and the congregation joined in:

Holy, Holy, Holy, Lord God Almighty!
Early in the morning our song shall rise to Thee,
Holy, holy, holy, merciful and mighty!
God in three persons, blessed trinity.

Holy, holy, holy, all the saints adore Thee,
Casting down their golden crowns around the glassy sea.
Cherubim and Seraphim falling down before Thee,
Who were and are and evermore shall be

As in the procession, the song that was used to usher the Holy Spirit into the church was a well-known Anglican hymn that had been translated from English into Yoruba; this was based on hymn #280 from the Church Missionary Society Hymnal, and was written by Reginald Heber in 1826. Again, the lyrics feature the repetition of the word "mímọ́" three times. As in the first hymn, no "local" drums were used in the performance of the song, although the tempo moved along at a somewhat faster pace.

Movement during this performance, while less controlled than in the procession, was still constrained by the structure of the hymn. There was the same bowing of the head during the repetition of "mímọ́" as in the processional hymn and there was no dancing. However, the men's movements during the performance of this song were deliberate. Standing in two lines in the central open area before the church altar, Ẹgbẹ́ Fògo members acted out the words of the hymn, literally saying and doing at the same time: thus when the lyric sung was "Casting down their golden crowns around the glassy sea, Cherubim and Seraphim bowing down before thee" the men removed their caps, placed them on the floor in front of them, and bowed down so that their foreheads touched the floor. Although the rest of the congregation did not perform this, they were active and attentive participants in the performance: singing loudly and gesturing broadly toward the front of the church with arm movements expressive of worship and adoration. Proof of the Holy Spirit's entrance was apparent by the end of the hymn, as around the church people became ẹlẹ́míi (in a spiritual trance), many of them shouting and speaking in tongues.

In both of the hymns performed during these entrances, the lyrics were those that the angels sing before the throne of God in heaven: "Holy Holy Holy, Lord God Almighty." By acting out the lyrics of the hymns, Fògo and the entire congregation became the embodiment of angels in heaven worshipping before the throne of God. Their clothes, movements, and words were an attempt to replicate what was referred to in the Fogo anniversary program as the "ideal standard of worship in the Church on earth as it is in heaven." Indeed, the repetition of the word "mímọ́" throughout this phase of the performance served to inscribe these words— written on the walls of the church—into the spaces of the church and the bodily practices of the congregation. Further, the performance of the second hymn was identical to performances observed by both Peel (1968, 151) and Omoyajowo (1995, 115) in Cherubim and Seraphim churches during the 1960s and 1970s, suggesting that this hymn was a historical practice of the Cherubim and Seraphim in general. Fogo's performance was an act of historical mimesis that linked the performers to the founders of the church.

This symbolic process of bodily transformation required the performance of a certain kind of music. The songs sung during this phase of the ceremony were both hymns, taken from the Cherubim and Seraphim hymnbook and performed in a distinct musical style. Church members understood hymns and hymn performance to be linked to the church's history. Hymns indexed and activated the spiritual power of the church's founders, achieving a connection with the past that enabled church members to act in the present. This was particularly important for the Fògo ritual, which was envisaged as being a ritual practice from "time immemorial" and thereby capable of transforming church members into angelic beings.

Repetition also played a central role in hymn singing, and aesthetically reinforced the spiritual practices of the Fògo ceremony. Hymn performance was distinguished from the performance of other kinds of songs in the church by the practice of "lining out." Two or three women in the choir acted as hymn heralds, by announcing each line of the hymn before the congregation sang it. Lining out facilitated participation in singing for those in the congregation who did not have a hymnal or could not read. In addition, lining out entailed a practice of repetition that reinforced the message of the hymn, producing an overlapping aesthetic that drew attention to the meaning of the words.

Prophet Korode, the choir master of the Ayọ̀ ni o Church, explained the reason for using a hymn herald to line out the hymns:

> When [the song herald] calls it that way, the message is set, so when you verbalize it in song, it's doubly settled in the person singing. I've always said that repetition is the power of the inner mind. The more opportunity you have to repeat something, the more perfect you become at doing that thing. So, when the song herald calls it, and the singer sings it, you discover that you have twofold verbalization of the articles of song, and at the end of the day it's a lot more internalized by the person that is actually vocalizing it. So that's one of the essences of the song herald.

In his explanation of the importance of lining out hymns in performance, Korode articulated a significant way in which Cherubim and Seraphim worship "practicalized" church doctrine and made it real for church members: the repetition of practice makes perfect, reproducing one's subjectivity in line with belief. Finally, the repetition and overlap between the Hymn Herald's call and the congregation's response added to the sonic density of the performance, filling the air with the sound of the ritual.

Furthermore, the hymns used in this section of the ceremony were performed in a distinctive musical style, one described by church members as "worshipful." Songs sung in the worshipful style were often described as "solemn songs that carry you to spirit," or "music for sober reflection." The worshipful style was understood to be more effective in drawing down the Holy Spirit into the space of the church. Most songs sung in this style were hymns, and typically Anglican or Methodist hymns rather than those composed by the Cherubim and Seraphim.

An important musical characteristic of the "worshipful" style was that no so-called "local" drums were played; and here my informants used the English word "local" to specifically refer to the *gángan* (small, hourglass-shaped tension drum), which, in addition to adding to the complexity of the rhythmic texture through performing interlocking rhythms, was able to "speak" fragments of Yoruba texts by manipulating the tonal characteristics of the Yoruba language. There are three tones in the Yoruba language—low, mid, high—and the drum imitated those tones to "speak" fragments of text: usually formulaic bits of text such as proverbs. As one of the instrumentalists from the choir explained, in the "worshipful" style, these drums were not played because "with local drums they start dancing, and they do not focus on the content of the words." Note here the important role of the talking drum: in addition to being linked to "locality" it also produced a particular mode of movement—dancing—and it was the absence of this drum and dancing that particularly distinguished the "worshipful" style, a style which is less worldly and more heavenly.

Action

Once these entrances were accomplished, the working phase of the ritual began. In this segment performative utterances of Biblical texts alternated with the performance of hymns in order to mediate the space between the church and heaven and between the fleshly bodies of church members and the spiritual entities of angels. This series of hymns and prayers produced and delimited the reciprocal devotional obligations between God and the congregation as praise and worship were offered in exchange for God's blessings.

As the last phrases of "Holy, Holy, Holy" were sounded, the Worship Leader ("Asíwájú isin") for that day's service read from Isaiah 6 in Yoruba; a text describing angels worshipping before the throne of God:

> Above [God's throne] stood the seraphim: each one had six wings; with two he covered his face, and with two he covered his feet, and with two he did fly.

> And one cried unto another, and said, "Holy, holy holy is the Lord of hosts: the whole earth is full of his glory." (Isaiah 6:2–3)

The passage goes on to delimit the difference between humans and divine beings, emphasizing human sinfulness along with the ability of God to purge sin for those who transform their lives for God's purposes.

As he read the passage, the worship leader stood inside the Holy of Holies, facing the altar. The entire congregation also stood and faced the altar during the Bible reading, with the exception of the Fògo members who remained in two lines facing each other along the open space in the front of the church. Members of the congregation confessed their sins quietly under their breath, with the exception of a few individuals who were ẹlẹ́mìí. These individuals, both male and female, stood rocking back and forth in a trance-like state and occasionally lapsed into periods of glossolalia, speaking in tongues under the influence of the Holy Spirit.

In contrast to the vision of heaven presented in the ritual up to this point, this verse served as a reminder of the worldliness of men. The worship leader read the phrases of the passage from Isaiah describing the sinfulness of man: "I am a man of unclean lips and I dwell in the midst of a people of unclean lips." The reciprocal relationship between God and the church was also outlined: God heals Isaiah by removing sin and guilt, and in turn Isaiah agrees to be used by God. Note as well that the passage described the actions that had taken place in the church that day. In the Bible passage the seraphim's praises of "Holy, holy, holy, is the Lord of hosts" precede the entry of God. These words echo those sung in the hymns that preceded the Bible reading; "Holy, Holy, Holy," the words that made up the choruses of the previously sung hymns. Thus this point in the ceremony was a prime moment for sins to be confessed and cleansed, a step that was necessary for church members to submit their prayer requests soon after.

The pivotal moment of this portion of the ceremony was the delivery of Ẹgbẹ́ Fògo's thanksgiving offering to the altar. As the flags, banners, and the offering were carried to the altar, the congregation sang "We Speak of the Realms of the Blessed," an Anglican hymn with lyrics that had been translated into Yoruba:[1]

We speak of the realms of the blessed
Of the country so bright and so fair
Often they speak of its glories
How sweet it would be to get there

We speak of its pathways of gold
Of its walks decked with jewels most rare
Its wonders and pleasures untold
How sweet it would be to get there

The performance of "We Speak of the Realms of the Blessed" represented a transition in the ceremony. During this song Ẹgbẹ́ Fògo's banners, flags and, most important, their anniversary offering—a sum of money wrapped in white lace and displayed on a tray—were carried forward to the altar. Musically, while the talking drum was not used, the performance differed from the worshipful style heard earlier in its use of what church members identify as the reggae style. The church's reggae style was dominated by the bass guitar and featured the distinctive percussive strumming of guitar strings on the backbeat; however, it was performed at a much faster tempo than typical of Jamaican reggae. In the church, songs performed in the reggae style were usually shorter and conveyed only one idea or theme. Finally, in contrast to the worshipful style that I have discussed thus far, dance steps were associated with reggae style: a bouncing, almost running-in-place movement, with upper bodies held erect and arms pumping the air in front of the body.

An additional difference in this performance from earlier hymns in the ceremony was that the offering hymn was one typically performed during wake keeping and burial ceremonies, resonating with the important symbolism of heaven in this ritual. When I asked Abiodun why they used music typically performed at funerals during the Fògo ceremony, he said: "Of course they use that song because Fògo is of the heavenly court!" emphasizing the angelic qualities of Fògo and its practices. Though the "heavenly" implications of this song were strong, the purpose was actually for the living, to help them remember the purpose of their life, the meanings of their actions in the world, and to help them along their journey through life. Abiodun further explained the significance of wake-keeping songs as follows:

> By the time one is born into the world, God knew that you were coming to this world. He has brought you into the world for a particular reason. So, by the time somebody dies, actually he is going back to the creator. It is better for that type of occasion to have a sort of song that will be reminding of us, not the person that has died, but the people that have yet to die. You want to tell them that if they die, this is what they are going to face, this is what will happen.

Thus, it was significant that this song—a heavenly wake keeping song—was used not only to accompany the offering to the altar, but also preceded congregational prayers: the song opened up a space that was particularly conducive to making prayer requests. This use of funereal music implied a symbolic death and rebirth, producing a liminal ritual moment, one that articulated the cyclical nature of Yoruba conceptions of life (*iyè*) and destiny (*orí*) as one struggled through life's journey to make one's way in the world. In addition, it also evoked a space of passage, one in which power was drawn downwards, and life progressed upwards, in a transaction with the divine. Thus this performance opened up a space of possibility and critical reflection in which the congregation made their prayer requests; in this liminal space healing could occur, material and spiritual wealth was sought, and most significantly, the bodies of church members were remade in line with the church doctrine's ideal imagining of subjectivity.

Exit

In this part of the ceremony, Ẹgbẹ́ Fògo members performed song and dance in order to revert back to their usual, human selves, infused with spiritual power.

They returned to their everyday selves with a better understanding of the world and their place in it, having made sense of the world through the performance.

As the congregational prayers ended, the tone abruptly shifted as the chorus began the final hymn of the Fògo ceremony

> This is the foundation of Truth that Jesus laid
> Which the Baba Aladura follows
> Let no one think that
> He derailed from it, he stands on Christ the Rock
>
> Chorus:
> Cherubim rejoice, Seraphim rejoice
> We laid the foundation on the truth
> We laid the foundation on the truth
>
> Even if thunder sounds in thousands of deafening voices
> The children of Jesus will stand still
> Let man not despise the ark of Noah
> The ship sailed safely, the children of Jesus are saved
>
> Stephen was persecuted, Peter was persecuted
> Our Lord Jesus was persecuted
> Moses Orimolade was persecuted
> Let us all be watchful
>
> Spiritual Father rise and put on your girdle
> To meet the Cherubim
> God has glorified His work from heaven above
> The crown of salvation shall be yours
> Even though the world slights Moses, the angels approve of him
> The God of Abraham approves of him
> The Hosts of heaven hear his prayers
> God the trinity

The performance of this hymn marked a shift in musical style from what had been sung earlier. Again, a hymn was performed, but in contrast to earlier hymns, this was one unique to the Cherubim and Seraphim Church. A member of the church composed the hymn in the past, although the precise dates and nature of composition were not known. The lyrics of the hymn commemorate the founding of the Cherubim and Seraphim Church. Furthermore, this was also the first hymn performed in the anniversary ceremony where the talking drums were heard. In the church three or more drums of this family were used, tuned to a single pitch by tying a rope around the tension strings. These tuned drums performed interlocking rhythms, while the lead drummer used the drum to "speak" fragments of hymns, songs or proverbs or other texts that support the message being sung.

The use of the talking drums thus produced a notable second difference in the style and feeling of the ritual: in bodily movement. During the performance of this hymn Fògo performed a unique dance. Holding two white handkerchiefs, one in each hand, they held the cloths before them and swung them from side to side. Staying in two lines, they danced around the open area in the front of the church, tracing out a figure eight pattern in this space. The congregation also performed this dance, drawing out the handkerchiefs that had been distributed earlier that day, and swinging them back and forth as they danced in their places in the pews. The celebratory mood in the church continued to rise as the verses and chorus of the hymn were repeated. The Fògo Captain stood facing the altar, dancing before the lines of men as they danced around the space of the church. He opened his arms wide dancing before the Lord, finally bending over at the waist and crouching on his knees, rhythmically thrusting his hips and holding his arms out open before him.

The lines of Fògo members swinging their handkerchiefs back and forth as they danced in lines around the church resembled nothing so much as angels flying around God's throne. But of course this iconic association had been produced through the ceremony up to this point, from the solemn procession with lit candles, to the members of the Fògo band "casting down their golden crowns around the glassy sea." The church program included two photos of the final dance being performed during earlier Fògo celebrations: the first depicts a Fògo member holding the handkerchiefs before him and is captioned "FÒGO TYPICAL DANCE" and the second is of Prophet G. O. Fakeye, the charismatic general leader of the church, dancing the Fògo dance, captioned with the following: "THE LEADERSHIP OF THE PRAYER HOUSE JOYFULLY DANCING BEFORE THE LORD, LIKE DAVID THE KING OF ISRAEL, AND THE LORD BLESSES HIS PEOPLE MIGHTILY."

What was especially interesting here, however, was that these iconic representations of heaven and angels invoked earlier through the performance of solemn hymns with their origins outside of Nigeria were merged with "local" Yoruba ways of being and acting. This was indexed by the use of the talking drum—the so-called local drum—in addition to the use of a hymn that specifically referred to the Cherubim and Seraphim Church's founding moment: the lyrics even mention Moses Orimolade, the church's founder, by name. In this transition from heaven back into the world, from angels into men, Ẹgbẹ́ Fògo members made apparent the truth of the church's practices and the efficacy of their actions by relating them to specifically local, Yoruba histories and performance practices.

This segment of the ceremony ended with Ẹgbẹ́ Fògo members exiting through the front doors of the church, in parallel with their entry through the rear at the beginning of the ceremony. Outside, they formed a semi-circle, and the Fògo Captain offered a final prayer: a fervent thanksgiving to God for allowing them to celebrate the anniversary:

In Jesus' name! In Jesus' name! In Jesus' name! Eternal God of truth; the God of Light, the God of Righteousness; the God of Cherubim, the God of Seraphim, the God of Moses Orimolade Tunolase. We thank you, we thank you, Holy One of Israel that resides amongst the Seraphim, we thank you. Thank you, your mercy endures forever. We thank you for assisting us thus far, receive our thanks. We have celebrated this year's anniversary. The farmer knows not his last day of working in his farm before his eventual death. May this year's not be our last. Preserve us until next year. Preserve us until next year. Do not let anyone be found dead in our midst. Hear and confirm this prayer. In Jesus' name we have prayed. Amen.

With this statement, the leader linked the historical performance of the ceremony to the group's prosperity in the future. The prayer for the continued life and happiness of the group was contingent on the successful performance of the ceremony, in which the practices through which members of Fògo glorify God were exchanged for blessings.

Coda

Inside the church the congregation used musical praise and worship to thank God, further completing their reintegration back into the everyday world. Through this final dance the lessons learned in the ceremony about "the right kind of worship" was transformed into embodied knowledge, and heavenly ways of being and acting were translated into Yoruba modes of movement and expression. To complete this transformation, the choir segued from the final hymn into songs and choruses taken from the choir's 1993 album, *Take Control*.

Káábiyèsí o!
Holy and righteous, full of grace
Iyanu! (lit: miracle)
Káábiyèsí o!

Talking drum/chant:
I dread the King
Great King
The Great King who is like the dye
The King who is white as the new moon
Great King
I dread the King
Great King!

Call and Response:
Our Jesus is definitely coming back
Káábiyèsí o!

Káábiyèsí, which is typically translated as "your royal majesty" and literally means "may we bear living children (multiply in life) during your reign," is the customary greeting for the *ọba*, the divine king of Yoruba precolonial political organization (Apter 1992; Pemberton and Afolayan 1996). This praise name is used in combination with a talking drum formula typically used in Yoruba royal contexts to praise the *ọba*. However, here these formulae were used to praise the Christian God.

During the Fògo anniversary celebration a heightened form of Cherubim and Seraphim worship was performed ritually for the congregation by a selected group of male elders. As such, it was a highly condensed and controlled mode of ritual action as well as a conservative representation and reproduction of the church's ideal subject. To return to Abiodun's assertion that the Fògo anniversary celebration served to "practicalize" the church's doctrine, we can see that it did so by making real and embodying the religious beliefs and ethical stances of the church by using multiple media to enact angelic mimesis. In these performances church members were both saying and doing at the same time. They modeled a particular relationship and at the same time achieved that relationship. As the analysis thus far has shown, these actions were achieved through the use of a distinct musical progression, one that coordinated the bodily movements of church members and also organized their understanding of spiritual immanence and transcendence so that the space of the church was transformed into heaven and God's presence was felt by all who participated in the ceremony.

Cherubim and Seraphim Worship and Social Inequality

As this analysis has demonstrated, the Fògo ceremony was a node of mediation in which complex and profound aesthetic forms—including music, dance, oratory, and costume—came together in a compelling and dynamic ritual in order to coordinate participants' bodies, senses, and emotions. This organization of sense and sensibility worked to (re)produce conditions of possibility and modes of sociality that placed Yoruba moral values at the center of socioeconomic organization. Participation in the aesthetic forms and nodes of mediation of Cherubim and Seraphim practice connected church members to ethical norms and moral standards that promised to provide those who follow them with happiness and success. With their emphasis on the importance of hierarchy and hard work, these ethical and moral behaviors enshrined the importance of a set of values that were understood to be distinctly "Yoruba" by those who advocated them. This was how participation in "the right kind of worship"—as exemplified in the performance of the Fògo ceremony—was understood by participants to lead toward material success and well-being in the world.

At the center of the ideals emphasized in the Fògo ceremony is the importance of hierarchical social relations predicated on the importance of reciprocity. Those at the top of the hierarchy demand respect from others and are granted authority. However, the ability of those at the top of the hierarchy to have power is predicated on their willingness and ability to provide for their followers through acts of reciprocity. The hierarchical organization of Yoruba society has been noted by various analysts, from those who do so in in a conventional sociological sense (Bascom 1951, 1969; Eades 1980; Fadipe 1970), to those who emphasize how relations predicted on seniority rather than gender are important modes of understanding relationship between individuals in Yoruba society (Oyewumi 1997). The role of hierarchy and reciprocity in Yoruba religion has also been addressed, from the way in which worship in Yoruba indigenous religion is shaped in relation to the importance of both religious and social obligations toward and dependence on others for attention and support and (Barber 1981). These ideals are also central to Yoruba musical practice, as seen in Waterman's (1990) discussion of how jùjú music as performed at Yoruba celebrations serves as a metaphor for social order.

Waterman's analysis is of particular interest as it serves as an important point of comparison for the case discussed here. Both the styles of music that would lead to the development of jùjú as a genre and the forms of Christianity found in Yoruba independent churches arose out of the same milieus of colonial urban development and migration starting in the 1920s and were a product of the combination of communal Yoruba values and global forms of culture and media. Both of these religious and musical forms enabled the translation of communal Yoruba values into new contexts.

Based on his observations of Yoruba musical practices and modes of sociality in the period immediately following Nigeria's oil boom, Waterman writes:

> Suspended in and energized by a complex skein of localized patronage networks, jùjú portrays a traditional hierarchy mitigated by the generosity of the wealthy. This persuasive idealized image has helped to reproduce an ideology of cultural cohesion and universal opportunity, and thus, I would argue to obfuscate ongoing processes of social stratification in post-Oil Boom Nigeria. (Waterman 1990: 213)

Are the worship practices of the Ayò ni o Church, as exemplified in the Fògo ceremony, with its promises of salvation and redemption through the maintenance and recreation of Yoruba hierarchical social values, also obfuscating of processes of social stratification? Is the promise of salvation through worship an empty one; one that maintains the status of the wealthy and the legitimacy of their power without allowing for the processes of mobility and well-being enshrined in the ideals of hard work and reciprocity? The answers to these questions are not simple or straightforward. And in some ways, given the dependency of Nigeria's economy on oil and the way in which employment and quality of life in places like Lagos are dependent on fluctuations in the global oil market, these things are out of control of all members of the church, no matter how wealthy or powerful they are.

As I have argued in this book, Cherubim and Seraphim worship practices are productive of social ways of being and modes of organizing the world. The Fògo ceremony in particular, with its emphasis on the authority of male elders in the church to recreate religious and social worlds, works to portray an ideal form of society similar to that articulated through jùjú performance. And the issues of social stratification and inequality in Nigeria in the 1980s discussed by Waterman in the conclusion to his study echo similar dynamics that I observed in my research with members of the Ayò ni o Church in Lagos throughout the first decade of the twenty-first century.

Recall that many Nigerians saw their country's transition to democracy in 1999 as a moment of possibility in which previous economic and political woes would be overcome. Some of these so-called democracy dividends have since come to pass. Indeed, there has been an overall decrease in poverty levels in Nigeria. In addition, according to the World Bank, since 2000 Nigeria has experienced one of the world's highest rates of economic growth. However, that growth is mitigated by an increase in economic inequality that worsened considerably during the first decade of the twenty-first century. Because oil revenues were concentrated in urban areas, residents of Lagos benefitted from these economic developments, as evidenced by the expanding real estate market and other improvements to the quality of life. However, while these have resulted in vast wealth for some, and a more tangible grasp on the markers of middle-class status for many, there are still many in Lagos who live day-to-day and struggle to provide housing, food, and a good life for their families.

At the same time as the 2000s have represented a period of economic growth and rising inequality in Nigeria, it has also witnessed an explosion of religiosity as membership in churches and mosques have grown. The increasing visibility of Pentecostal churches in Lagos is a key example of this, made visible in the renowned traffic jams on the Lagos-Ibadan expressway when the Redeemed Christian Church holds their monthly revival services and tens of thousands of Christians throng to the church's "campground" for an all-night service. For many in Lagos religion has become both the explanation of their success as well as a means of succor for those in need (Marshall 2009; Ukah 2008; Wariboko 2014).

While the growth of Pentecostalism has resulted in the loss of some members of Cherubim and Seraphim churches to Pentecostal denominations, the Ayò ni o Church continues to attract new members. In 2005, the church added an additional weekday morning "Shiloh" service targeting the more impoverished residents of the community. Many came to these services seeking special prayers and interventions in their lives. Along with such special prayer and worship sessions, the church also offered free meals following the service to those in need, ran clothing drives, and opened a medical clinic which offered care to those who could not afford it on their own.

The example of Bayo, a man who I came to know through the church and whose life history stands in contrast to that of Senior Apostle Abiodun, shows how participation in church worship and the modes of sociality participation entailed enabled certain kinds of possibility at the same time as it curtailed others. I was introduced to Bayo toward the end of my lengthy stay in the field in 2003, by Mrs. Abidemi, a senior member of the choir who was also the matron of the Amos band. Bayo had joined the church six months prior to our introduction, and had recently been named to the Amos band by spiritual directive. Eight months prior to our meeting he had moved to Lagos from his home village in Ekiti state in search of opportunities. His brother had come to Lagos before him and found work as a driver and so it seemed to Bayo that there were more possibilities for employment in the city. So he came with his wife, and two young children. His wife was pregnant with their third child.

Bayo struggled to find work in Lagos, and the family relied on money that his wife earned from taking in laundry. Given that he had not finished secondary school, and that he had little technical training, Bayo's employment opportunities were limited. He worked briefly on a construction site, carrying planks and cement blocks, but it was painful work and he hoped to find something that was less physically demanding. That was where I came in. Another member of the church had offered to loan me a car they were not using, to help me get around the city in pursuit of my research. I was able to drive the car to church myself on Sundays when traffic was light, but during the week I preferred to leave the driving to professionals and take taxis and busses to my destination. Expressing concern for my safety on public transportation, Mrs. Abidemi saw an opportunity to help Bayo, something she was obligated to do as the matron of his band. She asked if I would be willing to hire Bayo to drive the loaned car to take me to my appointments and obligations.

I reluctantly agreed with her request. Although I enjoyed the opportunities for participant observation and lively conversations with people from all walks of life that taking public transportation afforded, I too felt the tug of obligation to fulfill a request made by a woman senior to me who had previously helped me in many ways. I met Bayo after church one Sunday. He was a small man, and looked down at the ground as he talked with me and Mrs. Abidemi. He promised that he was a hard worker and that I would not regret hiring him. Bayo arrived at my house the next morning ready to work. Unfortunately, the arrangement did not work out as planned. Neither Bayo nor I knew the city very well, and we frequently got lost on our way to a destination, or ended up hiring an okada (motorcycle taxi) to lead us to our destination. After two weeks I became frustrated with what seemed to be a waste of my time and money.

I asked to speak with Mrs. Abidemi after service one Sunday and explained my concerns. She begged me to continue to hire him, and told me that she would encourage him to speak with her driver, who would better orient him to the best routes through the city. She reminded me that the naming ceremony for his newborn baby was coming up and that the family was in desperate need of Bayo's income. I realized now that I was part of the hierarchy, obligated both to Mrs. Abidemi due to her previous kindness and assistance to me, as well as to help those in need who had less than I did. I agreed to give Bayo another chance. I also made sure to give his wife a large cash gift at the child's naming ceremony, which would help her to provide for the newborn and for the rest of the children.

My relationship with Bayo ended after eight weeks, when the car I had been loaned broke down and the owner decided not to repair it. For me, the loss of the car was not a big inconvenience. I returned to taking public transportation and relying on friends to get around the city. For Bayo the loss of this employment opportunity, even though he knew it was temporary, was potentially devastating. I went with him to the home he shared with his brother's family, bringing gifts for the children and bags of food to help them get by for a short while. I promised that I would recommend him for any subsequent opportunity he might find. He thanked me and said that he knew I would look out for him and his family.

Although I would see Bayo or his wife during or after church services during the remaining three months of my stay in Lagos in 2004, I lost track of him during subsequent visits. In the summer of 2010, when I returned for a short stay, I saw his wife after church. She had aged significantly since I had last seen her. She told me that Bayo had left the church and abandoned his family. He had temporarily found employment as a driver for a bank in Lagos thanks to another member of his band. But that job ended when the boss's cousin moved to Lagos and replaced Bayo. She thought that Bayo had moved to Port Harcourt to work, but she was not sure. She still struggled to feed her family, but she was able to find work cleaning or doing laundry and was able to manage. "We thank God," she told me, observing that the church was a crucial part of her life and her ability to survive in the world.

My relationship with Bayo is but one example of how the ideals of hierarchy, reciprocity, and hard work—embodied in the idea of home and recreated through Cherubim and Seraphim worship practices—had the potential to ensure the well-being of all members of the community. Relationships of obligation and care were articulated and reinforced through worship practices and the modes of sociality they entailed. Yet Mrs. Abidemi's dependence on the church hierarchy, or even my own, was of a significantly different nature than that of Bayo and his family. The church network could provide employment opportunities as in the case of Bayo or help one to see new possibilities for advancement in employment, as it did for Senior Apostle Abiodun, yet it was unable to create those opportunities wholesale nor to completely ease the experiences of poverty for those who were not able to find employment no matter how willing to work they were.

The opportunities afforded to Senior Apostle Abiodun could never be made available to Bayo, given the differences in their backgrounds and the times in which they sought to make their respective careers. Obfuscating this reality were the ideas articulated through the Fògo ceremony and the example of the lives of men like Abiodun: that the ability to be successful was linked to religious practice and observance, and that emulating those above one in the hierarchy both in life choices as well as in spiritual obligations was a key to success. Again, Waterman's study of jùjú, particularly his conclusions regarding the relationship between social inequality and musical performance are apt. He writes, "Viewed as a system of rhetoric arguing for a particular vision of society, jùjú simultaneously legitimates inequality and argues that all actors may become wealthy and powerful, a kind of African Horatio Alger ideology. In the face of widening disparities in wealth, education and health, music plays a role in the reproduction of hegemonic norms" (Waterman 1990: 227). The same could be said of Cherubim and Seraphim worship practices and the ethical and moral ideals embedded in them.

Note

1. I have altered the English version of the hymn to more accurately reflect the meaning of the sung Yoruba text; most notably the line "Y'o ti dùn to láti dé'bẹ̀," which I translated as "How sweet it would be to get there," which is supposed to be a translation of "But what must it be to be there?" The Yoruba text expresses a much stronger statement of longing than the English version does, especially because "sweetness" is a highly desirable embodied state of being: the expression of happiness in Yoruba is "inú mí dún," translated as "my stomach is sweet."

Epilogue

As I finish writing this book in 2016, the importance of singing the same song amid changing circumstances remains a central concern for church members. This is especially so given the profound changes to church leadership and organization that have occurred in the decade since I began my research with the Ayọ ni o Church. In January 2015, Prophet G.O. Fakeye, the church's general leader, died in a hospital in the United States. I learned of his death on Facebook where church members posted about their feelings of shock and their remembrances of a powerful man of God. Fakeye's death represented a turning point for the church: with the loss of such a charismatic and spiritually powerful leader, would the organization be able to maintain its size and place among other Cherubim and Seraphim churches? Would even more members leave the church to join Pentecostal congregations? Who would take over the leadership of the congregation and ensure continued spiritual guidance?

I viewed the mourning of church members and the controversy over succession from my home in Vermont, watching people post their photos of church services following Fakeye's death or comments about his life on social media, including Facebook and WhatsApp. Not visible to me from this distance were the deliberations and prayers that took place in countless meetings of church elders. The next leader of the church was chosen in secrecy by a group of church elders, in consultation with representatives from the Cherubim and Seraphim Church Movement headquarters in Kaduna. It was understood that their decision was mainly driven by spiritual consultation as they prayed and fasted for God to reveal the next leader of the church to them. However, this process did not prevent rumors and speculation from circulating among other members of the church. But most suspected that Prophet S. F. Korode, the church's choirmaster, was to be chosen. An early Facebook post asserting this as fact was quickly retracted out of worry that it would offend members of the church who held higher positions of seniority than Korode. Finally, in June 2015 an announcement made it official: Korode was the new general leader.

The selection of Korode as Fakeye's successor was evidence of Korode's own spiritual powers, as well as his charisma and leadership skills. While a handful of people asked in comments on the announcement or in private messages whether Korode had "jumped the line" and been promoted over the head of men who were senior to him, most celebrated the decision. Photographs of him circulated widely on social media between church members, with comments of congratulation and celebration.

A central argument of this book is that songs are central to understanding Cherubim and Seraphim Christianity, at least as evidenced in the Ayọ̀ ni o Church, because they are the media through which people are joined together to each other as a moral community as well as to a set of ethical practices that orient church members toward key values that enable them to navigate their lives in Nigeria. It should come as no surprise then that the man responsible for organizing musical activities in the church and spearheading its musical evangelism should be chosen as the organization's new leader; in many ways it affirms the arguments that I have been making here. *Singing Yoruba Christianity* asserts that any discussion of Cherubim and Seraphim Christianity should start and end with singing, as songs are the central media through which religious, moral, and social ideas become possible and real. Songs enhance all other aspects of Cherubim and Seraphim practice, through performance drawing together a variety of media such as the white church uniform, the Bible, prayers, bodily movements, and other aspects of worship that are recognizable as constituting Cherubim and Seraphim practice.

It is no coincidence that the high point of Fakeye's funeral was an all-night service of songs, performed by the Ayọ̀ ni o Church choir, on a large stage in a massive field in Fakeye's home town of Imesi Ile in Osun state, Nigeria. Thousands of people attended the event and stayed up all night singing together with the choir in order to ease their leader's passing from this world to the next. Again, as I chatted with people on WhatsApp about their preparations to attend the funeral and viewed photographs and read reports concerning the event on Facebook, the importance of everyone coming together to join voices and bodies in song in order to celebrate Fakeye's life and to acknowledge his transition to heaven was emphasized. Songs were the dominant media through which the community ensured their continuity after the demise of their leader.

Discontinuity and Unity in Yoruba Christianity

While the ideal of singing the same song and producing the same mind was the main part of musical practice in the Ayọ̀ ni o Church, the events and examples discussed in this book have also demonstrated that the production of unity via song was something that was not as simple as it might appear. Performances of any given song were contingent. Singing had to be done correctly, according to exact musical parameters and performance practices, thus forming an aesthetic of persuasion that bound church members together with each other as well as with their religious beliefs and ideals. As described in chapter 4, church members learned to cultivate a labor of immediacy that enabled them to successfully execute a performance that was effective at both drawing the congregation together and drawing God's power down into the church. Furthermore, as detailed in chapter 7, church members had to learn to listen in the right way, so that their spiritual power became oriented toward the Holy Spirit.

Indeed, even as choir rehearsals, Bible study sessions, and courses designed for members at various stages of membership worked to ensure that church members were correctly oriented in their worship practices, issues of belonging and worship remained in need of vigilance. Continued practice and discipline were required to make sure that the congregation worshiped correctly and with the appropriate ethical orientation toward their religious work. Through such practices, church members were able to create a moral vision of the world, and to delineate a set of ethical ways of acting within it, that was understood to embody Yoruba Christianity.

Even with all of this effort a great deal of disunion existed. The Ayọ̀ ni o Church was but one religious institution in a crowded field that appealed to members with the promise that they offered the best and most correct way of being Christian. New churches constantly appeared in Lagos, often led by a charismatic pastor who reached out to attract new converts and to draw members away from their current congregations, with the promise of life transformation and salvation. Young people left the Ayọ̀ ni o Church to join Pentecostal congregations while others joined the Ayọ̀ ni o Church when they found that their previous congregation did not meet their spiritual needs.

The Ayọ̀ ni o Church's leadership emphasized that it provided a particularly Yoruba way of being Christian, a practice and a spiritual orientation that appealed to Yoruba ways of being in the world. The "Yoruba-ness" of Ayọ̀ ni o Church worship was seen through the continued emphasis on reclaiming Yoruba values and integrating them into Christian practice via the singing of hymns as a historical practice, as discussed in chapter 1, or the inclusion of Yoruba "honoristic values" that emphasize hierarchy and social order as indexed through styles of dress and the organization of space as we saw in chapter 5. As the analysis here has demonstrated, for members of the church the linking of Yoruba and Christian was mutually constitutive. One was not prior to the other, but rather one's Yoruba-ness or Christian-ness was something that is enacted in relation to a particular context.

The Ayọ̀ ni o Church produced their version of Yoruba Christianity in a moment in which the "Yoruba" aspects of their practice had come under question by leaders and advocates of neo-Pentecostal churches, who argued that Nigerians needed to overcome and leave behind the "African" aspects of their identities in order to progress both personally and as a nation (Marshall 2009). Numerous scholars of Pentecostalism have discussed how churches in West Africa circulate, promote, and localize ideas related to political and economic globalization in an ever-widening public sphere. The use of electronic media by Pentecostal churches, combined with their use of English instead of local languages and their emphasis on modern forms of consumption (Meyer 1998)—all of which might be understood as more "Western" (or at least more globally oriented) and less "African"—is seen by some as helping to constitute new forms of identity outside of national and ethnic identities by linking Africans to wider global religious networks (Hackett 1998; Marshall 2007; Marshall-Fratani 1998). In addition to examining the political role played by neo-Pentecostalism in African religious imaginaries, analysts have also connected the shift to Pentecostalism to neoliberal transformations of African economies since 1990 (Gifford 2004). In many ways the prosperity gospel promoted by these churches, with its emphasis on individual success, resonates closely with neoliberal economic practices such as privatization—the privatization of media contributed to the ability of Pentecostal messages to dominate radio and television broadcasts in many places—and structural adjustment.

The case discussed in this book has complicated both the assumed link between Pentecostalism and the global, as opposed to the local, as well as the reliance on notions of rupture and conversion that are used to make sense of global/local relations in studies of the globalization of Christianity (see Robbins 2004). Through a focus on how discourses about the right ways of being Christian are taken up, responded to, and negotiated by members of the Ayọ̀ ni o Church—a Cherubim and Seraphim Church typically linked to earlier ways of being Christian in Africa and that self-consciously understood its version of Christianity as being especially Yoruba—this book has offered a corrective to what Matthew Engelke (2010) has identified as the "Pentecostal prejudice" that has characterized studies of Christianity in Africa in the past twenty years.

In particular, the analytic focus on music has allowed us to examine how discontinuity is enacted, overcome, resolved, or even perpetuated by a group of Yoruba Christians who, as members of the Ayọ̀ ni o Church, worked to create their own sense of belonging to a larger Christian community as well as to a set of ideas linked with being Yoruba. Because music is both discourse and practice, it enacts the process whereby contradictions are both produced and resolved, and unity and dis-union are made and unmade. The focus in this book on music and musical practices is therefore not coincidental. Indeed, it is in the negotiation of what kind of music is both Yoruba and Christian, or meaningful and efficacious for Yoruba people in their Christian practice, that we can see how a particular view of Yoruba Christianity itself is produced in relation to others. Thus Christianity—whether it is asserted to be Yoruba or Western, local or global—is not a thing, but a process.

The role of music in mediating discontinuity can be seen in the attempts of a group of leaders from a number of different Cherubim and Seraphim churches to come together to try to unify the disparate denominations of the church. Unification was understood as a strategy that would spiritually strengthen members of Cherubim and Seraphim churches by ensuring that they were all practicing the right kind of worship. Unification would also help to create a united front against the encroachments of Pentecostal Christianity by demonstrating the continued strength in numbers of members of Cherubim and Seraphim churches. It would also serve a need that was of historical interest to members of Cherubim and Seraphim churches: the overcoming of the disagreements and fragmentation that has characterized the Cherubim and Seraphim since the death of Orimolade, the churches' founder.

As Omoyajowo (1984) detailed in his study of the historical development of Cherubim and Seraphim denominations, a disagreement over church hierarchy and spiritual authority led to the creation of different Cherubim and Seraphim denominations. Numerous factions emerged, each of which claimed to offer the most effective approach to worship that would enable church members to achieve a good life. Even within a given Cherubim and Seraphim denomination divisions emerged along lines of church authority, concerning liturgical practices, or in relation to doctrinal issues. Church members that I spoke with frequently bemoaned these divisions, which they felt often served the worldly interests of church leaders and their desire for personal power rather than the spiritual needs of their followers.

When I visited the grounds of the Ayọ ni o Church in the summer of 2010, I noticed that a new sign had appeared on a building just to the right of the main entrance. This sign indicated that the building contained the offices of the Cherubim and Seraphim Unification Movement headquarters. Curious about what seemed to me to be a new development at the church, I made an appointment to meet with the director of the unification movement. I learned that the movement for unification of Cherubim and Seraphim denominations extended back to the 1970s, when members of various Cherubim and Seraphim churches came together as students on university campuses and began to discuss the situation of the church. The director explained that the goal of the movement was to reunite the Cherubim and Seraphim churches according to what they saw as Orimolade's original vision. As he put it, "The divisions between different Cherubim and Seraphim denominations are shameful to the organization. Because of our differences we were not able to speak in one voice. Large as we were there was no unity and we were being marginalized by other churches." Advocates for Cherubim and Seraphim unification believed that the churches needed to come together in order to have a stronger presence among Yoruba Christians.

Central to the organization's plans for unification was the development of a common liturgy; a shared order of service, uniform doctrinal beliefs, and a coordinated set of practices which streamlined everything from the styles of church uniforms worn by church members to the organization of members and the use of titles to indicate one's position in the group's hierarchy. However, the leader of

the movement explained to me that the difficulty they faced at achieving unification was how to make people want to adopt these new practices, to change from the
ways they had taken up randomly and for their own purposes, and to adopt the
official model that would standardize the correct form of worship for all who
claimed to be Cherubim and Seraphim.

It was not surprising then that music was of central concern to the leaders of
the unification movement. On the one hand, music was a part of the liturgical and
doctrinal standards advocated by the unification movement, and a standard
hymn book as well as an outline of minimal requirements for musical practices
in the church had been created. On the other hand, music was also a key means
through which unification itself would be achieved. To that end, a unification
choir had been created featuring members from the Ayọ̀ ni o Church choir to
help convince other churches to join the movement and to help implement their
changes. As the leader of the movement explained, "Music is an integral part of
practice and liturgy. Every church practices it. Music has a common language. It
is spiritual. It helps to lighten up the spirit so that you are able to open up spiritually
in the service. It is through music that we feel that connection to God."

Given the complex history of divisions between Cherubim and Seraphim
denominations, achieving unification is unlikely. However, it represents an important and continuing process that allows church members to characterize what
Cherubim and Seraphim Christianity is and how it is both part of as well as distinct from other forms of Christianity. Indeed, there is always a temporal dimension to singing the same song, even singing together about the importance of
unity and commonality. At some point the song ends and that experience of unison produced via singing together then needs to be made sense of in relation to
events yet to come. Different churches may sing a song in the name of unity and
yet fragmentation may still characterize how religion is institutionalized. This
should not be understood however as a failure of unification. Rather it points to
the ways in which religion itself is a process, something that is continually worked
out in context and adapted for particular reasons. Music thus enables both har-
mony as well as discord.

Old and New Media

My ability to follow the developments concerning Fakeye's death and the celebration of his life in song via social media brings me to the final point that I have
emphasized in this book. I have argued that mediation is a process that brings
together various media central to the religious life of the Cherubim and Seraphim: from the materiality of hymnbooks, church uniforms, and architecture, to
beliefs about the power and presence of the Holy Spirit. As I have shown, media
objects and processes of mediation are brought together in Cherubim and Seraphim

religious practice as a mode of angelic mimicry that enacts their cosmology. At the same time, media are central to the ethical orientations and disciplinary practices through which members learn to enact that cosmology correctly, so that their actions are effective.

Old and new media continue to be brought together by church members in ways that are both recognizable as well as innovative. The introduction of new media—particularly mobile technologies and social media—as a part of church worship in particular has been subject to much discussion and debate. When I visited the church in the summer of 2010, I attended a meeting with three of the elders in the choir concerning the use of the choir's recordings on mobile phones. The elders listened to an appeal from a member of the youth fellowship who wanted to create a selection of musical samples that church members could add as a call-back feature to their phones. If someone subscribed to this feature, anyone who called their phone would hear the song, rather than just the phone ringing. He argued that it would both enhance the evangelical capacities of the person who owned the phone, as well as the spiritual capacities of the caller who heard the songs rather than just a dial tone. This interruption of the mundane practice of calling someone on the phone with a sound fragment that was designed to bring a religious orientation into everyday life was seen as crucial to ensuring and maintaining ethical discipline.

The elders listened to the young man's proposal cautiously. They noted that the use of musical callbacks was similar to a highly successful text-message subscription service featuring daily spiritual messages from Fakeye that had been launched earlier that year. The representatives from the choir's executive committee present at the meeting cautioned the group that the songs used for these purposes had to be carefully selected: they should be uplifting songs, which would help to activate the hearers' spirits. However, the songs that were sampled should not be too spiritually powerful or one might risk sending a listener into a spiritual trance without their being properly prepared for it. The meeting ended with the elders agreeing to set up a meeting between the young man and representatives from the choir's record label to investigate what was involved in licensing and circulating samples in this way. Through such innovative uses of new media people's phones had the potential to become a new part of religious practice, one that furthered their ethical practices but that was continuous with older ideas about the kinds of religious work accomplished by various aspects of worship.

As emphasized in chapter 3 of this book, which detailed the choir's decision to begin recording and releasing their songs, the adoption of media forms was not always natural and inevitable. The introduction of new media itself often involved adapting worship practices in order to incorporate new objects or forms. At the same time, the way that any media form has been adopted has been subject to certain requirements and traditions of style and practice.

In chapter 8 I discussed the central role of the hymn herald, who lined out hymns as the congregation sang them, both for the practical reason of enabling those in the church who did not have their hymn books to know the next line to sing, but also for the purposes of doubling the intent of the hymn's message through repetition. When I had asked Korode early in my research about this practice, he emphasized its importance as part of the church's tradition as well as its use as a spiritual necessity. He explained that Fakeye had wanted to get rid of the hymn herald and instead insisted that all church members should own a hymnbook so they could read along with the hymns as they were sung. Korode had argued that the practice of using a hymn herald to line out hymns was a central part of worship and should be maintained even when new means of following along with the hymns became available.

With this knowledge of the disagreement between Korode and Fakeye over the use of the hymn herald, and Korode's insistence on this practice as crucial to worship, I was surprised to find that the voice of the hymn herald was no longer prominently featured during worship during a visit to the church in the summer of 2015, after Fakeye's death and the installation of Korode as church leader. Instead, closed-caption televisions and video-projection screens lined the church hall, broadcasting the scene at the altar or in the choir in close-up all over the church. The lyrics to the hymns were projected as the choir sang them instead of the hymn herald lining them out as part of the hymn's performance. Such a use of audio-visual technology was commonplace in most large Pentecostal churches and appeared to me to represent a radical change to a practice that in my experience had been insisted on by Korode. When I asked members of the choir about the change I was told matter-of-factly that it better served the large congregation who could now see all aspects the service. Furthermore, the use of televisual media as part of worship was more "modern." Church members with whom I spoke made a form over function argument: If the screens are going to be there, why not project the words. It just made sense.

However, this adoption of new media in the face of tradition was also made subject to that very tradition in particular moments. Later on in the worship service, the power went out in the middle of a hymn—a typical occurrence in Lagos where electricity supply was unreliable. Such events always produced an initial moment of discord as the choir adapted to the loss of their microphones and electronic instruments. In this case, the singers and drummers recovered quickly and were able to bring the congregation back into unison to sing the hymn. The generator was switched on quickly, and the choir was again amplified. However, there was a delay on the television screens, as the closed-circuit video system had to be restarted and cued up to the correct part of the service so that the lines of the hymn could be displayed again. In the face of this failure of new technology, one of the former hymn heralds in the choir picked up a microphone and began lining out the song. Out of necessity, the group returned to an old musical practice amid the new transformations. This example emphasizes the ways that the introduction of new technologies into religious practice involves both disruption as well as continuity. The use of new technologies as well as a memory of tradition ensures that church members remained adaptable to circumstances that continue to change, as stability is produced out of instability due to knowledge of the value of old ways in new circumstances.

Glossary of Yoruba Terms

àdúrà prayer, specifically Christian prayer.

agbáda item of Yoruba men's clothing, a flowing gown worn over a shirt and trowsers.

akọrin choir.

àkúbà single-headed drum modeled on the Afro-Cuban conga drum.

àlàáfíà Health, well-being. A general state of contentment.

Alàdúrà lit. "owner of prayer"; refers to Yoruba independent Christian churches that emerged in the 1920s and 1930s.

aṣo funfun white cloth, refers to the uniform worn by members of the Cherubim and Seraphim churches.

ayé the world, specifically the visible world of the living.

ayọ̀ joy.

Bàbá Alàdúrà lit. "father of prayer"; refers to male elders in Cherubim and Seraphim churches.

bàtá double-headed drum associated with Yoruba òrìṣà religion, specifically with the deity Ṣàngó.

dọbále male way of greeting elders and superiors; involves lying face-down on the floor in front of elder, casual form involves bowing one's head and touching the floor with the right hand.

dùndún double-headed, hourglass-shaped pressure drum that can "speak" Yoruba; "talking drum." Performed in Yoruba religious, political, and other social contexts but rarely played in Christian worship.

ẹgbẹ́ social club or voluntary association; refers to division of church members into smaller spiritual sections.

Èkó Lagos.

ẹlẹ́míì spiritual trance; to be "in the spirit" (lit. "owner of spirit").

Ẹ̀mí Mímọ́ Holy Spirit.

gángan small double-headed, hourglass-shaped pressure drum ("talking drum") used in Christian contexts.

ìgbàlà salvation.

ilé house, home.

inú inside, refers to one's spirit.

ìyè life.

jùjú a style of Yoruba popular music that influenced gospel music compositions and recordings.

kúnle female way of greeting elders; involves kneeling on both knees with hands behind the back.

ogo glory.

Olódumarè/Ọlọ́run supreme deity.

orin song.

òrìṣà generic term for Yoruba deities, refers specifically to indigenous religion not to Christianity or Islam.

ọba Yoruba sacred king.

ọjà marketplace.

ọ̀run heaven.

sámbà single-membrane wood frame drum used in early Yoruba Christian contexts.

ṣẹ̀kẹ̀rẹ̀ gourd rattle.

wòlíì prophet.

wọ́rọ́ 12/8 dance rhythm used in popular contexts and in Yoruba gospel music.

Bibliography

Abiodun Emanuel, Mrs. C. 1962. *Celestial Vision of Her Most Rev. Mother Capt. Mrs. C. Abiodun Emanuel, which Originated Cherubim and Seraphim in 1925.*Yaba: Charity Press.

Adogame, Afe. 1999. *Celestial Church of Christ: The Politics of Cultural Identity in a West African Prophetic-Charismatic Movement*. New York: Peter Lang.

———. 2000. "Aiye Loja, Orun Nile: The Appropriation of Ritual Space-Time in the Cosmology of the Celestial Church of Christ." *Journal of Religion in Africa* 30, no. 1: 3–29.

Ajayi, J. F. Ade. 1965. *Christian Missions in Nigeria, 1841–1891: The Making of a New Élite.* Evanston, IL: Northwestern University Press.

Anderson, Benedict. 1991. *Imagined Communities: Reflections on the Origin and Spread of Nationalism*. New York: Verso.

Apter, Andrew. 1992. *Black Critics & Kings: The Hermeneutics of Power in Yoruba Society.* Chicago: University of Chicago Press.

———. 2005. *The Pan-African Nation: Oil and the Spectacle of Culture in Nigeria.* Chicago: University of Chicago Press.

Askew, Kelly Michelle. 2002. *Performing the Nation: Swahili Music and Cultural Politics in Tanzania*. Chicago: University of Chicago Press.

Ayandele, E. A. 1978. "The Aladura among the Yoruba." In *Christianity in West Africa: The Nigerian Story*, edited by Ogbu Kalu, 384–390. Ibadan: Daystar Press.

Barber, Karin. 1982. "Popular Reactions to the Petro-Naira." *Journal of Modern African Studies* 20, no. 3: 431–450.

———. 2003. *The Generation of Plays*. Bloomington: Indiana University Press.

Barnes, Sandra T. 1986. *Patrons and Power*. Bloomington: Indiana University Press.

Basso, Ellen B. 1985. *A Musical View of the Universe*. Philadelphia: University of Pennsylvania Press.

Becker, Judith O. 2004. *Deep Listeners*. Bloomington: Indiana University Press.

Bell, Catherine M. 1992. *Ritual Theory, Ritual Practice*. New York: Oxford University Press.

Bloch, Maurice. 1974. "Symbols, Song, Dance and Features of Articulation Is Religion an Extreme Form of Traditional Authority?" *European Journal of Sociology* 15, no. 1: 54–81.

Brennan, Vicki L. 2010. "Mediating 'The Voice of the Spirit': Musical and Religious Transformations in Nigeria's Oil Boom." *American Ethnologist* 37, no. 2: 354–370.

———. 2012. "Take Control: The Labor of Immediacy in Yoruba Christian Music." *Journal of Popular Music Studies* 24, no. 4: 411–429.

———. 2013. "'Up above the River Jordan': Hymns and Historical Consciousness in the Cherubim and Seraphim Churches of Nigeria." *Studies in World Christianity* 19, no. 1: 31–49.

———. 2015. "Şenwele Jesu: Gospel Music and Religious Publics in Nigeria." In *New Media and Religious Transformations in Africa*, ed. Rosalind Hackett, 227–244. Bloomington: Indiana University Press.

Briggs, C. L., and R. Bautnan. 1992. "Genre, Intertextuality, and Social Power." *Journal of Linguistic Anthropology* 2, no. 2: 131–172.

Buggenhagen, Beth. 2012. *Muslim Families in Global Senegal: Money Takes Care of Shame*. Bloomington: Indiana University Press.

Cannell, Fenella. 2006. "The Anthropology of Christianity." In *The Anthropology of Christianity,* ed. Fenella Cannell, 1–50. Durham: Duke University Press.

Comaroff, Jean. 1985. *Body of Power, Spirit of Resistance: The Culture and History of a South African People*. Chicago: University of Chicago Press.

Comaroff, Jean, and John Comaroff. 1991. *Of Revelation and Revolution*. Vol. 1. Chicago: University of Chicago Press.

———. 2012. *Theory from the South: Or, How Euro-America Is Evolving toward Africa*. Boulder, CO: Paradigm.

Comaroff, John. 2010. "The End of Anthropology, Again: On the Future of an In/Discipline." *American Anthropologist* 112, no. 4: 524–538.

Corbin, Alan. 1999. *Village Bells: Sound and Meaning in the Nineteenth Century French Countryside*. New York: Macmillan.

Crumbley, Deidre Helen. 2008. *Spirit, Structure, and Flesh: Gendered Experiences in African Instituted Churches among the Yoruba of Nigeria*. Madison: University of Wisconsin Press.

Csordas, Thomas J. 1997. *The Sacred Self: A Cultural Phenomenology of Charismatic Healing*. Berkeley: University of California Press.

De la Cruz, Deirdre. 2009. "Coincidence and Consequence: Marianism and the Mass Media in the Global Philippines." *Cultural Anthropology* 24, no. 3: 455–488.

Dosunmu, Oyebade. 2005. "The Appropriation of Traditional Musical Practices in Modern Yoruba Drama: A Case Study of Wole Soyinka's Death and the King's Horseman." MA thesis, University of Pittsburgh.

Drewal, Margaret Thompson. 1992. *Yoruba Ritual: Performers, Play, Agency*. Bloomington: Indiana University Press.

Durkheim, Émile, and Karen Elise Fields. [1912] 1995. *The Elementary Forms of Religious Life*. New York: Simon & Schuster.

Eisenlohr, Patrick. 2009. "Technologies of the Spirit." *Anthropological Theory* 9, no. 3: 273–296.

Emoff, Ron. 2002. *Recollecting from the Past: Musical Practice and Spirit Possession on the East Coast of Madagascar*. Middletown, CT: Wesleyan University Press.

Englehardt, Jeffers. 2014. *Singing the Right Way: Orthodox Christians and Secular Enchantment in Estonia*. New York: Oxford University Press.

Engelke, Matthew E. 2007. *A Problem of Presence*. Berkeley: University of California Press.

———. 2010. "Past Pentecostalism: Notes on Rupture, Realignment, and Everyday Life In Pentecostal and African Independent Churches." *Africa* 80, no. 2: 177–199.

Essien, E. B., O. Fashina, and M. Ozuah. 1999. *Focus on Surulere District Sub-Headquarters*. Lagos: Seal of Life.

Euba, Akin. 1967. "Multiple Pitch Lines in Yoruba Choral Music." *Journal of the International Folk Music Council* 19: 66–71.

———. 1990. *Yoruba Drumming: The Dùndún Tradition*. Bayreuth: E. Breitinger, Bayreuth University.

Fabian, Johannes. 1971. *Jamaa; A Charismatic Movement in Katanga*. Evanston, IL: Northwestern University Press.

Famodimu, E. Olu. 1990. *Moses Orimolade Tunolase: Supreme Founder, Cherubim and Seraphim Worldwide: (from When He Was in the Womb to His Death)*. Kaduna: C&S Church Movement National Headquarters.

Fassin, Didier. 2008. "Beyond Good and Evil? Questioning the Anthropological Discomfort with Morals." *Anthropological Theory* 8, no. 4: 333–344.

———. 2012. "Introduction: Toward a Critical Moral Anthropology." In *A Companion to Moral Anthropology*, ed. Didier Fassin, 1–17. West Sussex: Wiley-Blackwell.

Fernandez, James W. 1978. 1986. *Persuasions and Performances: The Play of Tropes in Culture*. Bloomington: Indiana University Press.

———. 1982. *Bwiti: An Ethnography of the Religious Imagination in Africa*. Princeton: Princeton University Press.

Fox, Aaron A. 2004. *Real Country: Music and Language in Working Class Culture*. Durham: Duke University Press.

Freud, Sigmund. 1950. *Totem and Taboo: Some Points of Agreement between the Mental Lives of Savages and Neurotics*. New York: W.W. Norton.

Gifford, Paul. 2004. *Ghana's New Christianity*. Bloomington: Indiana University Press.

Greene, Paul D. 1999. "Sound Engineering in a Tamil Village: Playing Audio Cassettes as Devotional Performance." *Ethnomusicology* 43, no. 3: 459–489.

Hackett, Rosalind I. J. 1995. *Women and New Religious Movements in Africa*. Oxford: Blackwell.

———. 1998. "Charismatic/Pentecostal Appropriation of Media Technologies in Nigeria and Ghana." *Journal of Religion in Africa* 28, no. 3: 258–277.

Hannerz, Ulf. 1987. "The World in Creolization." *Africa* 57, no. 4: 546–559.

Harris, Hermione. 2005. "Continuity or Change? Aladura and Born-Again Yoruba Christianity in London." In *Christianity and Social Change in Africa*, ed. T. Falola, 307–334. Durham, NC: Carolina Academic Press.

———. 2006. *Yoruba in Diaspora: An African Church in London*. London: Palgrave Macmillan.

Haynes, Jonathan. 2000. *Nigerian Video Films*. Athens: Ohio University Press.

———. 2010. "A Literature Review Nigerian and Ghanaian Videos." *Journal of African Cultural Studies* 22, no. 1: 105–120.

Hirschkind, Charles. 2006. *The Ethical Soundscape*. New York: Columbia University Press.

Idowu, E. Bọlaji. 1962. *Olódùmarè: God in Yoruba Belief*. London: Longmans.

Idowu, Moses Oludele. 2009. *More Than A Prophet*. Lagos: Divine Artillery.

Keane, Webb. 2007. *Christian Moderns*. Berkeley: University of California Press.

Korode, Sunday F. 1995. *Cherubim and Seraphim Legacies*. Lagos: Immanent Illuminations Konsult.

———. 2002. *Where Do You Fellowship?* Lagos: Concept.

Kirk-Greene, A. H. M., and Douglas Rimmer. 1981. *Nigeria since 1970: A Political and Economic Outline*. London: Hodder and Stoughton.

Lambek, Michael. 2000. "The Anthropology of Religion and the Quarrel between Poetry and Philosophy." *Current Anthropology* 41, no. 3: 309–320.

———. 2010. "Toward an Ethics of the Act. In *Ordinary Ethics: Anthropology, Language and Action*, ed. Michael Lambek, 1–39. New York: Fordham University Press.

———. 2012. "Religion and Morality." In Didier Fassin (ed.), *A Companion to Moral Anthropology*, West Sussex: Wiley-Blackwell, pp. 341–358.

Larkin, Brian. 2008. *Signal and Noise: Media, Infrastructure, and Urban Culture in Nigeria*. Durham: Duke University Press.

Lawuyi, Q B., and J. K. Olupọna. 1988. "Metaphoric Associations and the Conception of Death: Analysis of a Yoruba World View." *Journal of Religion in Africa*, 18, no. 1: 2–14.

Luhrmann, Tanya M. 2012. *When God Talks Back: Understanding the American Evangelical Relationship with God*. New York: Vintage Books.

Mahmood, Saba. 2005. *Politics of Piety: The Islamic Revival and the Feminist Subject*. Second Revised. Princeton: Princeton University Press.

Marshall, Ruth. 2009. *Political Spiritualities*. Chicago: University of Chicago Press.

Marshall-Fratani, Ruth. 1998. "Mediating the Global and Local in Nigerian Pentecostalism." *Journal of Religion in Africa* 28, no. 3: 278–315.

Mauss, Marcel. 1973. "Techniques of the Body." *Economy and Society* 2, no. 1: 70–88.

Mazzarella, William. 2004. "Culture, Globalization, Mediation," *Annual Review of Anthropology* 33: 345–367.

Meyer, Birgit. 1998. " 'Make a Complete Break with the Past.' Memory and Post-Colonial Modernity in Ghanaian Pentecostalist Discourse." *Journal of Religion in Africa* 28, no. 3: 316–349.

———. 1999. *Translating the Devil*. Trenton, NJ: Africa World Press.

———. 2004a. "Christianity in Africa: From African Independent to Pentecostal-Charismatic Churches." *Annual Review of Anthropology* 33: 447–474.

———. 2004b. " 'Praise the Lord': Popular Cinema and Pentecostalite Style in Ghana's New Public Sphere." *American Ethnologist* 31, no. 1: 92–110.

———. 2009. *Aesthetic Formations: Media, Religion, and the Senses*. New York: Palgrave Macmillan.

———. 2010. "Aesthetics of Persuasion: Global Christianity and Pentecostalism's Sensational Forms." *South Atlantic Quarterly* 109, no. 4: 741–763.

———. 2011. "Mediation and Immediacy: Sensational Forms, Semiotic Ideologies and the Question of the Medium." *Social Anthropology* 19, no. 1: 23–39.

———. 2015. *Sensational Movies: Video, Vision and Christianity in Ghana*. Berkeley: University of California Press.

Meyer, Birgit, and Annelies Moors. 2006. *Religion, Media, and the Public Sphere*. Bloomington: Indiana University Press.

Muller, Carol Ann. 1999. *Rituals of Fertility and the Sacrifice of Desire*. Chicago: University of Chicago Press.

Ojo, Matthews A. 2006. *The End-Time Army: Charismatic Movements in Modern Nigeria*. Trenton, NJ: Africa World Press.

Olupona, Jacob. 2003. "A Sense of Place: The Meaning of Homeland in Sacred Yoruba Cosmology." *Experiences of Place*, Mary N. MacDonald, ed. Cambridge: Center for the Study of World Religions/Distributed by Harvard University Press, 87–114.

Omoyajowo, J. Akinyele. 1982. *Cherubim and Seraphim: The History of an African Independent Church*. New York: NOK.

———. 1984. *Diversity in Unity: The Development and Expansion of the C & S Church in Nigeria*. Lanham, MD: University Press of America.

——. 1995. *Makers of the Church in Nigeria*. Lagos: CSS Bookshops Limited Pub. Unit.

Onovirakpo, S. M. O. 1998. *The History and Doctrine of the Cherubim and Seraphim Church of Nigeria*. 2nd ed. Ibadan: Agoro Publicity Company.

Otubu, G. I. M. n.d. *Explanatory Notes to the "Order."* Pamphlet of the Eternal Sacred Order of the Cherubim and Seraphim.

Oyěwùmí, Oyèrónkẹ́. 1997. *The Invention of Women: Making an African Sense of Western Gender Discourses*. Minneapolis: University of Minnesota Press.

Parmentier, Richard J. 1994. *Signs in Society*. Bloomington: Indiana University Press.

Peel, J. D. Y. 1968. *Aladura: A Religious Movement among the Yoruba*. London: Published for the International African Institute by Oxford University Press.

——. 2000. *Religious Encounter and the Making of the Yoruba*. Bloomington: Indiana University Press.

Pemberton, John, and Funso S. Afolayan. 1996. *Yoruba Sacred Kingship: "A Power Like That of the Gods."* Washington, DC: Smithsonian Institution Press.

Pype, Katrien. 2012. *The Making of the Pentecostal Melodrama. Religion, Media, and Gender in Kinshasa*. New York: Berghahn Books.

Ray, Benjamin C. 1993. "Aladura Christianity: A Yoruba Religion." *Journal of Religion in Africa* 23, no. 3: 266–291.

Renne, Elisha P. 2004. "Dressing in the Stuff of Dreams: Sacred Dress and Religious Authority in Southwestern Nigeria." *Dreaming* 14, nos. 2–3: 120–135.

——. 2009. "Consecrated Garments and Spaces in the Cherubim and Seraphim Church Diaspora." *Material Religion: The Journal of Objects, Art and Belief* 5, no. 1: 70–87.

Robbins, Joel. 2003. "What Is a Christian? Notes toward an Anthropology of Christianity." *Religion* 33, no. 3: 191–199.

——. 2004. "The Globalization of Pentecostal and Charismatic Christianity." *Annual Review of Anthropology* 33: 117–143.

Rosenthal, Elisabeth. 2012. "Nigeria Tested by Rapid Rise in Population." *New York Times* April 14.

Sahlins, Marshall D. 2002. *Waiting for Foucault, Still*. Chicago: Prickly Paradigm Press.

Schulz, Dorothea E. 2006. "Promises of (Im)mediate Salvation: Islam, Broadcast Media, and the Remaking of Religious Experience in Mali." *American Ethnologist* 33, no. 2 2: 210–229.

——. 2012. *Muslims and New Media in West Africa: Pathways to God*. Bloomington: Indiana University Press.

Shaw, Rosalind, and Charles Stewart. 1994. *Syncretism/Anti-Syncretism: The Politics of Religious Synthesis*. New York: Routledge.

Shipley, Jesse Weaver. 2009. "Aesthetic of the Entrepreneur: Afro-Cosmopolitan Rap and Moral Circulation in Accra, Ghana." *Anthropological Quarterly* 82, no. 3: 631–668.

Silverstein, M., and G. Urban. 1996. *Natural Histories of Discourse*. Chicago: University of Chicago Press.

Smith, Daniel Jordan. 2007. *A Culture of Corruption*. Princeton: Princeton University Press.

Spitulnik, Debra. 1993. "Anthropology and Mass Media." *Annual Review of Anthropology* 22: 293–315.

——. 1998. "Mediated Modernities: Encounters with the Electronic In Zambia." *Visual Anthropology Review* 14, no. 2: 63–84.

Sterne, Jonathan. 2003. *The Audible Past: Cultural Origins of Sound Reproduction.* Durham: Duke University Press.

Sundkler, Bengt G. M. 2004. *Bantu Prophets in South Africa.* London: James Clarke.

Tambiah, Stanley J. 1981. *A Performative Approach to Ritual.* London: British Academy.

———. 1985. *Culture, Thought, and Social Action: An Anthropological Perspective.* Cambridge, MA: Harvard University Press.

Thieme, D. L. 1969. "A Descriptive Catalogue of Yoruba Musical Instruments." PhD diss., Catholic University of America.

Trager, Lillian. 2001. *Yoruba Hometowns: Community, Identity, and Development in Nigeria.* Boulder, CO: Lynne Rienner.

Turner, Harold W. 1967. *History of an African Independent Church.* Oxford: Clarendon Press.

Turner, Victor W. 1967. *The Forest of Symbols.* Ithaca: Cornell University Press.

———. 1969. *The Ritual Process: Structure and Anti-Structure.* Chicago: Aldine.

Ukah, Asonzah. 2003. "Advertising God: Nigerian Christian Video-Films and the Power of Consumer Culture." *Journal of Religion in Africa,* 33, no. 2: 203–31.

———. 2008. *New Paradigm of Pentecostal Power.* Trenton, NJ: Africa World Press.

Van Gennep, Arnold. 1960. *The Rites of Passage.* Chicago: University of Chicago Press.

Wariboko, Nimi. 2014. *Nigerian Pentecostalism.* Rochester, NY: University of Rochester Press.

Warner, Michael. 2002. *Publics and Counterpublics.* New York: Zone Books.

Waterman, Christopher Alan. 1990. *Juju: A Social History and Ethnography of an African Popular Music.* Chicago: University of Chicago Press.

Watts, M. J. 1992. "The Shock of Modernity: Petroleum, Protest, and Fast Capitalism in an Industrializing Society." In *Reworking Modernity: Capitalisms and Symbolic Discontent,* ed. A. Pred, 21–64. New Brunswick, NJ: Rutgers University Press.

Watts, Michael. 1996. "Islamic Modernities? Citizenship, Civil Society and Islamism in a Nigerian City." *Public Culture* 8, no. 2: 251–289.

Zito, Angela. 2011. "Body." *Material Religion: The Journal of Objects, Art and Belief* 7, no. 1: 18–25.

Index

Vicki L. Brennan is Associate Professor of Religion and
Director of African Studies at the University of Vermont.

www.ingramcontent.com/pod-product-compliance
Lightning Source LLC
Chambersburg PA
CBHW050352270326
41926CB00016B/3715